The New Nonprofit

The New Nonprofit

Six Models to Raise More Money and Accomplish More Mission

Dedication

To the nonprofits pushing on the long arc of history.

Contents

Foreword

By Roger Craver

This book could scarcely be more timely. It arrives at the very moment warning signs abound of the difficult days to come.

Today there are more nonprofits than ever, but revenue is not keeping pace with that growth. Despite the rising number of nonprofits we are witnessing a decline in the overall number of donors. Retention rates are down. Acquiring new donors is more expensive and less productive as we collectively pollute and overfish the same pond. Even digital and online fundraising, once considered a magic bullet, is flat-to-declining. In the words of Yogi Berra, “The future ain’t what it used to be.”

In this book Nick Ellinger makes it clear: the once-safe approach of sticking with the status quo has now become a strategic choice that carries with it high risk.

It’s time for serious fundraisers to chart a course from the Old World of Fundraising to a New World. These pages contain the navigational guide to get you from today’s Sea of the Status Quo to the New World’s lands of growth and sustainability -- all without fear of sea monsters or falling off the edge of the Earth.

Packed with fundraising research from behavioral science… fundraising case histories from organization breaking new ground… the book also includes fundraising results from 10 years’ of pilot programs, testing and proven campaigns conducted by DonorVoice. This is the donor experience and retention firm where Nick serves as VP of Marketing Strategy. In chapter after chapter this book highlights and explains the new mindsets, metrics and methods essential to transforming stale, same-old-same-old efforts into a vibrant, growing and sustainable program –all of which you can learn quickly and begin to apply immediately.

If you’re content with the current state of fundraising, this book is not for you. However, if you have the gnawing sense that there must be better ways to attract and hold on to donors, you’ll want to dig in and start highlighting or dog-earing pages. What you're about to feast on is the substance behind the over-used and little-understood term "Donor Centric."

For several years Nick has joined me in The Agitator reporting on new developments in fundraising and report on the DonorVoice team's research, testing, documenting and then sharing "New World" fundraising practices with our readers. Nick has now packed all this, plus much, much more into this book.

Revealed are the many proven opportunities that await you, as well as calling out those faux opportunities you should avoid. You don't have to seize every opportunity but you'll be making a real difference to your organization if you get to work on some. Among them:

- The immense benefits of becoming a Permission-Based Nonprofit.
- Why asking fewer times can increase revenue.
- The power—and results—of making your donors feel preferred and how to do just that.
- The essential importance of donor identity and why you're crippling your program without it.
- The secret segmentation weapon –Donor Commitment. What it is. How to use it.
- Why personas don't work and what you should be using instead.
- Why implementing a donor feedback program may be the lowest cost, highest yield investment you'll ever make.
- The deceptive and illusory fundraising promises of Facebook, Google, and Instagram.

The list goes on and on. The "what", "why" and "how to" of steps you can take for a far brighter future are all detailed—along with a generous helping of humor—in this book.

If you also sense that the time for change has come, but are not quite sure what actions to take, I recommend reading this book as Step #1. Step #2, of course, is to act on it.

Roger Craver, Chilmark, Massachusetts

Overview

"Oh, my sweet summer child," Old Nan said quietly, "what do you know of fear? Fear is for the winter, my little lord, when the snows fall a hundred feet deep and the ice wind comes howling out of the north. Fear is for the long night, when the sun hides its face for years at a time, and little children are born and live and die all in darkness while the direwolves grow gaunt and hungry, and the white walkers move through the woods."[1]

– George R. R. Martin

Winter is coming to nonprofits. Unnamed, faceless, cold, sparse, biting, relentless, gnawing winter. And not all will survive.

More nonprofits exist than ever before, with more coming.

The pie of charitable giving is expanding[2] but not as a percentage of GDP.[3] The pie is also not growing as much as the number of nonprofits is expanding, so the average nonprofit will lose revenues. What growth there is has slowed,[4] stopped or reversed[5] depending on the study.

Retention rates (when controlling for lifecycle) are declining.[6] Getting and keeping donors grow more expensive. Nonprofits increase the number of communications sent with both stamps and digital electrons. Communications increase in quantity of messages and decrease in quality of results.

As retention drops, the need for more acquisition increases, further increasing donor-by-donor pressure to give broadly and shallowly. The tragedy of the commons plays out in a million different households. Maybe ten million. To give to one is to be solicited by that one, then by the many. Most nonprofits do bulk acquisition from lists of people who give to other nonprofits. Few bring in new people to the idea of philanthropy, assuming it is easier to get the philanthropic to give more than to get the non-philanthropic to give at all.

The number of donors is decreasing, causing the giving of an average family to fall.[7] The relevance of nonprofits to donors wanes, leading The Blackbaud Institute to conclude "American donors are more valuable to American nonprofit organizations than the organizations are to the donors."[8]

Nonprofits flee to what we believe is quality, recapitulating what has worked for others. Donors see the playbook, whether it is address labels, false urgency, or a compelling story. The success rate keeps dropping.

The donor pool is now an apt analogy, as we are collectively polluting and overfishing these same waters with little restocking. Even those studies that show an increase in overall giving show a decrease in the number of donors,[9] making philanthropy a game for the wealthy instead of a broad-based good. These drops are not sustainable over the long term as quarters or halves of our donors fall out of philanthropy.

Winter is coming. And the only way to survive is to evolve.

You are right to insist on proof.

Surely, at least one of the many ways to measure philanthropy shows an increase in donor populations?

Unfortunately, no.[*]

We'll start with a study by *The Chronicle of Philanthropy*. They found that in 2015, 24 percent of taxpayers reported a charitable gift on their returns. A decade ago, 30-31% reported such a gift.[10]

Wait! We know fewer people itemize their deductions (and this number should decrease with the 2017 tax law). Perhaps they just aren't reporting it?

Well, we could ask them. That's what Indiana University Lilly Family School of Philanthropy does consistently. They found that the proportion of American households that reported charitable giving declined from 66% in 2000 to 55% in 2014.[11] Median annual giving dropped from $1,024 per year to $872 in a decade's time.[12]

---

[*] And don't call me Shirley.

Wait! People always lie to survey takers. That's Social Desirability Bias 101 – people say they want people to think about them.

However, social desirability would not change over time. People tend to lie to survey takers at consistent rates when you ask the same questions over time. So, while you can't take these percentages to the bank, you can likely count on the changes in these percentages.

Also, when you look at real donations, as measured by Blackbaud's DonorCentrics Index, from 2005 to 2015, not one single year had positive year-over-year donor growth.[13] This didn't stop in 2015; the 2018 Fundraising Effectiveness Project Report found that new donors **dropped 19 percent in one year; the next year, they dropped 7%**.[14]

Wait! Perhaps this is just a factor of changing demographics with a trough of people at giving age.

If this is your argument, you've never heard of the Baby Boom* or been to Florida.

Further, the decrease in giving is consistent across generations. Blackbaud looked at this very thing, finding that:

> "with the exception of Baby Boomers, each generation has seen a decline since 2013 in the percentage of cohort members who say they give to charity. The study's findings agree with a growing body of research suggesting that, even as total dollars donated are growing, the population of givers is contracting."[15]

Our generations are also shifting to be less advantageous for giving, as our most generous generation – those born before 1949 are entering their demographic sunset.

Wait! Generations are a false construct, invented by sociologists and grasped at by marketers who wanted to make phrenologists and fortune cookies look predictive. Maybe generations will adopt the behavior commensurate with their chronological age, giving more as their

* The demographic movement, not the 1987 Diane Keaton movie.

disposable income increases, as happens for about half of all generational "differences."*

So let's look at age ranges and see how people in those age ranges give over time. That will correct for people becoming their parents over time.

Sadly, every 10-year age group (30 and under, 31-40, 41-50, 51-60, and 60+) gives less now than they did in 2000.[16] Most dramatically, 58% of households led by fifty-somethings gave in 2014, down from 78% in 2000. Across every age group, fewer people are giving.

In addition, fewer people at every level of education are giving. Fewer people at every level of income are giving (although the drop is lowest among the wealthiest). Married, single, and cohabiting people are all giving less frequently. Religious and non-religious people are both giving less frequently.[17] Sadly, regardless of the color of your stats, skin, or hat, giving less frequently seems like the one thing all Americans now agree on.

Several good hypotheses have emerged as to why. One significant impact was clearly the Great Recession. Texas A&M economists Jonathan Meer, David Miller, and Elisa Wulfsberg looked at giving behavior and found the Recession caused the propensity to give to plummet. Further, when the economy improved, giving remained below previous levels.[18] Other research shows that economic shocks (in this case, using the Great Depression) mold the way people use money for the rest of their lives.[19] This is true for giving in particular – giving when you are younger builds a habit of giving that continues when you are older. So, likewise, does a habit of not giving.[20] A recession imparts non-giving ripples outward on a stagnant, fetid pond.

---

* The other half are genuine trends over time that are not specific to a generation. For example, generations are getting more and more technologically savvy, resulting in reports that "this is the most technologically savvy generation ever" by those with no sense of historical pattern recognition. There was a generation looked at as wunderkinder by their elders because they could work a printing press. There was probably a generation that figured out that most problems with fire could be fixed by turning it off, then turning it back on.

Another part of this involves changes in where the money is in the United States. The top .1% of households in the United States now has as much wealth as the bottom 90%.[21] The Institute for Policy Studies found in their report "Gilded Giving: Top-Heavy Philanthropy in an Age of Extreme Inequality"[22]...

Well, that sub-title totally gives away the results, no?

Anyway, from 2003 to 2013, itemized charitable deductions for those making more than $100,000 increased by 40%; they decreased among those making less than $100,000 by 34%. As a result, low-dollar and midrange donors have declined by 25% in the last decade.[23] This trend continues in 2018; overall giving increased 1.5%, while retention, donor numbers, new donor numbers, new donor retention, repeat donor retention, reactivation rates, and gifts under $1000 were all down. The only thing that went up was gifts over $1000: up 2.6%.[24]

This is not sustainable. Major donors are neither spontaneously generated nor immaculately birthed. They aren't created when a mommy major donor and a daddy major donor love each other very much and have a special sort of hug.

They first test you out with a gift. You grow on them. They grow on you. You learn about them. You build a relationship. Pretty soon, they don't know what they'd do without you. They are committed. And their giving moves from the transactional to the transformational. I'm sure someone has sent in a six-figure check to an acquisition package. I personally, though, have never seen it.

If our new donor numbers are down, our overall retention is down, our retention of new donors specifically is down, and our recapture rates are down, where are the major donors of the future going to come from?

Further, we should not aim for a nonprofit sector funded – and thus influenced – mostly by the very wealthy. Centralization of donations means centralization of control. Nonprofits have already faced pressures to change themselves to accommodate large funders (including grantors). Fewer donors means increased pressure to control the agenda; as the cynical version of the Golden Rule goes, those who have the gold rule.

In 2015, the Girl Scouts of Western Washington received a donation for $100,000 to help them support poorer scouts with a significant string attached: no support for transgender girls. The Girl Scouts rejected this assault on their values, returned the donation, and launched #forEVERYgirl, an effort to make up the difference in their funding. The campaign raised over $300,000.[25] This story would not have a happy ending without many individuals chipping in. Thus, as our donor files shrink, pressure increases. As that pressure increases, more nonprofits will go where money, not mission focus is.

Reliance on fewer funders decreases stability. Losing a few big donors can put a crimp in the good you do in the world. Because giving is instilled from a young age, we may reach a point where mainly the scions of the wealthy get those philanthropic values, solicited by a generation of fundraisers trained to cast narrow nets. In short, broad-based philanthropy is threatened.

Regardless of the cause, these trends toward fewer, wealthier donors have been apparent for years. Winter is coming. Like an ice age, though, it has been slow enough that we have continually readjusted to consider today our new normal.

But this normal isn't normal. If our acquisition and retention rates freeze at 2018 levels, we will lose 22% of our donor files over the next decade. If we continue down the current path with those acquisition and retention rates falling at the current rate, we'll shed 57% of our donor files.[26] Venerable organizations could go the way of Sears, Blockbuster, Radio Shack, pay phones, etc.* At that point, we would get to find out if nonprofits shutting their doors would mean fewer organizations for donors to spread their giving across or a poisoned ecosystem in the same way the behavior of bad actors leading to the financial crisis also harmed the good actors. After all, what does a co-op or a list exchange look like as nonprofits fail?

---

* Basically, anything featured in *Captain Marvel*.

We will not be able to change wealth distribution ourselves. Nor will we be able to un-Great-Recession the economy by reading *The Big Short* backwards.*

We've (mostly) contented ourselves with getting people who give to other organizations to give also to us. That's fishing in a shrinking pond. How do we change this?

Today's direct response fundraising is largely based on outmoded conventional wisdom. The process works like this: the nonprofit direct marketer selects the story she thinks will have the most impact, then pushes it out to a large group of donors and potential donors. For potential donors, she will likely rent or exchange lists of donors to other organizations, knowing they are most likely to donate. Her goal: to raise unrestricted funds to cover all activities of the organization.

There is a better way. This book questions every assumption in the preceding paragraph. Our future will be far brighter if instead we focus on:

- Sending these communications to only those who desire a specific channel and in the frequency they want within that channel, instead of pushing most messages to an undifferentiated mass audience.
- Communications differentiated based on the recipient, instead of a mass appeal based on what story the direct marketer thinks will have the most impact.
- Getting those who care for your cause to donate, instead of getting those who donate to care for your cause through list rentals and exchanges.
- Framing giving in ways that allows for donor preferences, instead of all appeals covering all activities of the organization.
- Empowering messages that come from supporters, instead of the direct marketer or even the organization.

---

* Fun fact: read any Michael Lewis book backwards and markets become less efficient.

- Sharing and associating among several nonprofits, instead of focusing on just one organization.

Any of the old, business-as-usual assumptions, if changed, could positively and productively alter the way we fundraise. In these pages, you'll see examples of organizations that have successfully dipped their toes into these waters, as I hope you will do. You will learn from those already swimming and those still on the beach.

More than anything, I want to convince you that change is necessary. From there, we can then agree that in today's turbulence that the safest path isn't the well-worn road.

The good news is that we are nonprofits. We've faced worse than winter and will do so again.

The permission-based nonprofit: Love requires consent

"We are very grateful that there has been an investigation into charity fundraising practice overseen by the Fundraising Standards Board and are pleased that there have been changes to the Code of Practice as to how charities fundraise, as well as changes to the law to prevent elderly and vulnerable people feeling pressured to give when they can't.

We want Olive to be remembered for her incredibly kind, generous and charitable nature. Far from being a victim, she was a strong believer in the importance of charities in UK society and local communities. She found great comfort in the knowledge that her support could help someone live a better life.

At the same time, she was concerned about the amount of letters and contact that she was receiving from charities and we are sure she would have been very upset to know that her personal details were being shared or sold by some charities who she had agreed to support. We are also pleased that a Fundraising Preference Service is going to be developed as this will mean that vulnerable people can put a stop to fundraising approaches in the future if they want to."[27]

– Olive Cooke family statement

Her name is Olive Cooke. People say she was killed by her kindness.

Olive began selling poppies for the Royal British Legion when she was 16. For those not familiar with the practice, poppies became associated with the sacrifice of soldiers during World War I with the publication of the poem "In Flanders Fields." The American Legion adopted artificial poppies after the end of the war to commemorate the soldiers lost. Shortly thereafter, the RBL began selling poppies both in honor of those lost and as a fundraising tool.

Five years later, Olive's husband was killed as a member of the Royal Navy in Italy, leaving her a war widow at the age of 21. She responded by redoubling her efforts. Over 76 years of her life, she sold more than 30,000 poppies to aid veterans. For her efforts, she had been honored by the Lord Mayor of London and the Prime Minister.

At the age of 92, Olive jumped to her death in the Avon Gorge near Bristol, England. Early reports claimed that she had been hounded to death by charity solicitors based on an interview she had given where she felt overwhelmed by requests for funds. More sober reflections found that she had left a note where she explained the reasons for her death as connected to depression and issues around her age.

Her granddaughter made a statement, which I'll excerpt extensively because of its power:

> "Nan would have wanted the work of charities to be promoted. It brought her great comfort to know she could help make a difference in a person's life by donating to charities and by her own charity work.
>
> She believed that charities are the backbone to our communities, that they can be the scaffolding for us in our times of crisis. She believed that charities give us support, hope and courage when we need it the most.
>
> I think that the amount of contact from charities was starting to escalate and get slightly out of control, and the phone calls were beginning to get intrusive, but there is no blame or suggestion that this was a reason for her death.

> She might have had up to 27 direct debits at one point and been a bit exhausted by all the letters, but she had decided which charities she wanted to give to.
>
> She had her favourites and was not bumbling along and letting them grow and grow. She was very on-the-ball with money and gave to charities because she wanted to and could afford to – it was a passion.
>
> …
>
> It would be nice if some good came from this, if people supported the elderly around them and offered them comfort and support.
>
> The contact from charities does need looking at, and obviously with the methods of fundraising there are issues that need to be addressed and are being addressed now, which has got to be a good thing.
>
> But their work should still be praised and they do such a great job."[28]

Personally, I can hope, and perhaps only hope, to be memorialized someday with "It brought him great comfort to know he could help make a difference in a person's life by donating to charities and by his own charity work."

In Olive's story, you see the positive and the negative of giving and asking. Olive believed in what she was doing. She was a sterling example of the power of an individual to make the lives of so many others that much better. It is an honor and a sacred duty to plant trees in whose shade we will not sit.

And yet, even though the fundraising appeals were not noted as a causal factor in her death, one does not say the deceased was overwhelmed by the quantity of correspondence as a positive thing.

To understand this fully, we must delve into the brain's ballet of chemicals when one donates or, more likely, doesn't.

Let's start when someone is reading your finely crafted appeal, starting with increasing oxytocin levels. Oxytocin is often called the "cuddle chemical" or the "hug hormone." Oxytocin is released naturally as a part of childbirth and is associated with maternal behavior and social attachment.

It goes much beyond this, however. More recent research has shown it is important in the formation of trust. People dosed with oxytocin are more willing to trust their money with strangers.

In this case, we, the nonprofit, are the strangers. When people empathize with a story, oxytocin levels are 47% higher on average.[29] People who receive oxytocin gave to 57% more causes and 56% more money after exposure to PSAs.[30] And this is where your finely crafted appeal comes in. And if you can arouse emotion as well, releasing a fast-acting hormone called ACTH*, you can increase giving 261%.[31]

This happens quickly. For donors who are interacting with charities repeatedly, this becomes subconscious behavior.[32] Neurologists say "fire together, wire together." This means if you do something repeatedly, the stimuli involved will tend to become associated and more efficient working together. Think of walking the same grass path day after day. Soon that path becomes almost as good as a sidewalk.

Now the oxytocin and the ACTH are pumping. That probably happened from the moment the donor saw your logo on the envelope, because the brain remembers how that logo made the person feel in the past. Visual stimuli have power; when we see a Coke can, our brains go to our hippocampus (for memory) and our limbic system (for emotion), assuming we have a history with the Coke brand.[33] Hopefully, when someone sees our logo, they have a wash of positive past history that adds up to "It's time to donate."

From fMRI data, we know when someone donates, the nucleus accumbens – the part of the brain usually associated with unexpected rewards – lights up and produces dopamine.[34] Dopamine is usually associated with pleasure. It produces the "warm glow" from giving.

---

* Adrenocorticotropic hormone. Hence the abbreviation.

However, pleasure is a side effect for dopamine. It is less a "liking" chemical and more a "wanting" chemical. Think of the classic rat-pushes-a-lever-and-gets-a-reward-experiment. That's what dopamine does. Do good. Get a dopamine reward. Most addictive drugs work through dopamine and most anti-addictive medicinal treatments repress dopamine. In fact, some people get addicted to giving, hooked on their dopamine highs.[35]

To oversimplify, when you present someone who wants to give an opportunity to give, you are giving them their fix. You are a dopamine merchant.

So now we know how your brain donates. Chances are, you knew much of this intuitively – the appeal and branding of an organization create an emotional state that a person satisfies by donating – even if you didn't know the names of the parts of the brain where it happens.

Let's look at the other side of this coin. Let's say you are getting a 1% response rate on average to your acquisition mail packages and 5% to your donor mail packages. If you are average, you are getting a .42% click-through rate on your emails.[36] So what's been described above happens in the distinct minority of cases.

The other 95-99.5% of the time, your communication is headed for a real or virtual trash bin.* But the potential donor has already been primed. The potential donor's chemical cocktail of oxytocin, ACTH, and dopamine kicked in when they saw your logo on the envelope or name on the email. Their mind is already preparing them to feel empathy. They're bracing to experience the emotional arc that comes from hearing about the difference they can make in another's life.

When donors have that build-up without release, what was going to be a warm glow turns into irritation. As more organizations solicit the same donors, this irritation mounds.

Donors believe they are good people. You'd agree, no? Good people do good things like donating. Yet, by consigning your communication to the waste basket (real or virtual), they are doing

---

* Or compost bin, depending on the nature of your message.

something inconsistent with their sense of themselves. Since humans strive for consistency, this conflict causes psychic pain.

This pain is "cognitive dissonance," the discomfort of trying to think two conflicting things at once (in this case, I'm a good person, but I didn't donate and thus am a bad person). When people feel it from two conflicting actions, beliefs, or identity, they generally change one of the items in conflict, create a justification for the action, or ignore or deny information that causes the conflict. This can happen in a matter of seconds, entirely at the subconscious or emotional level with no conscious cognition.[37]

The donor turns the dissonance back on the organization specifically or on giving generally. Instead of believing that they are a bad person by ignoring an appeal by a person, animal, or verdant place in need, they believe that the organization is doing a bad thing by appealing too much or in the wrong way. Clearly, this organization is not worthy of funds now. We move down a peg in the donor's estimation. Or, worse, the donor believes charities don't really need the money anymore. After all, the evidence is right in front of them.

In fact, 5.6% of lapsing donors say this pretty much verbatim: X organization no longer needs my support. Add in the 4.3% who said the organization asked for inappropriate sums, the 3.8% who found communications inappropriate, and the 2.6% who said the nonprofit didn't account for the donor's wishes and you have about a sixth of lapsing donors who are lapsing because of these communications.[38]

The pain that comes from turning down an appeal is the reason for a gulf of thinking between the fundraiser and the donor. It's a dangerous gulf and one not recognized or understood by conventional practice.

For the fundraiser guided by conventional practice, it is fine to send out 16 mailings, 36 emails, and four telemarketing campaigns asking for money and get 1.6 gifts per year. If donors renew their support at a rate in line with the stagnant or falling industry standards, you have more upgrades than downgrades, and can acquire more grist for the mill. Most fundraisers consider that a good day's work. If the donor doesn't want the appeal, they can trash/not answer it. Each appeal that doesn't work (allegedly) builds brand* and issue awareness and speeds the day the donor will give. Each snowflake in the avalanche pleads not guilty.

On the donor side, each unanswered appeal equals unwanted, unfulfilled brain chemicals and unnecessary psychic pain. Even if they throw it away, they can't just throw it away. When you actively solicit and receive feedback, you will see it in the comments. Donors conflate how many times they donate per year and how many times they should be solicited: "I give every June and December. Save your money and just mail me then."

Or, in other words, fundraisers think you must ask 50 times to get two gifts. Donors think you must ask two times.

Both are correct. Fundraisers look at truisms from the for-profit world like "you have to talk to someone nine times before they notice." We know if we were to tailor to the program to donor complaints, money would go out the door, followed shortly by us.

On the other hand, donors know their own behavior better than anyone else. They know this isn't the for-profit world. Nonprofit direct marketing has an even higher irritation rate than for-profit direct marketing.[39] This is likely since asking for something without individual benefit suggests an obligation on behalf of the recipient.[40] The fact that other people may need more communications doesn't sway them; they yearn to rise above the undifferentiated stew in which they've been placed.

Donors also use your communications as a proxy for how well their gift is being used. Some people read the acknowledgment letters and emails they receive and learn a little bit about where their gift has gone

---

* This is not true. Communications build brand for a while, then they build annoyance. Dutch charities found that a pulsing strategy of alternating heavy and off communications was optimal for managing this, stopping communication as soon as the brand versus irritation threshold was reached, from Naik, P & Piersma, N. (2002). Understanding the Role of Marketing Communications in Direct Marketing, from https://www.researchgate.net/publication/2496168_Understanding_the_Role_of_Marketing_Communications_in_Direct_Marketing. Note also the later discussion of the impact of reminder communications.

and what it is doing in the world. Unfortunately for many nonprofits, people also use the quantity and type of communications they receive to judge a nonprofit's effectiveness. People view excessive or inappropriate communications (for them) as a waste of money and thus as a proxy for what their donation is really doing. If your letter says they bought a mosquito net and your behavior says they bought 20 direct mail letters, which one are they going to believe?

Further, they make two leaps of logic: 1) everyone else is also receiving similar types or quantities of communications and 2) everyone else also dislikes getting communications in this quantity or medium. The first is an example of "availability bias" – people are swayed by, and extrapolate from, what is easily at hand and recalled. In this case, because communication schedules are not heavily segmented, it may also be true. Chances are if two donors are similar in amount and timing, they will receive similar communications.

The second is an example of the "other minds" problem. An important formative part of our development as children is figuring out that not everyone wants or likes the things that we want or like. The world is almost entirely other minds, each with their own different ways of thinking. Even once we have this insight, it's very difficult to put it into practice. One study indicates 18% of standup comedy routines and 37% of sitcom humor is based around our inability to understand the world from other people's points of view, most often centered around gender dynamics.

OK, I totally made that study up. But it feels true, no? We can watch the schlubby-looking guy and his implausibly attractive wife have a misunderstanding about the boss coming over for dinner and laugh because we see both points of view as an objective observer. Our Kevin-Jamesesque hero can't. He's in his own mind and can't understand someone else's.

We also laugh because we also identify with this. We are constantly guessing, and misguessing, what other people in our lives are thinking to our and their detriment. Even though we are trying to see things from their perspective, our starting point is our own mind. We then take that egocentric point of view and try to adjust that default to others. The better we know them, the more likely this is to be successful.[41]

In our case of the person who gets "a ton of mail pieces that I don't want – I give online," this person doesn't know other people at all. So all s/he can do is take her/his own point of view and multiply it by 100,000. Since this point of view is that they are receiving 18 mail pieces per year and they want six or three or one or zero, this person sees not only waste, but that waste is writ large.

The donor is not the only one with an "other minds" problem. You have it too. So do I. The goal of any donor is to make a difference in the world. As a nonprofit, you are making that difference for a donor. Our other mind problem is that we think we are communicating with acknowledgement letters and emails. However, when you are countering those thank-yous with communications that a constituent perceives as excessive or unnecessary, you may be turning them off from your organization.

This donor/donee gap is present -- and growing – as nonprofits work to volume their way into being relevant. This is a part of the cause of the crisis in fundraising, a crisis made no less dangerous by the fact that it is slow moving.

The way to close this gap is by following the guide of Seth Godin's two-decade-old formulation of permission marketing: creating communications that are personal, relevant, and anticipated.

Personal. The personalized and personal nonprofit's envelopes will be opened not for the free gift but for the joy they create and reinforce. Their emails will be read possibly for a nifty subject line, but mostly for a human connection. Their calls will be answered because they thank and thank well. Each communication is judged by whether it added to the well of the commitment each donor has to the organization and the mission.

Relevant. These wonderful donors are planting seeds. They are planting them so kids have a place to swing, so there is shade, so that people can breathe easier, or so we can have apples. But only one of these. Each donor has her own primary reason for giving. We owe it to the apple people to know they are in it for the apples. We owe it to them to avoid telling them about the tire swing or the shade if they don't care. Our story to them will be the deep moist flesh that children will pick from their tree and the juices that will stay on their cheeks until banished by a shirt sleeve. We will speak of shade to the shade people and tire swings to those who value kids on tire swings most.

Anticipated. We need to not just survive the winter; we must prevent winter for our long-term survival. We talk about converting people into the idea of giving. But our present tactics for acquiring donors aren't conducive to this; one does not ambush one's way into loyalty. Thus, like any healthy relationship-building exercise, we must build our efforts on enthusiastic consent.

This is not easy. Success depends on upending comfortable views of the universe:

- You can't always make more money with more communications.
- You can't only know donors by their actions.
- You can't permanently build on the sandy foundation that is interruption marketing.

The seven ages of direct marketing

We live in the seventh age of direct marketing. Once upon a time, the only customized marketing available was face-to-face (#1). For just a few coppers more, your horse could come with a saddle. This was discussed directly with your local equine merchant, who had no way of letting the rest of his* potential clients know about the free saddle deal (and reasonable financing options).

All other marketing was mass market, from the town crier or the newspaper with messages of the day ("LONDON STILL ON FIRE!"). No notices went specifically to the loyal customers of Gary's Olde Towne Tavern about the members-only happy hour. In other words, it

* Normally, I'd try to be gender neutral, but, in this timeframe, this is almost certainly a "his."

was a world with broadcast marketing, but no direct marketing other than face-to-face.

That changed when people got mail addresses (#2). Then phone numbers (#3). Then email addresses (#4). Each media and age started as something both completely mass market and completely individualized with nothing in the middle. In email, for example, your emails were either from your mom or from a wealthy Nigerian prince longing to give you a cut of the action.

We marketers branched out to cover the spectrum in between with segmentation, personalization, and modeling. In doing so, we increased our response and engagement.

This fourth age of addressability is where many nonprofits think the world lives. In fact, many of us are in denial about even this age. The only change in the denialists's control mail package is Dear [name]. The denialist's phone scripts ask for support for the same program regardless of what people have supported in the past. And because of time or tools available, the denialist will send the same emails to "everyone," ignoring histories of opening, donating, activism, or message interest. In many ways, they have taken the town crier's tactics and committed them to paper, phone wires, and fiber optic cables.

Time and tide wait for no cause. The fifth age came in the 90s, with cookies. The Web started like other media: a way to (slowly) get the same message as everyone else. Cookies changed the game: now a website could recognize the device accessing it and customize its experience based on what the device last did when it came to the site.

Cookies will only tell you what device has been on a Web site. This worked to address and adapt behavior when people had one main device for accessing the Internet. Now, we are awash in connectivity: desktop, laptop, work, home, tablet, phone, watch, game console, etc. Additionally, many of these devices are shared with another person.

Thus, in the fifth age, we expected a site would not know who we are when we switched computers. And we expected that we would see ads based on our loved ones' browsing histories, depersonalizing the online experience while easing Christmas shopping.

Today, our Facebook, Google, and Twitter logins follow us around the Web, ushering in the sixth age of addressability. These sites connect us to our browsing, our browsing to our email address, our email addresses to our relationships with people and organizations, and those relationships to customized experiences as we travel the Web device-agnostically.

In other words, online ads.

The seventh age is customized advertising across media. Netflix, Hulu, DirecTV, Spotify: all of them have your email addresses and robust knowledge of your preferences. Addressable advertising, which was a mere .1% of TV advertising in 2014, will be 13% this year.[42] I personally am excited about this. I'm a semi-avid football fan who does not drink beer and will never own a truck. Eighty percent of football advertising is wasted on me. It would be lovely to say to those companies "you save your money; I'll save my time" and part as friends.

When each of these media goes from general to direct marketing, our collective response shifts from excitement to interest to annoyance to numbed apathy.

The only way for sustained success is to create messages that apply directly to the recipient, rather than to an undifferentiated stew. These messages cut through the clutter. Personalization, customization, and differentiation start as novelties, transition to benefits, and end as requirements.*

As we enter the seventh age, nonprofits are still coming to terms with the second, third, and fourth addressability ages of mail, phone, and email. We even put up mental walls between channels. We think that anti-spam legislation online and opt-out abilities on the phone won't translate to people's thoughts about how they receive mail. Decreasing response rates across channels inspire us not to rethink our approach, but to try a different envelope color or subject line. Or, worse, we might

---

* My business school professors would ask that I describe this as: monovalent satisfier, then bivalent, then monovalent dissatisfier.

turn up the volume of our communications, substituting frequency for relevance.

So far, I've merely asserted that many people want fewer communications or different channels of communication. As I hope you'll see throughout this book, I'm a firm believer in "In God we trust. All others bring data." So where are the data?

DonorVoice looked at 27,000 pieces of feedback across a wide variety of nonprofits. Of these survey participants, 12,171 had free-response feedback. I personally read every single one of these and coded them to general categories of comments.*

Of these, the number #1 and #2 categories of substantive responses were that people were getting too many communications and that they were getting the wrong types of communications. These two items made up about 20% of all comments, making them the most common comments by a country mile.

Those who gave a reason fell almost entirely in three camps:

1. "I never asked for this." These were largely people whose relationship with the organization exists exclusively online. From their online profile, the organization then began sending them mail pieces and/or calling them. They never wanted these communications and didn't respond to them.

Mail removal requests were 81% of all channel removal requests, followed by phone at 16%, with email at 3%. Tellingly, the means of communication from which people wanted to be freed was directly related to whether they gave permission to start the communication channel and how easy it is to get off the communications channel. It's illegal to email someone without at least some level of consent; removing oneself is or should be as easy as clicking the link on the bottom. For phone, nonprofits will often phone append their file and

* This includes the nine people who said "I have no advice.", the three people who said "I have no advice. Thank you.", the four people who said "I have no advise.", and the person who said "I have no advised."

call donors without their channel consent but getting off the list is (or should be) as easy as saying "please put me on your do not call list."

For mail, however, nonprofits will often drop online constituents into the mail stream with neither notice nor consent.* One in, the mail stream is difficult to escape unless you write it on the reply device and find a stamp (that you pay for) or find the oft-hidden phone number buried somewhere on the organization's website. So mail rules the roost for removal requests.

2. "Why are you wasting your and, by extension, my money?" These folks are a variant on #1 – they didn't consent to be mailed or called – but with a twist. Because direct marketing is their primary communication vehicle with the nonprofit, they experience nonprofit waste. They may have the "other minds" issue. The tone of these comments is generally disappointed:

> "I don't need snail-mail reminders; email is fine. [Organization] doesn't need to waste paper and postage on me. Is there a way to be contacted by email ONLY?"

But sometimes pleading:

> "I am a committed [organization] donor. I regularly encourage others to donate to [organization]. Please stop sending me mailings. I will donate when I want to donate. Wasting paper and postage does not improve those odds. Please stop sending me mail! I am a teacher so my employer cannot match a donation. There is no reason to send me mailings. Please stop them! Please!"

3. "I tried, but this is too much." These are constituents who don't mind getting mail (comments here were almost all mail) – they mind

---

* In the United States, that is. Many of our European colleagues can't. U-S-A! U-S-A! U-S-A! (bald eagle screech) (firework explosion)

getting mail in what is to them an absurd amount. They were so turned off by the experience that they just wanted out of mail altogether.

You may say that you have this fixed by instituting mail codes and lines where people can call in to remove themselves. These are good and necessary, but they don't solve the problem. People are genuinely unhappy to be getting these communications. Here is a typical, unretouched response:

> "DO NOT SEND ME ANYTHING IN THE MAIL. PLEASE DO NOT. EVERY SINGLE TIME I DONATE I ALWAYS GET MAILERS. STOPPPPP!!!"*

And they vote with their wallets – many say they will stop donating if these undesired communications don't stop.

Most nonprofits are good about addressing these requests on a micro level as they come in – anyone who requests no mail gets no mail. However, most don't actively solicit this feedback and they don't address this feedback on a macro level by changing their solicitation practices to accommodate these comments.

One line in defense of these practices is for every person who voted against a communication by requesting to be taken off our list, dozens voted for it by clicking or donating. This would be compelling *except*:

1) We stack the deck by not actively soliciting feedback. A traditional mail solicitation makes it as easy as possible to make a gift: that's all the letter is about and all the reply device will accommodate. You naturally get more gifts than removals – that's what you are asking for. We actively discourage opting out.

2) The people who voice their displeasure are a small subset of the displeased. For every complaint an organization hears, another large number of people with a similar complaint stay silent.

---

* You can tell this person is serious because of the five Ps and three exclamation points. Would you even take this comment seriously if it only had two exclamation points or a mere four Ps?

From donors' perspectives, they are yelling that our present method of communication without representation is not satisfying them. Some are yelling it by not donating again. Others scrawl missives with all caps, poor spelling, and exclamation points galore!!!!!!! Others are yelling it over phone lines, which is why great donor relations people are worth their weight in gold.

Hopefully, this convinces you that unwanted communications irritate donors, some to the point of them not donating any more. But you may say our goal is not to make our donors happy. Our goal is to cure cancer. Or end drunk driving. Or prevent mistreatment of animals. Feed the hungry. Protect the abused. Light the fire of education. All this and more.

That said, to do these things, you need money. To get money, you need donors. To get and keep donors, you need your donors giving happily.

Thus, making our donors happy is a good goal. It's just not the end goal; if you had to choose between the mission and the donors, you should choose the mission. Thankfully, you don't have to make that choice. Permission-based marketing not only can make your donors happier, but also increase your revenues.

Reducing quantity

> *"The opposite of "more": It's not "less." If we care enough, the opposite of more is better."*[43]
>
> – Seth Godin

"What about our telemarketing program?" That was the big fear from a person who runs their nonprofit's telemarketing program: if we allow people to opt out of using the phone, could we kill our telemarketing program?

This is a natural fear. Asking people if they want to opt out means more people opting out. More people opting out means fewer people on list. Fewer people on list means less revenue.

So, permission-based marketing means less revenue. Q.E.D.

Significant flaws exist in this thinking, however. Most notably, t**he people opting out of a channel are not the people giving through that channel**. Some people will never give through their non-preferred channels. Never never never never never.

Think of the people you know. At least some of them – maybe even you – will not give through channel X for some reason. It could be they don't like their credit card information available on X. They may not know where their check book is.* They may think X is too costly or consumes too many other resources. They have their personal reasons. So do your donors.

This dislike goes beyond just communications that ask for money. One oft-recommended tactic is a thank you phone call, aimed at surprising and delighting your donors. Fundraisers predicted these calls would increase retention by 80%. The actual results were zero – no impact on retention over 500,000 thank you calls.† But that masks the real results. Those donors who had a positive interaction on the phone with the caller gave significantly more in the future; those who had a negative interaction gave significantly less if they give at all.[44]

What if you could take those who were going to have a negative reaction out of the channel? That is what encouraging donors to opt out of channels they don't want and into the ones they do does.

Taking those who don't like a channel out of it will cause your total number to fall, as you have fewer people receiving communications through that channel. But if someone doesn't like a channel, they are

---

* This one is me.

† It should be noted that these calls were 3-7 months after the gift and from telemarketers rather than senior staff. There is strong evidence that calls immediately after giving from nonprofit senior staff can increase retention overall, but the point still holds that these calls can turn off those who don't want them even if the calls are good in the aggregate.

unlikely to give through it. Thus, the people you are "losing" from the channel are of negative value to you in that channel. You are spending money to annoy them. An opt out can make you more efficient and increase net revenue.

So it's of benefit to you to have donors specify how they'd like to hear from you. How about how often they'd like to hear from you?

It's a bit heretical, but **less volume can sometimes mean more revenue.** How could fewer communications mean more net revenue? The trick is that every communication has some balance of persuading some people to make a gift and getting people who were already going to give to give to that communication. In fact, that balance is tilted toward the latter. Researchers found that 63% of a new mail piece's revenue isn't new revenue – it's cannibalized from the pieces around it.[45] In other words, if 37% of a new mail piece's revenue doesn't cover your costs, you are better off cutting the piece.

This is a conservative estimate based on European charities that mail less than once a month. Looking at a US charity that mails about twice a month, 75% of additional mail pieces' revenues weren't new revenues.[*] Thus, any mail piece with a standalone ROI less than 300% is a net loser for them.[†]

That's the simple illustration of how volume can cost you money. The more complex one is that you are turning off donors by communicating with them too frequently for their tastes, or through the wrong media.

Take the experiment done by one nonprofit with their new donors. That organization randomized their new donors to one of three conditions:

---

[*] How did we discover this? We ran a head-to-head test with two equivalent donor cohorts. One got fewer mail pieces. In the fewer-mail-pieces group, each of the mail pieces they did send got more revenue. We were able to track the revenue that should have been missing in a world where it was the mail piece that was doing all the work and compare it to the revenue difference that occurred.

[†] "Net loser" – also a description of my tennis game.

- No additional no-ask cultivation touches
- Six additional no-ask cultivation touches
- 12 additional no-ask cultivation touches

First, the obvious result—no one really wanted 12 additional cultivation touches. And looking at the aggregated data, no difference between no cultivation and six cultivation pieces appeared.

But wait! When these data were broken down by commitment level*, high-commitment donors had their retention go *down* by nine points when they got six additional communications versus none. They said things like, "Stop convincing me; I'm already convinced."

When we looked at low-commitment donors, the six additional communications corresponded to a 12-point increase in retention. These donors said things like, "I believe you do important work, but I actually don't know you well."[46]

Put another way, before this test, this nonprofit was paying extra money to *reduce* the chance that its best, most committed donors would donate again by sending them extra stuff they didn't want. (That's part of why it's so important to get feedback at point of acquisition, but I'm getting ahead of myself.)

Several organizations have proven you can reduce volume and increase revenues. One way is to change the program for everyone. The

---

* What do I mean by commitment? The term commitment is used in two different ways throughout this book. The first is the traditional concept of commitment: how much they care about the organization and how unlikely they are to leave.

The other is a measurement of this concept. DonorVoice asks three proprietary questions that it has found to be predictive of whether someone will stay or lapse. These are on a 0-10 scale. These are averaged for an index score, so a donor will have a Commitment Score on that 0-10 scale. Thus, in this case, "high-commitment donors" means donors whose Commitment Score is above the organizational average (and low-commitment donors have scores below the mean). This score is particularly useful in modeling which donors will stay with your organization.

Union of Concerned Scientists tested cutting their mail appeals from 12-15 per year to four. They:

- Had $8000 more in net income.
- Came within five percent on gross revenues.
- Had $2.60 higher average gift.
- Saved $32,000 in costs.
- Halved cost per dollar raised.
- Had $9.69 higher net income per donor.

Not only did net income go up in year one with a lower cost of fundraising, but they also improved the donor experience.[47]

Catholic Relief Services took a pilot group of 40,000 donors (against a control group of 40,000 donors of similar make-up) and tested decreased volume of both mail and emails by about 25-30%. Long story short, that reduced volume cadence became their control the next year because of its success.

In fact, with a 30% drop in email volume, their drop in online revenue was less than 2% – within the statistical margin of error.

That last 30% of their email communication volume gave them almost no additional value. Imagine what you could do with the extra time you save doing 30% fewer emails. My guess is it's better than "increase digital revenues by two percent."

A human services organization was challenged to mail 15% less and hit the same revenue numbers. The organization separated its donors into three tiers: one who could bear the most communications, one the least, and the remaining Goldilocks in between. From there, it was able to send its more marginal pieces only to its best donors and only its best pieces to its most marginal donors.

The organization didn't just stay where it was; it increased net revenue by 14% and decreased their cost to raise a dollar by 17%.[48]

You can probably, then, cut some volume and still increase your net revenue. The great news is that you may not have to cut volume across the board. By allowing your donors to call the tune, you can get rid of those people for whom volume, or an entire channel, is a waste. Considering that ten times more nonprofit professionals think we are communicating too little compared to the number of donors who think so, we can bridge this disconnect by asking for donor preferences.[49] So let's make an active effort to get people off your file who don't want to be there. This means asking how often, through what channels, and on what topics people want to get communications. Yes, you'll have fewer people on your file, but you'll be making them count for more.

Does this still hold true if you are a digital marketer? After all, contrary to mail or telemarketing efforts, almost everything you pay for in online direct marketing is a fixed cost. You need to buy an email platform, an online database, an advocacy platform, donation management, a content management system, etc. Once you have these things, they scale well with few marginal costs.

Thus, some online marketers are comfortable to pray and spray, counting on multiple emails to sway where quality of email does not. Similarly, if ads are cost-per-click or cost-per-acquisition, you can put out bad ads and wait for volume to save you.

These assumptions ignore the hidden marginal costs of online: time and attention. Time is the human resources you are putting into delivering and sending messages, which go up with the number of different messages that are going out. More importantly, the attention of your audience is a finite resource. Every time you deliver a message of importance to that person, you fill up that resource. Every time you deliver an irrelevant message, you draw from that well – until there's nothing left.

This does more than just burn that one constituent. Once upon a time, one could simply move to the next donor and try again. In the digital age, lack of response from one donor impacts your relationships with all your other donors.

When an email recipient repeatedly does not interact with (or even open) your emails, email providers are more likely to consider your emails less valuable for that person. If that happens with enough donors, those providers will consider your emails less valuable for all people.

I both am and am not talking about spam. I'm old enough to remember when Spam was a canned meat immortalized in a Monty Python song. Now, I know exactly what it is – sending emails that are unsolicited, misleading, or lacking an unsubscribe mechanism.

The problem is that is a legal and marketing definition. It is not the definition used by the people who receive our emails. A strong encapsulation of this is found in the book *Disrupted*, an account from a former journalist who then worked for Hubspot:

> "In training we're taught that the billions of emails that we blast into the world do not constitute *spam*. Instead, those emails are what we call 'lovable marketing content.' That is really what our trainers call it. That is the exact term they use. The convoluted logic behind this is that 'spam' means unsolicited email, and we only send email to people who have handed over their contact information by filling out a form and giving us their permission be contacted. Our emails might be unwanted, but they're not, strictly speaking, unsolicited, and therefore they are not spam.
>
> …
>
> To me this seems like complete bullshit. Of course we're creating spam. What else can you call it when you blast out email messages to millions of people?"[50]

To our end users, the careful distinction we make between spam and non-spam is non-existent. Or, rather, it exists in a different place for the marketee than the marketer. Just as beauty is in the eye of the beholder, spam is in the eye of the recipient: if it is a message I didn't want, it is spam.

Non-desired messages hurt your ability to reach your audience. That is bad. It's also the *better*-case scenario. The worse-case scenario is that constituents will hit the spam button (or whatever it is called on your platform of choice). If opt out provisions aren't visible, simple, and frictionless, constituents irritated by your communications will take this nuclear option. This blocks you from contacting this person. It also puts a black mark on your record for deliverability of other messages. Because you will not know you were marked spam, you will continue to send emails to a person who marked you as spam, which looks very much like the act of a spammer.

Once you have one email that triggers a spam filter for a donor, the more likely you are to go into that spam filter for that donor and to go to junk for other donors.

Deliverability is like trust – easy to lose, hard to gain back.

This has real impacts. A study by EveryAction[51] found that, in 2017, email providers filed more than 24% of nonprofit emails in the ol' circular filing cabinet as spam. This has a cost: the average nonprofit lost $29,613 to spam.

In fact, the study notes that for every one percent of your email going to spam (and every 100,000 names in your email file), you lose $1226. And most of this comes from indiscriminate use of email.

This volume of email is hurting responsiveness. Using M+R Benchmarks data[52], we find the more emails we send, the less people respond:

- Correlation between fundraising response rates and total number of emails you send: -.42.
- Correlation between fundraising response rates and total number of fundraising emails you send: -.42.
- Correlation between fundraising email click-through rates and total number of emails you send: -.42.
- Correlation between fundraising email click-through rates and total number of fundraising emails you send: -.47.

That's right. Increasing emails, and fundraising emails, correlates with decreases in engagement with those emails.

In M+R's email about these data, they say "Beyond a certain level, an overly-aggressive fundraising appeal schedule might cause supporters to turn away more than it encourages them to give." What these data show is that point isn't ahead of us; it's behind us.

But, you say, when I send a reminder email for end of year or a match or a deadline, I make more money. That's true in the short-term. One study showed that a reminder email increased revenue by 50%[53] (that is, the second email was half as effective as the first); another showed reminder emails were associated with a $2.18 increase in per donor revenue.[54]

That's not the whole story, however. The first study showed deadlines weren't effective and unsubscribes increased from the reminder email.[55] The second showed the real impact wasn't $2.18. The annoyance cost of the second email of lost future donations was $1.95, so organizations were making only $.23 in extra net revenue. And before you say "$.23 is still positive – I'll take the money," that was before researchers factored in the unsubscribers. Annoying people while giving them additional opportunities to unsubscribe leads to higher unsubscribe rates as surely as night follows day. When the loss of these constituents is factored in, the long-term impact of a reminder email is negative.[56]

Let me repeat that, centered, in bold, in its very own separate line, because it's important:

The long-term impact of a reminder email is negative.

Or, as the authors put it (emphasis mine):

> "The increasing volume of reminders, fueled by the encouraging results of previous studies, creates heretofore unanticipated costs for both receivers and senders. **A one sided and short-term analysis based solely on the intended behavioral outcome, as is common today, can lead to negative surprises in the long-run.** We encourage academics and policy makers to pay more attention to overall welfare effects."

And

> "It is easy to see that the higher the personal benefit of the reminder and the smaller the cost of the prompted action, the larger the utility from the reminder, irrespective of the potential annoyance costs. However, high frequency or very pushy reminders create a welfare diminishing cost even in these settings. Unfortunatcly, our data is not rich enough to estimate the optimal frequency of solicitations. Nevertheless, our model is the first inattention model that theoretically shows that **there is a limit to the amount of reminders** and thus provides a first step towards determining optimal frequencies."[57]

Thus, we turn away more donors and donations with our appeal schedules than we are picking up with them.

So how have nonprofits been able to have consistent online revenue growth? By growing our lists:

Year-over year change	Revenue	List growth
2011	14%	20%
2012	19%	21%
2013	21%	20%
2014	14%	22%
2015	13%	21%
2016	19%	16%
2017	14%	10%
2018	23%	15%

All told, online revenue increased 252%; online lists grew 277%; per constituent revenue dropped. That means increased email volume wasn't driving our recent revenue growth. (That's also why we'll later talk about lead generation.)

In email, as in mail, as in every other channel, we can't volume our way into being interesting. That's why we should be working to make sure our communications are anticipated (and desired). We should ask these preferences at point of acquisition and frequently thereafter to allow our donors to change our relationship.

So far, we've talked about permission-based marketing as avoiding negatives: annoyance to the donors, costs for us. A permission-based system also has active benefits: changes in consumer desires, changes in regulation, and the benefits from better data. We will cover these, hopefully persuading you to move as far as is practical from a permission system of benign (or malignant) neglect (opt-out) to opt-in practices.

Consumer desires

> *"Over time, all marketing strategies result in shitty clickthrough rates."*[58]
>
> – Andrew Chen's *Law of Shitty Clickthroughs*

In the seven ages of direct marketing, customers respond to a new form of marketing with excitement. Think how excited the villagers were to get the Wells Fargo wagon in *The Music Man*[59] compared to how excited you are to get the mail today. Or banner ads, the first of which had a **78% clickthrough rate**. Or early search engines, which could be hacked by repeating the text you wanted to have indexed over and over in the same color as the background.

The Law of Shitty Clickthroughs above shows this progress with any new medium or channel. Looking at banner ads as an example, two researchers asked users to find a piece of information on a web site. They randomized users to receive the information in text links or banner ads. When the information was presented as a banner ad, users were less likely to find it. When they did find it, it took longer on average. The researchers referred to this as "banner blindness."[60]

What's remarkable isn't that this happened; it's that the study is from 1998. The banner ad went from exciting to tuned out in four years.

People have only gotten better at ignoring ads: people even ignore sections of sites that look like ads or are next to ads.[61] The lesson here is if you ever need to hide a dead body, put it in a display ad. Our selective attention – the thing that allows us to hear our name from across a crowded room – largely tunes out the noise that is online advertising. One must be extremely focused on the ad recipient to get the click.

We start delighted ("You've Got Mail!"), then go to satisfied ("You've Got Mail.") to apathetic ("I've Got Mail?"). Sometimes, sentiment takes an additional step – from apathetic to hostile. This is especially true when the medium seems to be abused: impersonal, irrelevant, and without consent.

This hostility can be codified. (Here, I'm referring to legal code, although the use of adblocking software is another form of codification of norms against interruption marketing.) In the United States, 2003's Do-Not-Call Implementation Act and CAN-SPAM* curtailed the ways marketers could legally reach out with unsolicited phone calls and emails, respectively. Every year, state legislatures grapple with similar legislation for mail, failing largely because a non-governmental solution to opt-out of unwanted mail pieces already exists at DMAChoice.org. The trend is not our friend, however, with California leading the way to restrict both data and voice.

The reaction from Europe has been even stronger. One aspect of the much-discussed GDPR (General Data Protection Regulation) from the European Union is consent withdrawal. Once you have consent to communicate with someone through a channel or a pre-existing relationship with them, you need to be able to remove that consent swiftly. The consequences for non-compliance are up to 4% of your annual revenue or $22 million, whichever is greater, which would be a death knell for a great many organizations.

---

* CAN-SPAM stands for Controlling the Assault of Non-Solicited Pornography And Marketing. One wonders whether pornographers or marketers were more insulted by the implied equivalence.

People don't want to be interrupted by marketing and especially not by marketing that they didn't sign up for or isn't specific to them. That's the downside.

The upside is that the reverse is also true. Asking for channel preferences *increases* the likelihood of getting a donor. In two studies of what causes people to opt in, DonorVoice found donor communications control is the single biggest factor in whether someone will want to learn more from you. The more you let a person control, the more likely they are to become a constituent.

But wait (as the infomercial implores): there's more! In a joint study by DonorVoice and the DMA Nonprofit Federation, allowing donors control of their communications made them happier to donate.

Donors who give you their communications preferences are also worth more. In case after case, people using mail codes are more likely to donate and to give at a greater amount. The National Committee to Preserve Social Security and Medicare coded people who requested less mail and sent them half as many appeals as those who stated no preference. Those donors who requested – and received – half as many contacts gave more than the group that didn't express a preference.[62] Catholic Relief Services (CRS) found that donors who requested a specific mail preference gave 6-8 times more per year.

Granted, this may not be causal. That is, CRS didn't increase the *value* of their donor 6-8 times more by getting them to state a preference. Rather, it may be higher value donors who naturally give you their communications preferences. After all, they are the most engaged with you.

Think of the time and treasure you spend on figuring out who are your most valuable donors. By asking for preferences and honoring them, you not only identify those quality donors – you make them more likely to stay by listening and acting to serve them. Despite this being a benefit to both the donor and the organization, only ten of the top 100 nonprofit organizations (revenue-wise) ask for channel preferences upon email sign-up as of 2018.

The perils of external data

We have a phantom member of our family.

When my wife and I moved into our first house, one of the people who sold us the house was Kimberly-something. We immediately started getting mail for Kimberly Ellinger – her first name, our last. Our best guess is that a mailer assumed she either got married or divorced, changing her last name to the one that was now on the house.

That was 2003: five residences, three states, and two jobs ago. During that time, no one named Kimberly Ellinger ever sent in a donation, mailed back a comment card, or bought something through the mail. Because she doesn't exist. Never has.

But she followed us on all these moves. She loves Land's End catalogs. She clearly needs car insurance. She donates to animal and park nonprofits. She gets her AARP card yearly. And goodness help us, I think someone thought she registered to vote. She's more popular with politicians than my wife and I are. And I should stress this: we are real; Kimberly is not.

Clearly, this is bad data. But if you think the worst thing that bad data can do is run up your costs, au contraire, mon petit escargot.*

In 2014, a man received a letter from OfficeMax that was addressed to his name, with the second line of the address reading "Daughter Killed In Car Crash."

Yes, a year earlier, his daughter had in fact been killed in a car crash.

Both of these stories are emblematic of a third-party data ecosystem that aspires to signal, but delivers mostly noise. A July 2018 report from Deloitte looked at commercially available data. Considering the title of the report is *Predictably Inaccurate*[63], you can likely guess what's coming, but even I, a third-party data cynic, was boggled:

- 59% of people judged their data-broker data to be 50% or less accurate for demographic data, even for simple, easily available

* I should mention I don't speak French.

data like date of birth, marital status, and # of adults in household.

- 84% of people said data-broker data was 0-50% correct about their economic data. So beware that wealth append you just did.
- 75% said their vehicle data was over half incorrect, including 44% who said it was zero percent correct. (Consider that, in the United States, 22% of cars are white, 40% of all vehicles are SUVs, and 14% are Fords. Thus, if I guessed you drove a white Ford SUV, I'd only be completely wrong 40% of the time. Let me know if you want to hire me as a third-party data broker).

Cars aren't the only category where you'd want me to be your data broker. Less than 20% of people said their number of children was correct. Yet, 41% of mothers have two children[64] (yes, this assumes the person has children, but even correcting for this, you'd be better off guessing two than using a data broker).

The report is worth reading if only for some of the free responses, which include the gems:

> "It said I was single (I am married), I have no children (I have six), and I vote Democrat (I often vote Republican)."

And

> "If my data is representative, this seems pretty useless."

Most third-party data brokers are drawing from the same well, especially the data provided by the big three credit reporting agencies. So you can see exactly how accurate third-party data is for you at aboutthedata.com from Acxiom. (You do have to register, but what's the worst that could happen in the safe hands of one of the big credit reporting agencies?[*])

Mine says I:

- Have half the number of children I do.
- Vote for the other major political party.
- Have the date of my house purchase right, but number of years in the house wrong.[†]
- Am in the market for female apparel (those who have seen my sartorial stylings know I don't even spend on **male** apparel).
- Don't donate to anything but political causes (a bunch of nonprofits would be surprised by this…).
- Like cooking magazines (the International Criminal Court is split on whether my cooking constitutes a crime against humanity).
- Love gardening and crafts – doing them, reading about them, buying stuff for them. Gardening and crafts are on a very short list I have called "things I'm worse at than cooking."

All demonstrably untrue. And yet these are the things we are feeding into our models. One cannot expect to put garbage into a model and not get garbage out.

How did big data get so polluted? The report covers that as well:

- Outdated information that isn't worth the cost of updating.
- Incomplete information that isn't worth the cost of completing.
- Incorrectly collating multiple data sources.
- Incorrect inferences (think of what happens to your Amazon recommendations when you forget to mark something as a gift).
- Incorrect models.

---

[*] Don't answer that.

[†] This very minor error seems the most emblematic of third-party issues to me. They have the day I closed on my house. But rather than do the subtraction, they have a separate field in a database somewhere that only gets updated every so often.

- Corruption by malicious parties.

Allow me to summarize these reasons: **lack of financial incentives to do better**.

Most models are black boxes. You put your donors/constituents in, you get a score out. Easy peasy lemon squeezy. And when we get it wrong, we don't know because the constituent who starts getting ads in Spanish or honor/memorial solicitations doesn't care enough to report back that they haven't lost a loved one or spontaneously learned a new tongue. I know because I get both these ads from nonprofits. For most nonprofits, it's Good Enough.

So this is a peek into how the sausage is made. Turns out some Upton-Sinclair-level* stuff is going on back there. And it has real emotional impacts. (A warning to those who have had a stillborn child – you may want to skip down to the bolded line a couple of pages from now.)

Gillian Brockell knows this pain first-hand. Her son, Sohan Singh Gulshan, was stillborn. Her story:

> "let me tell you what social media is like when you finally come home from the hospital with the emptiest arms in the world, after you and your husband have spent days sobbing in bed, and you pick up your phone for a few minutes of distraction before the next wail. It's exactly, crushingly, the same as it was when your baby was still alive. A Pea in the Pod. Motherhood Maternity. Latched Mama. Every damn Etsy tchotchke I was considering for the nursery.

---

* A British colleague warned me this reference does not survive the Atlantic. For those who never had Mr. Gunn's American History class, Upton Sinclair was an investigative journalist in the early 20th century. This specific reference is to his book *The Jungle* that documented practices in the meatpacking industry, including some workers being ground up with other animal parts.

> And when we millions of brokenhearted people helpfully click "I don't want to see this ad," and even answer your "Why?" with the cruel-but-true "It's not relevant to me," do you know what your algorithm decides, Tech Companies? It decides you've given birth, assumes a happy result and deluges you with ads for the best nursing bras (I have cabbage leaves on my breasts because that is the best medical science has to offer to turn off your milk), DVDs about getting your baby to sleep through the night (I would give anything to have heard him cry at all), and the best strollers to grow with your baby (mine will forever be 4 pounds 1 ounce).
>
> And then, after all that, Experian swoops in with the lowest tracking blow of them all: a spam email encouraging me to "finish registering your baby" with them (I never "started," but sure) to track his credit throughout the life he will never lead."[65]

She also talks about how a system smart enough to divine that she was expecting should have been able to turn this off. She searched for things like "baby not moving." She posted an update with keywords like "stillborn" and "heartbroken."

But knowing someone is pregnant and/or has had a baby is profitable. Less profit exists in knowing they are not and have not. It's the same reason that Siri started out directing people who said they wanted to shoot themselves to the nearest gun store, not a suicide hotline. A machine programmed for commerce delivers commerce.

Even when Brockell figured out how to turn off parenting ads, she got adoption ads, another round in the meat grinder.

I can't claim to know her pain – we all grieve differently. But I knew and loved Gwendolyn Annette Ellinger. She too came into this world stillborn. This was many years ago, before ads were so personalized. But that didn't stop every ad from feeling designed to trigger me, replete as ads are with happy, smiling, healthy children.

I remember watching these ads in our living room, staring vaguely at the TV and vaguely at the wall, crying as a wall clock ticked off the seconds.

Later, as part of my healing process, I beat that noisy clock to death with a hammer.

I can't imagine how much more painful it would have been if advertisers had thought I was in the baby market and bidding eagerly to show me cribs. Passive consumption was bad enough, where every snowflake in the avalanche can plead plausible deniability. Active targeting must be excruciating.

This doesn't happen in a permission-based, first party data system. If you require, and get, an opt in, you won't mail Kimberly Ellinger repeatedly. If you base your customization on data users give you willingly for that purpose, you also won't remind people of one of the worst days in their lives. The Kimberly Ellingers of the world show that current donor-centrism is ineffective. If we pay, pray, and spray at someone who doesn't exist, what hope do those of us who do exist have?

Another reason these third-party data are largely wrong is, as consumers, we don't want them to be right. In the Deloitte study mentioned earlier, only 37% of people who found something wrong in their data-broker data corrected it. People preferred their data to remain private or they didn't care about getting it right. Two great open-ended responses from the study:[66]

> "I like that the info is wrong. It might save me from certain types of mailings…"

And

> "I'm skeptical and cautious about what could be done with this data. Even assuming the best of intentions and integrity by people who might consume this data, I

> cannot imagine a scenario that would also be in my or my family's best interest. I would actually prefer less personal information about me to exist publicly. So, obscure, inaccurate, or unreliable data is what I consider to be the next best thing."

The best-case scenario is that people think these data don't matter; the worst-case is that they are angry you have them without their consent. Clearly (he said sarcastically) this is the type of data you want to be using.

The idea that people are gathering data on you without your knowledge or consent seems creepy, even when the data are relatively benign. So some push back against our abilities to use these data. For example, Apple is under fire from advertisers for blocking cookies on its mobile devices and Safari browser. While there is a debate on this, since Apple doesn't make its money from ads and two of its largest competitors do, I'll wager the debate won't change Apple's mind.

This means that remarketing, open rate data, and personalization within our websites won't work (in many cases) on these devices and browsers.

This isn't just online, nor is it just for for-profits. Where rage and apathy mingle, as they do in privacy debates, politicians cannot be far behind. Large British charities like RSPCA and the British Heart Foundation have been fined for "snooping" on their donors.[67] Their crime: doing a wealth append to their donor file. That is, they were fined for using external third-party data. Broader EU-level discussions have come to the same end.[68]

Here in the US, wealth appending is a common-ish practice. (We tend to believe that if you outlaw wealth appends, only outlaws will append wealth data.) But in culturally similar countries, donors were so angry about this practice, they banned it. It is cold comfort to know as you purchase your third-party data appends that what you are doing is not illegal *yet*.

Not only must we gird against this coming to the United States, but we must also remember we have European folks on US distribution lists.

Thus (while I am a not a lawyer and this is not legal advice) we are subject to these regulations as we send out fundraising appeals.

We must prepare for a future without these external data. The safeguard is data that is personal to your organization and provided by the donor.

This means cultivating your own data garden. Places like Facebook are called walled gardens. You can play all you want in the garden while you are there, but everything stays in the garden. From a marketer's perspective, however, Facebook is more like a Roach Motel: data checks in, but it doesn't check out.

It's not just Facebook. Try to use the major ad platforms nowadays. To get your results, you must give them any data you want to build into the model. They combine it with second, third, and ninth-party data* and eye of newt to create your model, then use it with no visibility into the inner workings. Imagine having to show up at a restaurant with raw chicken thighs, sea salt, and fennel. The cooks then tell you how good the meal they cooked with it was.

In addition, all the data you don't bring to the table – second and third-party data – can be used by anyone using the platform. Thus, if you work at the Loving Shephard Foundation, your mortal enemies at the Shoving Leopard Foundation can work from the same hymnal as you. Competitions are not won with common resources and common models; differentiators must be different.

The answer doesn't lie in welcoming our new data overlords. It can be found by asking your donors for information about themselves.

At this point, two objections usually present themselves: "Aren't we going to turn off people by asking them questions?" and "What about people who don't answer?"

---

* Ninth-party data, as defined by the classic Ferris Bueller's Day Off: "My best friend's sister's boyfriend's brother's girlfriend heard from this guy who knows this kid who's going with the girl who saw Ferris pass out at 31 Flavors last night. I guess it's pretty serious."

To the first, witness how much people hate when you get this *without* their consent. The alternative is dire.

But it is still a concern. That's why donor questions must be asked within the right context. The book *Factfulness* had an interesting tale about this very issue:

> "I was interested to know whether some STDs were more common in some income groups, and so I asked them to include a question about income on their forms. They looked at me and said, 'What? You can't ask people about their incomes. That is an extremely private question.' …
>
> Some years later, I met the team at the World Bank who organized the global income surveys and I asked them to include questions about sexual activity in their survey. … Their reaction was more or less the same. They were happy to ask people all kinds of questions about their income, the blank market, and so on. But sex? Absolutely not."[69]

Context matters. People expect a gynecologist to ask about sex, not money. People expect economists to ask about money, not sex. People know approximately how each question is going to be used.

Likewise, people expect a charity to ask what their favorite charity is. Further, questions that assess commitment, satisfaction, why they give, and preference all benefit the donor. If a donor lets you know your donation form is nearly unusable, they presume they might not have to go through it again. Asking you to contact them by email instead of by mail may relieve their clogged mailbox. Telling you about why they give means they may not be asked to support something irrelevant.

If you are asking questions to customize donors' experiences with your organization and can show that as a benefit, your response will be higher. And even those who don't answer won't take offense that you asked.

You can also get this information by giving donors something of value for it. This value can be information and content – we'll talk about this more later – but we must show value. People's information is like any other resource; like labor or time, people will trade it for resources.

This is a different view of privacy than is sometimes taken. Often, privacy is thought of as a categorical no-no: people will let you in only so far, but no farther regardless of the remuneration. But that belief just isn't so.

In 2014, a Danish travel agency saw the statistics – birth rates were at a 27-year-low. Danes were not reproducing at a rate sufficient to replenish the population. They also saw surveys: 46% of people do more special hugging whilst on vacation. Ten percent of Danes were conceived on vacations.

And so the "Do It for Denmark" campaign was born.* The message was simple: more travel, more hugging, more Danes.

Wait, there's more. You could get a discount on your travel if you (or your travel partner) were ovulating during your trip. And were conception to happen, you could win three years of baby products and a family-friendly vacation.

What about customer retention? How about a "Do It Forever for Denmark Loyalty Program"? The more Danes you made, the bigger discounts you got.

The Danish National Statistics Bureau reported births increased 14% year-over-year in 2015.

So now when someone in your organization worries "will people answer that?", you can answer that you can get almost any information with the right incentives. After all, for a discount on travel and an opportunity to win some diapers/nappies, Danish people gave up their ovulation schedules. And they gave up when they got down.

---

* There are no footnotes for this because many of the sites that talk about this do so with pictures and details. Feel free to Google. I recommend the incognito browser.

This will always, however, be incomplete. What about those tricky people who don't answer additional questions? Not everyone will answer despite your best efforts.

That non-answer is itself an answer. Donors who don't answer surveys have consistently lower retention rates. Of course, that could just be because people who don't answer surveys don't get customized appeals. Thankfully, this has been studied without this variable with the donors of DonorsChoose.org, a crowdfunding site for classroom projects across the United States.* The site asks for additional, optional personal information. This variable turned out to be very predictive of donor value and future giving. Those who gave additional information had a first-year retention rate of 37% and an average gift of $61. Those who didn't had a retention rate of 14% and an average gift of $43.[70] Put simply, someone less willing to tell you about their interests is far less likely to donate again.†

Now, this is correlation, not causation. The authors can't say, and I won't opine, whether getting additional information from a person caused them to return or both additional information and retention are caused by some other variable.

But that's also irrelevant. Think how much effort you put into knowing which donors are more likely to retain. You are likely paying for at least one solution right now that purports to have a glimpse at this answer. It could be a list co-op, an external modeling firm, or even RFM analysis. If you aren't paying for modeling, you are paying by not having modeling. Whether someone gives additional information is highly predictive and thus is a valuable add to your models. It's also a datum that no one else will have; thus it can be a source of competitive advantage.

---

* Because nothing says "functional democracy" like teachers having to rattle a can to afford textbooks.

† The study defines disclosing personal information as uploading a picture, disclosing location, or both.

So, we know that the right questions in the right context will be answered and those who don't answer questions are less valuable anyway. These data are also a defense mechanism. Get them from the horse's mouth and you won't have to pay for them and can't be regulated away from using them.

They also have the advantage of being 99% accurate (one must allow a bit for user error). If Facebook says someone is interested in environmental causes or interior design or cinema of the Ukraine, they are X% certain that is true. X is close enough to 100% that people will pay to target that segment and not a percentage point more. As we've seen, it matters more whether it makes money than whether it causes emotional distress.

But if people say they are interested in environmental causes, it's true. They won't mind if you target them based on that information – they gave it to you.

No longer does the cynical Golden Rule – those who have the gold rule – hold sway. Those who have the *data* rule, because they charge gold for it and even those with gold need it. You need to own the constituent, the relationship, and the information about the constituents that makes them valuable and allows you to speak to them like they want to hear from you. And thus you must be a strategic accumulator of data, lest you have to sign a check and say "mother, may I" to communicate effectively.

The solution

> *"Privacy means people know what they're signing up for, in plain English, and repeatedly. I'm an optimist; I believe people are smart, and some people want to share more data than other people do. Ask them. Ask them every time. Make them tell you to stop asking them if they get tired of your asking them. Let them know precisely what you're going to do with their data."*[71]

– Steve Jobs

Picture if, for some reason, you had to tell donors the truth.

Stamped on your reply envelope, or in your telemarketing script, or on your donation form, you had to print the following:

- When you donate, you will receive somewhere between zero and literally hundreds of communications per year.
- These communications could be through your original channel of communication or others if we can get the data appends.
- We won't tell you what you will get in advance. You will not be asked if it's what you want.
- Once you start getting communications, your ability to change will be minimal and rarely, if ever, solicited.
- We will gather information on you from third parties, append it to your record, and use it to build models about you.
- We will divine your interests from your actions and from third-party data rather than asking you for explicit preferences.
- Your contact information will be rented to or exchanged with other organizations both individually and en masse through co-ops.

My guess is your response rate would drop. If donor ignorance is what you are relying on, it's time to rethink your business model.

Happily, giving donors a measure of control over their communications makes people significantly more likely to want to opt-in – usually by a 2:1 margin or more. In fact, it's the most important factor in whether they wish to opt in. People prefer to choose channel(s) over frequency, but either is better than nothing. Additionally, this can be a sequential ask – finding out in what channels someone wants to hear from you, then (in that channel) asking about frequency or topic selection.

This is how, as mentioned, the National Committee to Preserve Social Security and Medicare and Catholic Relief Services found those more valuable donors specifying their donor preferences. Let's zoom out and look at an organization that is substantially wagering on permission-based marketing.

In January 2017, Oxfam took a new step in Europe with an app allowing donors to control their donations. This acknowledges a characteristic of donors not often discussed: they change. The people who thought they wanted your mail newsletter realize after three issues it's not their cup of tea. Or the people who liked your acknowledgement so much they are now willing to try you out on email. They get married and/or divorced. They move. They have children. They die. They want to increase, decrease, or end their monthly gift. The app allows Oxfam to change with the donor.

This isn't the only feature. The app allows the donor to move their monthly gift up, down, or off. It tracks all the donor's giving, translating donating of items to currency and translating donating of currency to impact. And, of course, it allows the donor to give, sometimes in ways she may not have considered.

In this way, Oxfam is taking a cue from so many service operations. I remember two decades ago in business school* debating how and whether things like automated airline ticket kiosks, electronic banking, and self-service grocery checkouts would take off. As we students hypothesized, if both parties don't want to be in an interaction, it is better automated.

For picayune details, you don't want to have to deal with a donor services representative, as lovely as these professionals are.† You would prefer the organization just *know* that you throw all the mail away, that it was a typo when you entered your name as Robret, or that you live somewhere else now. To contact donor services is a cost of time, effort, and mental energy that you will undertake only if the other costs (e.g.,

---

* For those trying to divine my current age, remember I graduated business school at age nine.

† Any implied comparison between these fine folks and airline customer services, bank tellers, and grocery checkers is entirely disavowed.

binning your mailed missive along with the car insurance offers, pretending Robret is your code name, not hearing from you again) are more painful. Often, they aren't. If you can open an app, perhaps they are.

But, you say, I can't do an app like this because (pick one or more):

- I don't have an Oxfam-like budget. I squeeze a nickel until Thomas Jefferson begs for mercy.
- My board is so bad at technology, they think Android was in Star Wars: Episode VIII.[72]
- I fear syncing anything else with my database, because the difference between trying to get an effective database sync and my last highly invasive gender-specific medical procedure is that the medical procedure is over.
- Other reasons, both compelling and "compelling."

You don't need to create a separate app to give your donors some influence over how they interact with you. It can be something you have on your web site, where someone can see their donations and make these types of changes. This was frequently requested in our donor feedback research but infrequently done.

As for cost, let's look back at the automatic ticket kiosk at the airport. This technology takes care of the mundane items so that fewer people can focus on more specialized inquiries and on adding additional value. Same for this. How large would your donor services team have to be if people could take care of their own basic inquiries?

Or, if you kept donor services at its current size, how much else could they be doing to cater to your higher value donors? After all, a donor services rep who is changing an address for a $10 mail donor is one who is not talking to a monthly donor about their satisfaction and whether they would like to increase their gift amount. And vice-versa.

Or you can ask with some frequency in their medium of choice. Whether you create an Oxfam-like app, or a donor services center online, or are just diligent about asking and respecting donor preferences, the key to getting to this point isn't budget or time. It's the will to do so. It needs to be something you need to do.

Many direct marketers worry about what happens when donors can customize their communications: will donors select options that diminish or eliminate their giving? As we've seen, the research evidence says the reverse: people are more likely to donate when they have an active role in communications. You can give that to them and create a permission-based marketing organization.

You may argue those organizations that have gone to permission-based marketing at the behest of the EU's General Data Protection Regulation (GDPR) or similar privacy regulations have seen file sizes and revenues drop. I would agree. However, this is a reason to embrace permission marketing before it is mandated, rather than under the gun.

Why you want to do this voluntarily instead of by mandate

GDPR, and the response from the charity sector in the UK and EU, has often been muddled. Some believe that compliance means that everyone needs to have opted-in; others use "legitimate interest" as a reason to keep contacting their supporters.

Those who chose an opt-in framework often choose unwise methods and messages to re-recruit donors, making it hard for donors to opt in and suppressing response rates. As file sizes waned and deadlines for GDPR compliance approached, charities become ever more panicked to gain that elusive tick in their opt-in box. As a result, a regulation that was intended to diminish unwanted communications caused people to be deluged with more and more communications as compliance day drew closer. Anyone who could not have predicted unintended consequences from legislation has no knowledge of governments, or works in government, or both.

Increasing volume is one thing many nonprofits do when they have a communication problem. The other is to think about the nonprofit's needs and desires, forsaking the donor's needs and desires. Consider this GDPR message received by a colleague of mine:

> "We would love to continue to keep in touch with you by mail, phone, email, SMS, and other electronic means to let you know about our latest news, events, education, awards and other benefits. Please be assured that we will treat your information with the utmost care and will never sell it to other companies for marketing purposes. And, you can ask us to stop at any time."

It continued in that manner for a while. I defy any reader to guess which organization sent this. My guess is even if the person who wrote it is reading this, they don't recognize it because they thought they released version 17 with the legal department's proviso that we might also want to contact people by fax, telegram, or carrier pigeon.

It lacks any expression of why my colleague would care. Yes, the organization wants to keep in touch with her. Presumably, it would like to keep in touch with all people through all channels. But why would she want them to keep in touch with her? On this, the message is silent.

Those who have gone to opt-in only have seen significant bumps in the road. Cancer Research UK found that telephone fundraising had sub-10% opt-in rates. Mail was at 20% and email was at 45% (presumably because most emails are already obtained through opt in).[73] These low rates were the result of trying to go opt-in on a timeline and trying to compensate through volume (they deployed 150+ different communications).[74] They also didn't embrace legitimate interest for communications; if someone has been a mail donor for 20 years, they are likely OK with the channel.

The picture I hope you are seeing is that government-led permission marketing systems can be messy and operate on artificial timelines. Those not already covered by this regulatory regime give you the advantage of creating your own rubric. For example, you may determine that anyone who has donated to you twice or more by mail should receive mail. You'll of course give the donor copious clear ways to opt out – by ticking a box, using your app, going to your web site, etc.

– and continually checking in with her. But you have a legitimate reason to believe this person wants to receive this communication.

On the other side of the coin, new donors are… well… new. You can start with a clean slate and operate off an entirely permission-based opt-in system for communication media, frequency, and topic preference. Over time, those in the old system will age out of your file and you will have transitioned into an opt-in system gently.

The goal, then, is to start now. You can start small or start big, but the more you meet your donors on their terms with their permission, the more you will raise from them, the more of them you will have, and the more you will differentiate yourself from those who do not.

You want your donors to love you. No good love story happens without mutual consent.

The preferred nonprofit: Going deeper, not wider

The tragedy of the commons

> *"Adding together the component partial utilities, the rational herdsman concludes that the only sensible course for him to pursue is to add another animal to his herd. And another; and another... But this is the conclusion reached by each and every rational herdsman sharing a commons. Therein is the tragedy. Each man is locked into a system that compels him to increase his herd without limit--in a world that is limited. Ruin is the destination toward which all men rush, each pursuing his own best interest in a society that believes in the freedom of the commons. Freedom in a commons brings ruin to all."*[75]
>
> – Garrett Hardin

For years, the conventional wisdom counseled frequent communication without consent through all available channels as an effective practice. Why? Because people mostly give when asked. Therefore, we should ask them repeatedly to get them to give more. This speaks to a clear confusion between necessary and sufficient conditions: it is necessary for people to be asked to give; it isn't sufficient.

It also forgets that our donors are human. What can be a bombardment of the physical mailbox and virtual mailbox, leaves donors feeling they must defend themselves against appeals.

People who get a greater number of solicitation requests say they:

- Write down when they gave to a charity last.
- Try to find out when last they gave before donating.

- Limit their giving to charities of a certain type.
- Put the "maybe" solicitations in a box or pile for later reference.

The more mail they get, the more they agree with the statement "I feel I must protect myself from the mail I get from charities." This cumulative exposure to nonprofit appeals erodes donors' likelihood of donating.[76]

Perhaps you think I'm being melodramatic when I say donors want to protect themselves, despite drawing here from a research study called "Defensive Responses to Charitable Mail Solicitations."[77] Listen to some actual donor statements in interviews with the University of Kent:[78]

> "Somehow or other your name gets on a list and you are bombarded. It's amazing what comes through the door, and you've got no means of making an objective judgement."

> "I'm afraid what I do now is say I've selected the charities to which I'm contributing, and I'm not adding to my list."

> "It's just an impossible amount of stuff [that comes through the door] and I couldn't possibly support them all, even though I'm sometimes sympathetic to the requests."

> "It's a bit like when you get 500 applications for a job and you've got to find some way of weeding it down to a manageable number."

> "I'm not rich enough to be able to support every cause that I approve of."

These are the comments from people who are being solicited by more charities than they wish. *Moreover, these are the people who continue to give.* One must imagine those who have said a plague on all our houses would be even more salty.

This might be forgivable if it were a net positive. However, as I mentioned earlier, 63% percent of revenues from a new mail piece are cannibalized from the mail pieces around it from that organization, meaning that only 37% of a new mail piece's revenue is new to the organization.

An additional 10% of mail revenue isn't new revenue to the sector; rather, it is cannibalized from other organizations in the sector. Thus, only 27% of a new mail piece's revenue are new to nonprofits generally.[79]

This is the tragedy of the commons. Between 27% and 37%, an organization has an incentive to add a mail piece because it increases their net revenue and where that mail piece <u>decreases</u> the overall net revenue for the sector. Thus, the tragedy of the commons has a compelling financial rationale. We communicate more even though it hurts giving generally.

A better way exists. We can go deeper instead of broader, learning about the donor and getting more out of each interaction with him/her.

The power of being preferred

It would be wonderful for you if all your donors gave only to your organization. Rationally, they should. They would look at all the organizations out there, pick the one with the biggest impact for the buck, and give everything they plan to give.*

---

* Actually, if we were fully rational utility maximizers as envisioned by sophomore econ, the idea that you would send a check to help anyone else is laughable. Some of these people helped don't even share your genetic material! But asking classical economists to predict human behavior is likely trying to figure out how many people fit

Researchers would *really* like us to behave like this. Consider this opening to a paper on donor behavior:

> "Charity could do the most good if every dollar donated went to causes that produced the greatest welfare gains. In line with this proposition, the effective-altruism movement seeks to provide individuals with information regarding the effectiveness of charities in hopes that they will contribute to organizations that maximize the social return of their donation."

Why don't people take this rational utility-maximizing approach?

Researchers have two hypotheses as to why people give: 1) donors want to do good in the world and 2) donors want the feeling of doing good in the world. Often, these go together. Consider though, whether you would rather give to an efficient organization who doesn't make you feel good about your own personal impact versus a slightly less efficient one that does. That conflict is often present in thinking about giving.

The truth is somewhere in the middle. Researchers looked at how much enjoyment people got out of paying a tax that they knew would go to a positive end versus freely donating the same amount. It turned out they liked having a positive impact either way, but they preferred to donate rather than be taxed.[80] Donors wanted to be the hero of the story.

Despite some scholars separating us into emotional altruists (bleeding hearts) and effective altruists (Spocks), most live somewhere in the middle. If given $100 to donate to charity, people don't give it all to our favorite charity. Nor do people give $1 to 100 different charities just to receive 100 wonderful thank-you notes.

A study by Infogroup found that donors gave to three charities in the past year and 10 over their lifetime. Further, at least ten percent of donors donated to at least six other nonprofit categories.[81]

---

in a room and assuming all the people are cubes – you'll get an answer, but the assumptions are flawed.

To some extent, we must accept this fickleness as the price of doing business with humans. Coke is a company that has customers so loyal that the time it messed with its formula is still synonymous with "marketing failure." Yet 72% of Coke customers also buy Pepsi.[82*]

As a result, Coke is not trying to get people to drink more liquid. Coke drives for "share of throat" – what portion of what you drink can Coke own? By using this metric, they know if they can increase your loyalty and experience, they can increase their revenue (with you still not giving them your unswerving obedience).

The same is true for nonprofits. At the risk of getting the Tautology Police involved[†], charitable people do charitable things. Our donors are good people who do good things in the plural sense. Almost all of them support multiple causes and organizations. That's fine. What we want to be able to do is create an experience for the donor that makes them want to give us more "share of donations" than other nonprofits.

We must accept that our donors will be promiscuously charitable. Personally, I've been touched by family and friends impacted by Alzheimer's, autism, cancer, depression, discrimination of various stripes, drunk driving, fertility issues, heart disease, kidney disease, MS, sexual assault, suicide, and more. As a donor, I have ties to several of these causes and spread my giving among them.

Conversely, if a person's connection to an issue came through the college roommate you last saw at the reunion four years ago, the issue likely diminishes in importance.

It is not good enough to be liked; we must be loved.

It is not good enough to be loved; we must be preferred.

We must be a part of our donors' "why" for giving. It is the core of how you differentiate yourself from your fellow nonprofits. "I feel that other causes are more deserving" is the number two reason people cite for lapsing.[83] Being preferred keeps you on the list.

---

[*] My wife wants it known she is in the 28%.

[†] Motto: Our motto is our motto.

Donors can get their warm glow anywhere…and they do. Other than pleading poverty, the number one reason people offer for not giving to an organization any longer (at 36%) is "I feel other causes are more deserving."[84] Think of this as code for "another organization touches me more deeply than you do."

You save lives? You change lives? So does everyone else.

You save the lives of the people I care about? You change lives around the issue that I feel in my heart? Tell me more.

Over 1.5 million nonprofits exist in the United States. Let's say a third of those you'd find to be a waste of time and money. And let's ignore the rest of the world for the moment.[*] So we have "only" one million nonprofits to which you'd feel good donating.

The point of all of this is when you are in a meeting where someone says "our target audience is people who want to do good in the world," you are nothing but "generic." A few nonprofits may be able to get away with this because of some combination of size, inertia/history, and good branding. But that's about .001% of nonprofits.[†] If you are in the other 99.999%, you must pick your donors or, more accurately, give the donors you aim to attract a compelling reason to pick you.

Your organization can't out-generic the United Way. I've been that guy who sows the wind, putting tchotchkes into envelopes trying to get someone, anyone, to sign on the line that is dotted. I've also reaped the whirlwind. Those donors go the same place customers with low preference and low switching costs go: away. If your acquisition strategy was "anyone will do," when you ask again, your donors will reply "anyone will do."

We've seen this en masse in an international relief charity. They surveyed their donors on their level of commitment to that organization and to other international relief charities. They came in fourth place in commitment level *among their own donors*. That meant when times get

---

[*] Because I'm an American – "ignore the rest of the world" is our foreign policy.

[†] This is likely an overestimate. Even behemoths like ALSAC/St. Jude can benefit from differentiating among people's reasons to give.

tight for these donors, these donors cut the low commitment organization before other organizations.

This is an untenable place to be, because retention is the most important variable for fundraising. Let's say you stumbled across a genie who could increase gifts per donor per year, average gift, or retention rate by ten percent. You should choose retention rate, because it compounds. Using some simplified assumptions*, you will bring a baseline of $3,110,817 over five years. Having a 10% increase in average gift or gifts per year is nice, bringing in an extra $311,082.

But in these scenarios, you end the five years with 3,888 donors. If you can increase retention by 10%, you have 6,262 left at the end of five years. Those donors bring in $820,889 over the baseline and over $500,000 more than the other 10% scenarios. So you tell the genie you want to increase retention and walk away happy.

Here's the catch: genies don't exist. Or rather, the genie was inside you the whole time. So the overarching question for your organization is how to move from broad, shallow support to narrower, deep support. Who should choose you, among the million nonprofits they could choose? Who should be more committed to you than to any other organization?† And how do you prove to them you are perfect for them?

The University of Kent looked at this in a report titled *How Donors Choose Charities*.[85] Through in-depth interviews they found four reasons a person will choose an organization. Two of them – efficiency and personal impact – can be achieved by any nonprofit for any donor. The other two are:

---

* Assumptions:
- Retention rates of 30 % of first-time donors (sadly high as an estimate) and 60% of multi-year donors.
- Average gift at acquisition of $20 and an increase in average gift of 20% per year.
- 1.5 gifts per year per donor.
- 100,000 donors.

† One is reminded of Jack Welsh's GE mandate that they be first or second in a market or exit. Not a bad rule of thumb here either.

> "[P]eople do not give to the most urgent needs, but rather they support causes that mean something to them… [1.] Donors' tastes, preferences and passions, acquired as a result of an individual's social experiences. These motivate many giving decisions, even among donors who perceive themselves to be motivated by meeting needs… [2.] Donors' personal and professional backgrounds, which shape their 'philanthropic autobiographies' and influence their choice of beneficiaries."[86]

In other words, it's about the donors and who *they* are. These are the donors who will stay with you through thick and thin:

- "My son had meningitis so I give to the Meningitis Trust."
- "My brother died of bowel cancer so I give to cancer research."
- "My mother became disabled and needed wheelchairs and things like that, and I realised what a difference it made, so I've been keen to give to charities that provide wheelchairs in the third world."
- "[My husband and I] work for the music business and so we support music charities and music causes."[87]

Trying to determine who will retain by looking at an RFM analysis or demographics is to ignore these most salient of points. At best, transactional variables are an exercise in begging questions: these people are more committed because they gave; they gave because they are more committed. Only by asking donors about themselves will you get data on which you can act.

People are bad at logic and reason. People care but care specifically. People care so specifically that donors will ignore the effectiveness of their gifts. Researchers tested effectiveness data with donors and found that, sure enough, donors will pick the most effective organization every time…

… *provided* they don't know which organization is which. However, when specific causes are listed, they will largely ignore effectiveness. Let's let the disappointed researcher from the beginning of this section tell it:

> "[I]f you give them a choice set that consists of a variety of causes, and you provide that same information on effectiveness and make it really easy for them to understand that information, those are the cases in which people ignore the effectiveness information. The reason is because they care about it, but not enough to sacrifice their own personal preferences when choosing a cause to support."[88]

Being preferred matters. You won't get all your donors' giving, but you'll get the plurality of it. Tying your cause to why your donor gives matters more than how effective you are.

Some may argue that they are already doing this. The evidence suggests otherwise. As we've already mentioned, many organizations try to volume or technique their way to relevance. As a result, communications become an undifferentiated stew of sameness, a mediocrity morass.

I recently received an email addressed to:

> Hi {!Lead.FirstName},

From an organization large enough to know and test better.

Our alleged "thank-yous" are little better, seeming as though some were written by an unholy hybrid of Sgt. Joe Friday and a platoon of gun-shy lawyers:

At 1430 hours, the suspect made a donation.
It was tax deductible pursuant to 26 US Code 170.

Lest you think I'm exaggerating, here's an anonymized[*] thank you letter I got from a nonprofit for a donation:

> "Dear Nicholas Ellinger,
>
> Anonymous Organization gratefully acknowledges your generous gift(s).
>
> Thank you for your generous donation. To learn more ways you can help our organization, please visit our website at thisisnotarealwebsite.org.
>
> Sincerely,
> Someone who should know better"

Wow, really warms the cockles of your heart, doesn't it? Even if you aren't sure what heart cockles are[†] and why you would warm them,[‡] this fails on two levels: it could be about any organization and it sure isn't about the donor.

For fun, I signed up for the email newsletters of the 100 largest charities in the United States.[§] Here are the subject lines from most of the emails I received on Giving Tuesday:

- A special Giving Tuesday challenge for you
- Alert: Triple Match
- DEADLINE: #GivingTuesday gifts doubled!

---

[*] I believe in the organization – they fit with one of my identities –and thus have no desire to publicly shame them.

[†] The ventricles. It comes from the Latin cochleae meaning shells because of their shape.

[‡] Etymologists appear to be unsure, other than warming the heart generally being seen as a good thing.

[§] I have a warped sense of fun.

- Don't miss this, Nick
- Double your impact for #GivingTuesday
- ENDS TONIGHT: Now up to $15,000 available!
- Every donation doubled today!
- FINAL NOTICE: Match expiring
- FW: Alert: Triple Match
- fwd: [until midnight] TRIPLE your impact
- #GivingTuesday challenge
- #GivingTuesday is here!
- #GivingTuesday: Your gift DOUBLES
- Good news: match EXTENDED
- Happening now: TRIPLE your impact
- Hours Left: Help Meet Our #GivingTuesday Match Goal
- Hurry Nick – triple match!
- It's not too late: 2x MATCH
- Last chance: 3x Match
- Last chance for Giving Tuesday
- MATCH: 3x
- Match! Make Bigger Change This Giving Tuesday
- Only a few hours left
- Reminder: Give on #GivingTuesday!
- There's still time to help – #GivingTuesday
- This #GivingTuesday your gift doubles!
- Triple Match Alert: Time is running out
- TODAY ONLY: Gifts Doubled!
- UPDATE: We're So Close to Our Goal!
- URGENT response needed: All gifts DOUBLED!
- Your gift can be matched on #GivingTuesday
- Your #GivingTuesday gift

Most of these emails are snoringly generic. I bet some of the people who wrote those subject lines don't remember which is which. They are looking at the list saying "did we use '#GivingTuesday challenge' or '#GivingTuesday is here!'?"

At best, these subject lines talk about "when" to give, not "why." And when you do that, you don't raise much new money – you cannibalize revenue from other communications. This is because the primary pitch is the time of year, rather than the good the donor's gift can do.

November's Giving Tuesday was not an anomaly. In December, these organizations sent a total of 632 emails (about ten per). Ninety-four of them—one out of every seven emails—referenced a matching challenge grant in their subject line. This only intensified as the month went on—during the last two days of the year, this grew to one in three. In fact, 10 percent of the organizations extended their match deadline; one organization extended their deadline twice.

For perspective, only 85 emails mentioned Christmas, Chanukah, or the holidays. And only four—less than one percent—said any form of "thank you."

Here's an actual December email, with only the name of the organization, the amounts, and the signer taken out:

> "All gifts doubled. Give now >>
>
> December is a big fundraising month for XXX, and right now, we're behind. The 15th of the month is almost here, but we've only raised YYY—leaving us ZZZ behind.
>
> Will you help?
>
> 20XX is going to be a big year for us, but only if we can hit our goals. The mid-month milestone is a pivotal

> moment for our fundraising. And if we start the second part of the month behind, it will be hard to catch up."

If you can guess the organization that sent this, you are a better person than I. It's not about the organization. And it's not about the donor. I've run many digital campaigns for nonprofits. In all these years I couldn't get the person two desks down from me to care where digital revenue was for the month of December (just like I didn't care about their work on the letterhead procurement process). Why would I ever think that would be compelling to a donor?

I don't want to fill a bucket with my donation. I want to light a fire. I want either to save a life or change a life in a way that reinforces who I believe I am. I do not want to be .037% of whether Kris makes her December revenue goal. This organization-centrism is endemic. I read a donor newsletter the other day from a nameless organization (to protect the guilty) that mentioned the donor once, on the third page, second story, eighth paragraph. That's a sin, and not a minor one.

Contrast this with:

> "Your generosity gives hope to XXX cancer patients, like Kenlie, Devon and Marleigh. Thanks to friends like you, families like theirs will never receive a bill from XXX for treatment, travel, housing or food—because all a family should worry about is helping their child live."

Of course XXX is St. Jude; if you doubt this, Google the phrase "never receive a bill." Of course it does a great job of laying out why a donor would give to them.

I've seen the results from neither campaign. But I will bet the entire non-plastic contents of my wallet* that the second outraised the first. I say this because I've seen the results from a seven-email, matching-gift

* $7.35, three metro cards from cities I don't live in, and seven receipts I haven't yet processed for reimbursement.

campaign that one organization ran. The difference among the emails was wild. Some emails performed five, even 10, times better than others.

This nonprofit explained that the better performing emails used some of their most effective messaging from earlier in the year. The less effective emails used messaging it was simply trying. All the emails had been adapted to use a matching gift.*

In other words, strong message, impact, focus on the donors' identities, and powerful story beats technique every time.

Some call this shift from an organizational focus to a donor focus donor-centrism. It is the first step in donor-centricism, to be sure. But just because it is necessary doesn't make it sufficient. Saying your focus on donors is getting out of your own head and realizing they exist as

---

* A brief aside: a match is a strong technique with serious limitations. Two forces are at work here: One is self-selection. If you frequently run matches, you will attract donors who want their gift matched. The other is that you train your donors who are ambivalent that they should be looking for their gift to double or triple. This leads to what I call the Men's Wearhouse effect. Whenever you see an ad for that store, you see that you get one, two, or three suits free when you buy one. Why would you ever buy something regular price there without a free suit?

Now, look at your competition. They are doing matches, too. They just went to triple match from double match. They are doing a 10-time flash match.

You become like a coupon-centric retailer, a charitable J.C. Penney. You won't sell much at full price because you don't have those customers anymore. You are competing on price. That's a spiral that doesn't go upward.

Also, there's some evidence that talking about a lead gift works better than a match (because some people count the match as part of their gift and give lower average gifts). And triple matches don't work better than 100% matches (which may not work better than 50% matches). Also, they tend to work only for active donors – lapsed donors and non-donors respond better to pitches as to why to give.

So match with caution and only to the extent that it doesn't block getting an actual reason why someone should give.

separate beings is like saying your astronomy is My Very Educated Mother Just Served Us Nine Pizzas as a mnemonic for the nine planets.* To focus on the donor, we must focus on the donor individually, not as a donor-Borg collective. We must know why they give and reinforce that reason for giving every time we ask.

This preference is how we can expand the pie of charitable giving. As a sector in the United States, we have been stuck at two percent of GDP for the seeable past.[89] All our efforts to get people to donate haven't brought in new money; they've shifted it.

Research explains this, finding that donors have a mental budget for their philanthropy. Like any mental budget, it's allocated in amount, in timing, and in beneficiaries. Generally, people substitute one charitable act for another, not for a non-charitable act. The allocation is only moderately malleable.[90]

This is a little weird. After all, part of the point of money is fungible: your picture of a dead president and/or founding father on special paper can be exchanged for rent, coffee, donations, whatever. American money says as much right on it: THIS NOTE IS LEGAL TENDER FOR ALL DEBTS, PUBLIC AND PRIVATE.

But that's not how people think about money. People have special categories for each type of expense. Think of it as separate jars: $1400 for the mortgage, $800 for food, etc. They experience mental pain every time they must rob from one cookie jar to put it into another, so they try not to violate their mental budget.

How do you get donors to rob from Peter to pay you? How do you make the pie bigger?

You make donors happier. Research shows that the happier people are with their giving to you, the more they are willing to give. This sounds obvious, but when someone enjoys giving to you, they are willing to dip into other jars (like entertainment) that may not normally be open to you.[91] This is something I'd argue the effective altruists miss

* Yes, I include Pluto in there! Clearing your orbital path is overrated! #Pluto4ever #itsroundandorbits #PlutoTruth

– the gifts they receive may be more effective, but if yours have more heart behind them, you'll receive more overall.

This happiness occurs when giving speaks to your soul, your core nature. So let's get started by talking about who your donors are.

Becoming preferred by speaking to your donors' identities

> *"Individuals used to identify their lives most closely with a place, an ethnic group, a particular culture or even a language. The advent of online engagement and increased exposure to ideas from other cultures means that identities are now more fungible than previously. People are now much more comfortable with carrying and managing multiple identities."*[92]
>
> – Klaus Schwab

People have many identities that they inhabit and move through in their daily lives. In a matter of an hour, you might move from worker to voter, from child to parent, from professional to Packers fan,[*] from alumnus to amateur author[†] – all based on what situation you are in and what identities have been primed. If you doubt this, try using your Packer fan identity in your next parent-teacher conference or performance review and see how that works for you.

When I talk about a donor identity, it is one or more of those core conceptions of who a person is and how it intersects with an organization's mission. It is the "why" of giving.

The most basic donor identity is "I am a good person doing a good thing." I vote in every election. I do this despite knowing in my brain of brains (as opposed to my heart of hearts) that it made no possible difference. Everyone I voted for will win or lose by a healthy margin.

---

[*] You are a Packer fan, right?

[†] YMMV on how amateur this author is.

Even if my one vote could be the margin for victory, it wouldn't be, with recounts and lawyers and such.*

But I vote because I believe 1) being a voter is good, 2) I am a good person, and therefore 3) I will be a voter. It's so much a part of my identity I would think differently (and worse) about myself if I didn't. Like all humans, I desperately want to think well of myself.

Note that I mentioned neither candidate nor party. Whom I voted for was just a means to my end of expressing my identity and beliefs. Our donors are very similar. Nonprofits are the conduits through which good people do good deeds and reinforce their own identities.

That is the basic "why" for why people give. Through their gift they have said "I am a good person doing a good thing." And yet some nonprofits don't reinforce the identity of that donor as a good person, as they are so busy talking about themselves.

Even priming the most basic donor identity of "donor" can help your fundraising. The American Red Cross primed a donor's identity as a donor. They added, "Previous Gift: [Date]," to the top of its letter to lapsed donors. That one change increased response rate by 20 percent.[93] Giving someone a positive identity can cause them to want to live up to that identity. For example, random citizens told they were above average citizens likely to vote and participate in civic events, were 15% more likely to vote than citizens told they were average.[94]

Texas A&M and the Seattle Seahawks call their fans the 12th Man for a reason. Even though it is highly unlikely that someone will be called out of the stands to play (although Buffalo Bills fans are waiting by the phone as I write this), this idea of a person that helps the team on the field gives these fans something to aspire to and a role to play. In fact, the U.S. Olympic and Paralympic Foundation have institutionalized this, calling their supporters "The Team Behind the Team."

---

* Please vote. Yes, one vote may not make a difference, but together, those votes are powerful. The world really is a better place when there are more voters in it. For all those who have died to get the vote and for all those around the world who would do so given the chance, please vote.

This is the most basic level of donor identity. But it only scratches the surface of the reason why people give. What you are looking for is an identity that only some people have and one that has special meaning for people related to your organization.

As Seth Godin puts it:

> "People like us do things like this: There is no more powerful tribal marketing connection than this.
>
> More than features, more than benefits, we are driven to become a member in good standing of the tribe. We want to be respected by those we aspire to connect with, we want to know what we ought to do to be part of that circle.
>
> Not the norms of mass, but the norms of our chosen tribe."[95]

You are looking for this tribe. For an identity to have importance, it must be something that not everyone has. An appeal letter that starts out "As a fellow less-hairy ape" probably doesn't work that well, because that's all of us.

So, for example, if all men behaved like all other men, and all women behaved like all other women, and those two groups really were from Mars and Venus, that would be a perfect segmentation. (Respectively: they don't; they don't; they aren't; it isn't.)

Consider romantic comedies. Demographics and stereotyping would say they should be marketed exclusively to women. This misses men who like romantic comedies and women who hate them. Netflix, wisely, markets romantic comedies to people who watch romantic comedies. That's why Todd Yellin, Netflix's VP of Product Innovation said:

> "There's a mountain of data that we have at our disposal. That mountain is composed of two things. Garbage is 99

percent of that mountain. Gold is one percent...Geography, age, and gender? We put that in the garbage heap. Where you live is not that important."[96]

The reason these segments don't work out is simple: there's more difference within these demographic groups than between/among them. Consequently, they are not predictive (or, at best, they are not nearly as predictive as they could be.)

You also want to avoid identities not linked to the donor's reason to give. Any organization could access these identities and thus they give you no long-term advantage for capturing this donor's heart.

So the first three rules of ideal identity are:

- They act differently from people in other identities.
- The identity must be knowable by asking.
- The identity must be linked to their reason for giving to your organization.

Now, the tricky bit. In addition to acting differently and being knowable, an identity for your nonprofit also must:

- Give you better results by segmentation and customizing based on that identity AND/OR
- Be worth a different amount than another identity.

Remember, identities are nearly infinite; you must use the ones that give you value in the knowing. Let's say you think there's a religious identity: people who are giving to your organization for religious reasons even if your organization is secular. If those giving for religious reasons are worth the same as those who aren't, reply to the same pieces as those who aren't, and don't respond any better when you add religious messaging to the mail package, then the religious identity is worthless to you.

Let's take a simple and anonymized example of a valuable identity. An animal-focused nonprofit had (not surprisingly) cat people and dog people who donated. When the organization asked donors whether they were a cat person or a dog person at the beginning of an inbound telemarketing call and had that information played back to them later in the call (e.g., "As someone who loves cats, you should know that…"), donation rates and average monthly gifts went up 15 percent each.[97] Plus, that nonprofit then had this donor information to do likewise in all its communications.

Even more disparate were the types of donors to a health care charity. It turned out substantial differences between those who had received direct services from the organization and those who had no connection to the organization existed. More obviously, those who received direct services had significantly larger lifetime values and were more committed to the organization. This means the organization could spend more to acquire these donors (and less to acquire others).

Less obviously, those two groups had entirely dissimilar reasons for giving. For those with a direct connection to the organization, 60 percent of their relationship came from wanting a deeper involvement with the nonprofit. They cared about the nurses who gave medical care at home and supported the families of their patients. Those with no connection to the organization were not interested in a deeper involvement and didn't care about home nursing at all. In fact, mentioning these two things as the impact made these donors less likely to give. One size fits no-one.

Despite this, as generally used in conventional fundraising "your impact" messaging is not only one-size-fits-all; it's based on what the staff would like to talk about, rather than what the donor would like to hear. It's like preparing to go fishing by taking worms, grubs, caterpillars, rat-tailed maggots, etc., and tasting each one personally to see which bait to use.

Our fundraisers' tastes differ from those of our donors. An international relief organization once had their staff rate 20 potential appeals; it then asked donors to do likewise. The top three appeals according to donors were ones the staff ranked in the bottom seven.

And the staff's favorite appeal was the donor's second worst. Even if we know we aren't the donor, we can't necessarily replicate the donor.

This understanding is essential to crafting your communications. It isn't just understanding why donors give to your organization generally; it's understanding why *each* donor gives to your organization.

Picture an oversimplified disease charity with a dual mission – prevent the spread of the disease and help those who have the disease.

Usually, such an organization will have something like this somewhere on page two of their control annual fund appeal:

> "And not only are you helping defeat this dread disease, you are also helping support those who have it in their time of need."

Or

> "And not only are you helping people who suffer from this disease, you are also preventing people from getting this disease in the future."

The majority – probably the vast majority – of their donors have a reason they give to the organization. A reason. Singular. They care more about one of these mission areas than the other. Yet we often message everyone the same regardless of their identity. We may talk about what the organization is doing with their gift, but we don't take care to make sure the impact is one the donor wants to make. And yet for some this is still called loving your donors.

This is (from my experience) partly an organizational compromise. The people who work there believe in all parts of the mission and want everyone to do likewise. Every department wants representation. And no one wants to offend the prevention people if only services are mentioned or vice versa. It's easy for the direct marketer to satisfy everyone and throw it all in. But the purpose of direct marketing is not to be easy for the direct marketer.

We already segment, but it's just usually by transaction data like RFM (recency, frequency, and monetary value). But if you worked for a disease charity, how would you slice and dice these segments?

1. Someone who has the disease and last donated to you 23 months ago
2. Someone who has the disease and last donated to you 25 months ago
3. Someone who doesn't have the disease, doesn't know anyone who has the disease, and last donated to you 23 months ago
4. Someone who doesn't have the disease, doesn't know anyone who has the disease, and last donated to you 25 months ago

A purely transactional segmentation puts the 23-month donors together and splits up the common identities. What we should be grouping together are the common reasons for giving and adapting our message to the donor's identity.

You can start in broad strokes and still have an impact. For some organizations, it will be the difference between "I have this disease," "I love someone who has this disease," and "I just want to help." For others, it's the difference between dog people and cat people. For still others, there may be a segment that is looking to make amends for something they did in their past.

For each of these identities, a more compelling, tailored "you" statement will work better than the kitchen sink approach. I wouldn't urge you do to this if matching the donor's identity to the ask didn't increase results. It does. Take one of the few times demographics are a valid identity. Researchers created four different appeals for a university: need-based, merit-based, first generation to go to college, and LGBTQ person who had been cut off by their parents because of their LGBTQ status. They also randomized the gender and race/ethnicity of the student. As you probably guessed, people were more likely to give when their gender and race/ethnicity matched the student discussed in the appeal.

Beyond that, women and those with marginalized identities (race and sexual orientation/gender identity) were more likely to support other marginalized people, whether there was a match or not. Those same people were more likely to give to the LGBTQ appeal.[98] Both the student and the message work because they are tied to a core reason for supporting the university.

A wilderness conservation organization discovered two identities: conservationists and users of the land. The former are folks who advocate for the protection of the land and environment for its own sake and for the sake of future generations.* The latter are those who were using the land for their vocation or avocation: hikers, bikers, campers, etc. Using Facebook ads†, DonorVoice advertised to both audiences with two ads. The only differences were whether the ads started with "As a conservationist" or "As an outdoor enthusiast" – literally the simplest version of identity priming. This simple addition increased click-through 12-14% because it showed the prospective donor the organization knew them and why they would donate. A mismatch of donor identity (e.g., showing the conservationist ad to the outdoor enthusiast) decreased click-through. Thus, you can make prospective donors feel preferred from the very beginning of the donor's journey – literally before acquisition – by knowing donor identity and catering to it.

So you are looking for a donor identity that describes only some people, is knowable, is linked to the donor's reason for giving, and gives you better results when you prime it or segment by it.

Once we know our donor identities, we can imbue the identities with positive characteristics. The NRA, for example, takes the gun owner

---

* These were actually sub-identities: conservationists who are doing it for ecosystems and the flora and fauna versus those who are doing it for future generations. But we're simplifying, since this was a test of the top-level identities.

† While third-party data is inherently worse than first-party data, when I say it's just good enough to use, I mean that – it is usable data for the purposes of attracting new constituents, then learning more about them yourself post-acquisition.

identity and wraps it in patriotic, freedom-loving, safe, self-sufficient, etc. Everyone likes to be positive things. Through repetition, they stick.

Associating a cause with an already existing identity also helps accrue the existing benefits from that identity. You've heard of people talking about motherhood and apple pie; consider what Mothers Against Drunk Driving (MADD) has done. During debates in the 80's on drunk driving legislation, Congressman James Howard was said to remark "How do the mothers feel?" referring both to the organization and to mothers themselves. One identity can also be used to co-opt an existing identity. The Chesapeake Bay Foundation wanted to expand the types of people who would think of giving to them. So it went after an animal lover identity.

Yes, really.

The mail package teaser read "Because your pets will drink any water they see… there is something you should know." with a pet tag premium. This doubled the response rate in co-op lists and produced a 30% lift to animal lists[99], opening a new potential universe for acquisition.

Not all the manifestations of a donor's identity will have occurred even to that donor. The Chesapeake Bay Foundation gave pet owners a reason that their responsibilities to their furry love – their basic identity – could also include watershed protection. Given the increases in response rate, that's a connection those donors would not have made on their own. Granted, the Foundation will now have to treat these donors differently within the organization to retain them, but that's a "great problem to have."

Understanding a donor's identity also allows for greater persuasion and loyalty. Newton's First Law applies to humans too: an object at rest tends to remain at rest. Unless humans are acted upon by the outside world or consciously try to change ourselves, they are very comfortable with consistency and default. Their minds go out of their way to "protect" us from information that challenges our identities and predispositions, arguing against them or even filing an opposing piece of information away for later retrieval.[100]

This natural human reaction results in "filter bubbles." Anything that will make us unhappy, make us do something we'd prefer not to, or cause damage to our identity or way of thinking is ruthlessly dispatched.[101]

The good news is that when you understand a person's identity, you can get inside their filter bubble. This is not often done, however. In a study on political argumentation, researchers found three things:

1. Communicators tend to argue from their own moral values, rather than their target audience's values.
2. You are more effective when you argue from your target's values; arguing from your own values is largely ineffective and often counterproductive.
3. This holds true even for some of the most contentious issues of our day in the United States, including same-sex marriage, universal health care, English as the national language, and more.[102]

Filter bubbles come into play when trying to persuade a constituent to take an action or care about a topic. For example, child sponsorship charities often have a portion of their donors who are parents who sponsor a child so that their own children have an opportunity to learn about what another culture is like and teach them value of compassion for those who have less. These donors are entirely distinct from those without children.

Moreover, lest you think this is a demographic approach, they are also dissimilar from parents who don't involve their children in their philanthropic decisions. Even if you know a person is a parent, you wouldn't know the right message to get them to give or keep giving – should you talk about the impact they are having on a child halfway across the world or the one that lives in their house? Getting the message that fits the identity allows you to be on the inside of that constituent's filter bubble looking out.

We've talked mostly about focusing on donor identities that are worth more, like those with direct connections to your issue. It's also worth knowing what donor identities are worth **less.** One of the most infamous of these identities involves disaster donors. These donors want to do something when an immediate and urgent problem makes the evening news, which is great. (We'll talk about acquiring and retaining them later.) That said, those who pop up only for disasters are notoriously difficult to retain or refocus on systemic fixes. It is (potentially) an identity that is worth less than other identities; thus, you would pay less to acquire them than a non-disaster donor. You would also send messaging to them that is largely disaster-focused, making it a valuable identity to know, even if it's a less valuable identity to acquire.

Similarly, when researchers looked at DonorsChoose.org donors, they found two types of donors: those who came in because of a teacher-referral (and thus were likely to support a specific teacher) and those who came in without a teacher-referral (presumably to support public education generally). Teacher-referred donors had a $47 average gift and a 22% first-year retention rate; site donors, those not referred by a teacher, had a $55 average gift and a 28% retention rate. Lower average gift and lower retention rate is a brutal combination.[103]

Of course, in this case, if you are DonorsChoose.org, you are still going to acquire these teacher-referred donors happily. You want teachers using their networks to introduce potential donors to the site. But if you are planning a remarketing or co-targeting campaign to reacquire lapsed donors, where would you best invest?

Knowing donor identity opens messaging opportunities that may increase the value of these donors. If someone comes in through a teacher, they likely are going to be more interested in that teacher's (and school's) opportunities, versus site donors who are likely more agnostic toward school specifics. For these types of donors, it's about understanding their motivation so you 1) don't waste your breath and 2) use that breath for the few things that may turn them into more loyal donors.

Hopefully now you are convinced. You want to discover what identities work for your organization. First, you need to get a list of potential identities to test (after all, if not all identities work, you may go through a few before you hit the best option). Here are some non-exhaustive thoughts for brainstorming identities:

- Direct impact (e.g., I have the disease; I have been poor myself) versus indirect (I love someone who has the disease/has been poor) versus none.
- Currently receiving services from your organization versus previously received services from your organization versus no services received.
- For religious organizations: "I give to live out my X religious identity" versus "I am not an X, but you do good work."
- Religion, even for non-religious organizations. You may roll your eyes, but some animal organizations have reported that they have a segment who respond differently to subtle cues like "helping all God's creatures."
- Interacted with your organization directly versus not. e.g., behaviors of people who have adopted an animal from your shelter are often different from those who haven't.
- Interactions with your mission. Similarly, someone who adopts an animal from a shelter may respond differently to an unrelated animal organization.
- Volunteers versus non-volunteers.
- Relate to volunteers versus relate to those served. Let's say you are Habitat for Humanity – you may have a segment of people who wish they could be out there swinging a hammer, but who are doing so vicariously through your volunteers. A traditional appeal emphasizing the plight of the homeless may not work as well for this group.
- I've used cats versus dogs repeatedly as an example because 1) it is simple and 2) it works. What's your organization's equivalent?
- Especially for cultural organizations, have they been to the museum/opera/library/monument/park or not? One such organization reports that the average lifetime value of a donor is

cut in half once you get more than 50 miles away from their site (one of the few relevancies of location).

- Content patterns. What program(s) do you tune in to your PBS stations to watch? (Answer: for me, British people killing each other: Sherlock, Poirot, Miss Marple, etc.; for my wife, British people not killing each other: Downton Abbey, Victoria, Pride and Prejudice, etc.) Is there a difference in donors by what content they consume?
- For environmental/nature organizations, do they like to experience nature outdoors or indoors? I'm in the latter group – I like nature if and only if I don't get any on me.
- An interesting quirk of crime victim organizations is a small subset of donors who may have committed the crime or an antecedent in their past.
- Disaster versus non-disaster donors. Identity in these types of donors is usually based on how they came into the organization rather than by self-identification. Sometimes a person may have donated to a mail package because it was in front of them when a disaster hit and they are actually disaster-only donors. Or someone who donated to a disaster but is willing to support other efforts.
- Globalists versus "here firsts." If you serve both populations, you will likely have some donors who want to go as far as to restrict their donation to their home country… or to anything but their home country. Clearly different behavior.
- Parents versus non-parents. We've also seen a variant on this where parents who involved their kids in their philanthropy are different from parents who don't.

To any of these ideas, add in anything that you are seeing often in open-ended feedback.* A simple "why did you donate today?" question

* You are actively soliciting feedback, right? More on this later.

will not allow you to create an identity then and there (you'll get answers like "because you mailed me," guaranteed). But it will give you hypotheses to test.

I want to give you some ways to do this yourself but will also alert you to an alternative provided by DonorVoice, the company for which I work. This is unavoidable since we provide solutions that will discover identities and their values. But if you will be sullied by solutions that require some payment, I'll warn you so you can skip ahead.

The central challenge of testing identities is that they are often self-reported. Thus, you must collect them from your donors before you know if they are valuable. Ugh. And you must collect them in quantity for any sort of significance. Double ugh.

So if you want to start testing identities on the cheap, start with pre-existing identity data. You may already know identities like:

- Who has received services from you.
- Who has volunteered with you.
- Interactions with the organization like pet adoption.
- Content consumption patterns.
- If they've been to your museum/opera/library/monument/park.

To that, you can add proxies for identity:

- People who downloaded your brochure "So you have spoy in your fleep" are likely spoy-fleep sufferers.
- Repeated action alert senders are likely advocate identities.
- While more difficult, you may be able to determine preferences like cat versus dog by click pattern in emails.

None are as good as self-reported data, but they are OK if you bake in some skepticism with your results. That is, code these tentatively, then ask for real data.

So now, we test? You sure can. Just split your identity files in half, sending half identity version A and half identity version B. For example, if you have cat and dog people, send half of the cat people cat messaging and half dog messaging. Same for the dog people. If cat people like cat messaging and dog people like dog messaging, you are in. (If both prefer one messaging or the other, maybe you have a new control!)

But let's say you have a largely offline donor file. You won't be able to test without incurring significant cost. Instead, you can use your existing file, looking at lifetime value by identity segment.

Some identities, like the cat versus dog example above, are likely at the same value. Rather, the increase in value by employing identity will come from matching the message to the donor.

For those, you can start backwards – with the communications. Simply go through all your communications to a select set of donors and code them as to what identities you'd think these communications appeal to.

Ha ha ha ha ha ha! Yes, I was kidding about "simply."

This is a painful, laborious process. I've done it. But capturing key information about the communications related to identity (e.g., is there a petition involved? is the story about someone helped or about the volunteer doing the helping?) will allow you look at people's previous activity.

This is messy data, because we don't always know if the communication is the direct reason for the gift or an incidental one. I once did this with people who had donated 10 or more times in five years. Of those donors, about seven percent of them donated to 80% or more of the mail pieces with petitions attached (which accounted for about a third of pieces). The odds of this happening by chance were vanishingly small; these donors became the starting point of an advocate identity.

This process works for information you have. But what if you don't have data for an identity you want to test? Here I'll advocate for something I rarely advocate for: telemarketing. Using a telemarketing script, you can ask an identity question up front (ideally, only one) then branch off with customized scripts based on their answer. You'll get your answer as to who has what identity and whether this identity matters in the same phone call.

But these are relatively blunt instruments. That's why I advocate …

Warning: this is where I talk about products and solutions you can buy. If you want to remain unsullied by commerce, skip ahead to the bolded line on the next page.

…for a Pre-Test Tool or Commitment Study from DonorVoice.

A Pre-Test Tool is A/B testing on steroids. It breaks your messaging down into concrete segments (e.g. tone and type of voice, who you help, what the donation does, identity statement, type of gift – whatever is most important for you to learn about), then creates five different versions of each segment. Next, donors receive a survey where they go through about eight different questions that work something like your optometrist's eye test: do you prefer A or B? Since A and B are both made of different versions of each attribute, you can quickly understand not only what version people prefer more, but what attributes matter most.

Additionally, you can place questions about identity at the end of the survey and, from that, determine if different identities prefer different messaging. All without peeling one stamp.

A Commitment Study goes into depth with your donors about all their touchpoints with you: brand positioning, donor relations, fundraising asks, cultivation, channels, messaging, etc. It also asks about their identities and their commitment to your organization. By marrying their answers with your transactional data, you can see what touchpoints cause commitment and those that don't. This allows you to scale up touchpoints that matter, fix the broken ones, and drop those that do not increase retention and donor value.

Moreover, by asking identity questions, DonorVoice can tell you which of your identities are different in value and commitment, plus what makes your donors tick. It's an essential step in creating different journeys for different types of donor.

(It's now safe for the pitch-adverse to continue reading – told you I'd be brief.)

Once you have your golden identity or key split of different identities, this identity-first thinking must go throughout your organization. It screams first and foremost for a tearing down of the barriers among channels.

The problem begins, as usual, in a spreadsheet. You must budget direct marketing and your board will not accept something with three lines: revenue, expenses, and net. How then to split your marketing programs?

Naturally, you do this by channel, since that's how you'll be spending money. A rational decision spurs an irrational implication: thinking about digital donors, mail donors, telemarketing donors, et al, as if it is the channel that defines the person. Pretty soon, it's how your strategy is organized, zooming in on ever-smaller channel fractals (e.g., direct marketing to digital to social media to Facebook to Facebook Custom Audience to Facebook Custom Audience look-alike sectors).

All because of a @#)($*&@#()$ spreadsheet. This would be fine if 1) channels were the best ways to organize donors, 2) strategies were best developed for channels, or 3) channel thinking were a benign influence.

None of these is the case.

Audience identity is a far better way to organize donors than channels. Ideal groupings of donors would have similar commitments to the organization, reasons for supporting the organization, and financial benefits. Or, put another way, you want to segment to maximize the similarity of the people in the segment or cell with a clear difference from those outside it.

Channel doesn't do that. Here's an example from a health charity (some numbers have been tweaked for anonymity):

- Mail donors' total giving was $400 and their overall commitment score was 7.6 (out of 10).
- Event donors' giving was $325 and commitment was 7.8
- Digital donors' giving was $275 and commitment was 7.9.

Pretty thin gruel here. What you might learn here is that mail donors are a bit more valuable. But when writing the appeal, you have no idea what to say for the mail group that is different from digital.

Now let's look at this same audience, but by whether they were a direct beneficiary of services, indirect beneficiary, or no connection:

- Donors with a direct connection had total giving of $500 and their overall commitment score was 8.6.
- Those with an indirect connection gave $400 and commitment was 7.9
- Those without connection gave $250 and commitment was 7.1.

Now we have some actionable findings. Direct beneficiaries are the most valuable and most committed by a significant margin – they are more different from each other than those differentiated by channel. They are also more likely to attend your events. Each of these donors has a mailbox, email box, and phone number and it's just a matter of their preference by which they give.

They also have different reasons for giving, as discussed earlier. So not only do you know what group is most valuable, you also know what to say to them. Yes, this takes a study of commitment and identities, but it is well worth it for this type of value-boosting intelligence.

Strategies are best done around audiences. You can already see why -- audience groups are far more different from each other than simply people giving via different channels (especially when the channel used to acquire someone can be an accident of history, not an actual preference).

But it's also because channels are ephemeral. I was reminded of this by a piece written more than a decade ago called "MySpace.com: A Place for Donors?"[104].

If I'm remembering 2007 correctly, we also discussed whether Second Life was a relevant channel for nonprofits and how much experience is necessary to become president. It was a different time.

The reason that MySpace and Second Life came up then and Snapchat or TikTok comes up now is that the channel is the new and shiny toy. *What is constant is the audience.*

Since a large part of strategy is determining what *not* do to, "how do I best reach this set of people?" will yield better fundraising results than "what do I do with this channel?" in the same way that "how do I build a bookcase" yields better home improvement results than "what fun thing can I do with this hacksaw, a plastic coat hanger, and welding set?".

Channel thinking is actively destructive. Should you mail your event donors? If you are letting channel drive your decision, you can answer this three ways: 1) no, 2) yes, 3) yes, but take channel into account when you are doing your RFM selects so you aren't going as deep into lapsed audiences. The data would say don't try too hard: most event donors don't donate in other ways.

But consider if you did this by audience. You would go deeper into direct connections than those with no connection to your organization and come closer to the ideal mix for your program. As the evidence shows, event donors will donate if they are of the right identity and asked in the right way.

Channel thinking also hurts campaign structure: because different people are working on different programs, they may be deploying different messages to the same audience simultaneously. Working in silos has been roundly condemned. But still it persists. This leads to cases where, for example, your Google Grant keywords won't include the subjects of campaigns you are running. In this fragmented system, you can't benefit from the collective intelligence of everyone involved in your program.

You also miss opportunities when you view your channel as having an audience, rather than your organization having an audience through various channels.

A simple example of this was NPR's decision not to promote the NPR One app or NPR podcasts on its terrestrial radio stations. They wouldn't ask for downloads or mention podcast hosts in an endorsement-like way.[105]

Part of this is understandable. Radio stations pay the bulk of NPR's bills. These stations want to hold on to their share of ears and make sure that people listen to radio stations. They exert pressure; NPR folds.

But this suggests Theodore Levitt's Marketing Myopia, where you think you are in a different business from the one you are in:

> The railroads did not stop growing because the need for passenger and freight transportation declined. That grew. The railroads are in trouble today not because that need was filled by others (cars, trucks, airplanes, and even telephones) but because it was not filled by the railroads themselves. They let others take customers away from them because they assumed themselves to be in the railroad business rather than in the transportation business. The reason they defined their industry incorrectly was that they were railroad-oriented instead of transportation-oriented; they were product-oriented instead of customer-oriented...[106]

A virtual show of hands. Who here thinks that NPR's long-term future is in traditional terrestrial radio? OK... OK... thank you. Hands down.

Now who thinks their long-term future is in online radio, podcast, and things we haven't even thought of yet? OK... OK... keep them up... there are a lot of you to count...

Exactly. Because of territoriality and present revenues, they are potentially mortgaging the future for the present. What business is NPR in? The radio business or the informing (or entertaining or thought-provoking) business?

They've answered this with their public engagement numbers. In 2017, they had 41 million users per month on NPR.org, 37.7 million unique listeners (and static) on broadcast radio, and 20.4 million unique (and growing) podcast listeners. They are moving broadcast shows to podcast and vice versa.[107] To hazard a guess, part of their audience is channel-specific – they only listen to broadcast or only to podcasts – and part is channel-fluid. In other words, their business, and value proposition, transcends medium.

The same thing is true for your nonprofit. Your audience is your audience.* You should be trying to engage them in as many ways as they desire, as deeply as they desire. Each medium should be a means not only of trying to get the next donation or upgrade, but also to connect through additional media.

So, let's bid a fond farewell to channel thinking and bury it next to MySpace as a fundraising platform.

This identity-first thinking must also be a part of your brand. You often see an organization rebrand without thinking of who their donors are and what they want from you. I've been through this drill. I've also been through prostate exams. And I'd rather go through the latter than the former if push comes to shove.† Those organizations who want to mess with their name or logo better have a compelling reason for doing so. We're talking "we at NAACP don't want to spell out what the CP stood for," as compelling, not "I hear teal is all the rage for logos this year." You are going to face short- (and potentially medium- and long-) term fundraising pain as people learn your new mark or name.

A refocusing of a brand can come without having to change the wallpaper. Your brand is more than your logo and your name. It's the totality of the psychological associations people have with your organization. Thus, you and your rebrand can help fundraising by adding positive associations, subtracting negative associations, or working with your donors to make the positive associations they have more relevant.

This starts with knowing your donors as they are, not as you might wish them to be. While identity works as a direct marketing concept, it's also something you can build your brand around. Take, for example, the U.S. Olympic and Paralympic Committee. It used to run a premium-based program: front-end, back-end, and probably in-between if such a

---

* Can I hide out at your place if the Tautology Police read this?

† A rather unfortunate use of this expression.

thing were possible. If you donated $20, you could get a jacket or a hat or whatever piece of merchandise was available.

Two things made this untenable: 1) the obvious cost factor – more than 80% of their revenues were eaten up by merchandise and fulfillment costs; 2) sports gear is profitable – giving away a low-quality jacket made it more difficult to sell a high-quality, higher profit jacket.

So it did a Commitment Study of their donors. It found that (somehow) they had acquired a section of donors who were not in it for the merch. They had genuine philanthropic intent. What they wanted was to feel a part of Team USA. Now, it talks about its donors being the Team Behind the Team. If a donor donates $100 or more per year, they become part of The Sixth Ring, a key part of the Olympic moment. And most of their appeals are now from athletes, telling donors how the donor was a part of their Olympic journey. With these changes, they've increased annual gift frequency from 1.6 to 2.4 gifts per year and substantially increased their net revenue, revenue per donor, average gift, and response rates in year one.[108]

Similarly, Catholic Relief Services found donors were living out their faith with their gifts, but some of its appeals could have been for any relief organization, only featuring "Catholic" in the name of the organization. It also found their donors had negative associations about the frequency of solicitation (almost 30 times per year in the mail alone for the best donors).

As discussed earlier, it tested a pilot program that reduced the number of appeals and focused on their donors' identity. The reduced frequency worked; it rolled out what was the test version to all its donors. It communicated this roll-out to their donors and asked how they were doing. Many donors said it was a step in the right direction, but not far enough. So it is now capturing donor preferences, customizing their mail streams, and taking the opportunity to discuss recurring giving ("you've said you'd like to hear from us only quarterly – would you like to set up a quarterly gift?").

Many donors are reporting how nice it is to have CRS seek their advice and to take their views into account. CRS is taking what was a negative association for some of their donors and eliminating it, leaving the positive associations you would want for a fundraising brand.

These are the ingredients that go into a successful focus on identity. The process doesn't have the flash of a new logo or a new name. But it will have the positive impacts you want in your fundraising, because it starts with the donor. You speak to a very specific audience or audiences with the words that make them trust you and commit to you. We still love those donors who send a $20 check every year to do generic good. But they aren't what this is about anymore.

Identities are not personas. Personas are not identities.

> *"The reason personas failed to achieve true personalization is that they were too simplistic to reflect the unique attributes that differentiate individual customers and prospects from the mass of other similar customers and prospects. And that is the essence of true personalization."*[109]
>
> – TIAA CMO Connie Weaver

In talking about donor identities, marketers will often say they've tried personas and they haven't worked like the marketer thought they would. Therefore, they aren't going to invest more in seeking donor identities.

Donor identities and personas are fundamentally different. Personas are usually created from cluster analysis of demographic and transactional factors with psychological and attitudinal constructs mapped on top.

So, as a result, you may end up with:

"Anna and Ben are 32-year-old Millennials who are drawn to the advocacy portion of your mission. They live in a growing hip urban area (Seattle? Portland? Nashville? Austin?) and volunteer locally. They try to shop at local stores and are more likely to buy from companies that are socially responsible. When they give, they give in lower amounts, but want to see a concrete impact from their gift. They want their giving to be easy, likely online, and their nonprofit activities to be fun."

The nice part of this is that you get a picture of Anna and Ben (and Ethel and James and the other eight personas you were given). They help you remember that you are not the donor and help you put yourself in another person's shoes.

If you've done persona work, this persona may look familiar to you. If that's the case, know that I generated this by taking one demographic variable (young) and extrapolating things that Millennials are more likely to do as shown in survey data and stereotype.

In other words, I completely made up this persona in two minutes while sitting on a park bench in Washington DC waiting for a meeting. If you have a persona that looks like this, the person who gave it to you made it up too.*

In case you think I'm exaggerating, here are three real descriptions of PRIZM social groups based on demographic data. While reading, think about what different approaches you would make in your messaging to one group over the other:

> "Big Sky Families – Scattered in placid towns across the American heartland, Big Sky Families is a segment of young rural families who have turned high school educations and blue-collar jobs into busy, middle-class lifestyles. Residents like to play baseball, basketball and volleyball, besides going fishing, hunting and horseback riding. To entertain their sprawling families, they buy virtually every piece of sporting equipment on the market."

---

* They may or may not have been sitting on a park bench while doing so.

> "Mayberry-ville – Like the old Andy Griffith Show set in a quaint picturesque berg, Mayberry-ville harks back to an old-fashioned way of life. In these small towns, middle-class couples and families like to fish and hunt during the day, and stay home and watch TV at night. With lucrative blue-collar jobs and moderately priced housing, residents use their discretionary cash to purchase boats, campers, motorcycles and pickup trucks."

> "Blue Highways – On maps, blue highways are often two-lane roads that wind through remote stretches of the American landscape. Among lifestyles, Blue Highways is the standout for lower-middle-class couples and families who live in isolated towns and farmsteads. Here, Boomer men like to hunt and fish; the women enjoy sewing and crafts, and everyone looks forward to going out to a country music concert."

Let me emphasize – these are **different** groups. Allegedly.

It just intuitively feels right to ask a series of global questions on how people feel (e.g. about your cause and supporting charities, etc.) and then group them based on the responses. *The primary challenge with these personas is the difference between groups is not related to why they give to the charity.*

Personas never go far enough to say why they support your specific charity and what that group (much less an individual person) needs, specifically, from your charity. For example, just because group A is 17% more concerned with climate change than group B, it doesn't follow that you should focus on climate change for group A – either or both groups may believe from a more persuasive messaging point.

More importantly, even if you know that Person A (vs. group A) cares about climate change, it is not digging deep enough, we need to know why. This "why", the one that sits below your brand, your messaging and your mission is the centerpiece of being donor-centric, it is the supporter's "why" and unless you dig that deep you'll forever be scratching the surface.

That's the downside of personas. You are given a name and a cluster, but the data is all demographic and transactional. Those can tell you "what" and a bit about "who." They can't tell you why. This severely limits how you can use them in marketing, untethered as they are to giving behavior. So the costly persona binder gathers dust on a shelf.

But perhaps even worse than not using personas is trying to implement them. In *Technically Wrong*, Sara Wachter-Boettcher highlights some "When Personas Attack" scenarios, like Etsy asking women what they were going to get "him" for Valentine's Day, when the recipient's partner was a "her." But one stuck out to me. She was working with a CMO to put names to personas, a common exercise to help create empathy for the user. He agreed with all their choices until:

> "We reached the last persona, "Linda." A stock photo of a fortyish black woman beamed at us from above her title: "CEO."
>
> Our client put down his paper. "I just don't think this is realistic," he said. "The CEO would be an older white man."
>
> My colleague and I agreed that might often be the case, but explained that we wanted to focus more on Linda's needs and motivations than how she looked.
>
> "Sorry, it's just not believable," he insisted. "We need to change it." …
>
> Back at the office, "Linda" became "Michael" – a suit-clad, salt-and-pepper-haired white guy."[110]

You could say don't throw the baby out with the bathwater – we should not throw out personas just because of one (expletive redacted). But there is no baby. Even if the persona had stayed Linda, it would have put everyone who had a set of needs into a demographic bucket. It is how Etsy "knew" its female users wanted to buy gifts for Ben, not Betty.

Identities are based on *first-party data*, not third-party data like personas. Identities are tied to why people give to you, not what they believe about life in general. Identities allow for specific messaging, while personas give you vague ideas of what a person in that cluster might be slightly more likely to want at best and unusable stereotypes at worst.

It is knowing the donor's core reason(s) for giving that is key to getting the right donors and retaining them for the long-term. To do that, we must listen in all channels at all times, then work to customize to our donor's desires. Having talked about this customization, let's now talk about the listening.

Staying preferred through donor feedback

> "As a manager, how do you seek out dissenting opinions?"
>
> *"Well, when I hear about them..."*
>
> "But by their nature you may not hear about them."
>
> *"Well, when someone comes forward and tells me about them."*
>
> "But Linda, what techniques do you use to get them?"
>
> *(No response)*[111]
>
> – Discussion between a Columbia disaster investigator and Linda Ham, the Mission Management Team Chair for the Columbia space shuttle mission

So how do you get this mystical identity once you know what you are looking for? *You ask right at the point of acquisition, along with other information that will help you retain them.* As the above quote shows, you will get the level of feedback you actively solicit.

Think about the most common donor interaction people have with your organization. If you have anything under 50% retention of new donors, and chances are you do, that most common interaction is:

- Someone donates.
- You talk to them some more and ask for donations repeatedly.
- You don't hear from that donor again.

Maybe you could have done something to retain their support. But you'd never know that unless you ask them.

You can barely move in the for-profit world without getting asked for your feedback. In tracking a week's worth of transactions, I found that half of all my transactions had direct feedback outreach (including a hotel where the desk clerk was asleep with a towel over his head). Another third had passive asks for feedback (including the link to a survey on my receipt at the post office). Only one-sixth of my transactions didn't ask for any feedback:

- The airport parking lot.
- A local Chinese restaurant. In fairness, the characters at the bottom of my receipt may be a request for feedback, but as I don't read Mandarin, it likely isn't a good ask for feedback.
- An airline that for the sake of anonymity I'll refer to as Definitely-Not-Canadian Airlines, who cancelled my Washington to Nashville flight for weather problems, despite clear skies between Washington and Nashville and the flight originally being delayed for mechanical issues. This phantom thunderstorm is important because it means that Definitely-Not-

> Canadian Airlines would not pay for the hotel in Charlotte[*] at which I had to stay for six hours before flying back to Nashville.

If your nonprofit isn't asking for feedback, I'm not saying that you are as bad at customer service as Definitely-Not-Canadian Airlines. You, dear reader, have never forced me to go to Charlotte against my will while paying for the alleged privilege.[†]

I am, however, saying that if you aren't asking for feedback, you are:

- As good at getting feedback as DNC Airlines.
- Worse at it than a hotel where the desk clerk is asleep.
- *Worse than the United States Postal Service* (shudder).

The preponderance of for-profit companies asks for feedback. (And for-profit companies represent the vast preponderance of our experiences, so this has become expected).

Feedback can also help you see issues you wouldn't normally see, like our sleeping hotel desk manager.

You probably know a decent number of your donors' pain points just from unsolicited feedback. In years of cataloging feedback for nonprofits, DonorVoice has found that some things cut across almost all major nonprofits as pain points – things like wanting fewer mailings, the desire to designate gifts, or problems with honor/memorial gifts.

And yet, each organization has its own unique challenges, things like:

- An acknowledgment email that was four pages long. People were printing it for their records and shocked that the basic data couldn't fit on one page.

---

[*] How did Charlotte get involved in this? This is an excellent question to which I've never received a satisfactory answer.

[†] Therefore I default when possible to Definitely-Not-Northeast Airlines.

- A temporary glitch where all donations, big or small, were acknowledged as $40 gifts.
- Anger[*] about having to put in a title on the donation form – it was a required field for that organization
- A confirmation email that had last name with no title, so it would say (for example) "Dear Ellinger,".
- Asks that led with a string in the message starting at $15. Yet, the smallest amount on their donation form was $50.

Thankfully, these organizations were able to fix these errors, as well as some of the issues that cross organizations like PayPal and designating gifts. All were simple to fix. All were discovered by people whose experience was bad enough that they either did not give or said they would not give again.

Without feedback, you're burning donors. Not passively failing to retain them – actively burning them.

Yes, you should secret shop your own processes. But if you designed it, you are probably more in the know than your prospective donor. This is the curse of knowledge: when you have knowledge, you can't effectively place yourself in the role of one who does not know. Plus, that donor may have desires or needs you can't imagine. I once had someone want to know how he could donate a cow.[†]

The only way to discover how the people who didn't donate or aren't going to donate again got burned is to ask them. Because you have something like the $40 glitch or the last name bug or the confirmation email that prints like Tolstoy or a form that refuses to autofill. You may just not know it yet. And that's burning donors.

Even the act of asking helps retention: people like being asked for their opinion. People who are asked for feedback are more likely to do business with you again even if nothing was done about their feedback.

---

[*] NOT an exaggeration.

[†] Not all feedback can be accommodated.

You can improve retention just by hearing people out (and you can do even better if you do something about it).[112]

So how do you do feedback well?

I take a lesson I first read about in Jordan Ellenberg's *How Not to be Wrong*.[113] During World War II, the Allies puzzled about where to put armor on their bombers. Strategic attacks needed these flying fortresses, but this necessity also made the bombers a prime target.

Armor is heavy. Heavy is flight's mortal enemy, as anyone knows who has run down the sidewalk flapping their arms while wearing a cape.* It sounds like a simple problem – look at where enemy fire hits the bombers and put the armor there. Officers went to Abraham Wald, a mathematician working for the Allied cause, and asked him how much armor to put on those spots.

Abraham Wald said none. He said the opposite: you need to put the armor where no bullet holes are showing. In this case, it was the pilot compartment, engine, fuselage, and fuel system.

I'll spare you some speculation: Wald was right; the officers were wrong. Decades later, Wald's paper on the subject was released to the general public because "not only as a matter of historical interest but also because the methodology is still relevant."[114]

But why was his counterintuitive answer right?

Because of the missing planes.

The Allies could only look at the planes that made it back. The places that were observed to have more bullet strikes – a wing, for example – could take more hits and still survive. Put that same level of fire on the pilot, the engine, or the highly combustible parts of the plane and that plane would no longer be available for observation.

So they armored the places with **fewer** bullet holes. As a result, more planes made round trips.

So where are your missing bullet holes? Four places come immediately to mind:

1. Any place where you aren't seeing donor feedback. Are you:

---

* Tried last week. Still didn't work.

- Reading donor comment mail?
- Asking your telemarketers to forward any comments to you?
- Reading all the email responses that are coming into your e-newsletter's reply account?
- Mingling at events to hear the chatter?

These are the easiest places to start. While it seems obvious, too few organizations listen to everything they are being told. The challenge here is that these are the things that your supporters will expect you to know – after all, they told you.

2. Any place where you aren't actively soliciting donor feedback. If you are listening to what people are saying, you have taken the first step. However, while necessary, it isn't sufficient. Hearing what is said will only get you the loudest voices, but not necessarily the most important ones.

If that doesn't work for you, remember that people don't give you credit for not knowing something. Rather, people tend to use something closer to the legal standard "knew or should have known."

Did Ken Lay know what skullduggery was going on at Enron? Doesn't matter. He knew or should have known. Ten felony counts say so.

Did NASA officials know about the O-ring problem that led to the Challenger disaster? It was sued by a widow from the flight who alleged that it "knew or should have known that the segments of the righthand solid rocket booster would not properly seal."[115] Even if it just failed to ask the right questions, it was liable.

Is Weinstein Co. liable for Harvey Weinstein's conduct? Lawsuits say the board "knew or should have known that Weinstein would lure young aspiring actresses into compromising situations."[116] Weinstein Co. is no more.

You are a nonprofit marketer. You live in a very different class from felonious execs and negligent administrators, but the question that faces you is the same. It isn't whether you know your donors' preferences;

it's whether you know or should have known them. Even if you just fail to ask the right questions, your donors will hold you liable as if you knew but failed to honor them.

3. When you don't have an organized response. Even if you are asking for feedback, then reading your comment mail, getting telemarketing comments, and reading your email responses, you are still not fully taking advantage of feedback.

Picture if the Air Force had analyzed each plane as a separate incident. Without aggregated information, not have been enough information would exist to act. You'd be at the whim of whatever plane the general happened to see the day he did his tour, which would be counterproductive unless he saw the general exception – a plane that took engine fire and survived.

Yet that's what often happens at a nonprofit. The mail folks respond to the mail comments, the online folks handle the online comments, and the telemarketers deal with the phone comments. Donor services staff help each person individually without big-picture visibility. To use the old analogy, people fight alligators all day instead of taking the steps to drain the swamp.

At best, it takes longer to bring up problems because everyone must recognize the pattern in their own area then elevate it. This makes it so that the pain points that cause systemic problems and donor loss are dealt with slowly. At worst, systemic issues don't get brought up at all.

Thus, it's important to have this information in one place and be able to respond to it methodically. Ideally, all your feedbacks requests flow into the same system and donor relations folks address individual cases while as the individual cases add up to real data.

4. When you are only listening to your fans and not your former fans. This is the true "missing bullet holes" problem. Everything that your current donors and supporters bring up as problems are the things that those people have survived. The problems that former donors and supporters have are the things that will kill you.

When you are looking at feedback platforms, you need to also reach out to people who have left the organization, either passively (by lapsing) or actively (by requesting to leave). Many people who leave still believe in the mission and think your organization is important. Either they didn't think it was as important anymore or didn't like the experiences they had with you. If it's the latter, they may want to tell you about it but didn't bother calling.

In addition, good feedback systems:

- Are systems.
- Are simple and standardized.
- Give donors a reason to participate. It doesn't have to be a gift card or a cookie, but even having a "because" phrase in there (we want your feedback, because we want you to be happy with your experience) is powerful.
- Allow the user to pick the channel. Do you want to talk or not talk? Go online or stay offline? All options should ideally be available to someone who may want to leave an anonymous tip or yell at someone for a while until they feel better.
- Have follow-up.

What is it worth to you to be able to address any questions, doubts, problems, etc., that these donors are having? For the YMCA, the answer was millions of dollars… except they had spent it in the wrong place. From *The Power of Habit:*

> "[T]he accepted wisdom among YMCA executives was the people wanted fancy exercise equipment and sparkling, modern facilities. The YMCA had spent millions of dollars building weight rooms and yoga studios. When the surveys were analyzed, however, it turned out that while a facility's attractiveness and the availability of workout machines might have caused people to join in the first place, what got them to stay was something else. Retention, the data said, was driven by emotional factors, such as whether employees knew members' names or said hello when they walked in.

> People, it turns out, often go to the gym looking for a human connection, not a treadmill."*[117]

From 150,000 YMCA member surveys, you see a few key things:

- What gets someone to join isn't always what gets them to stay.
- What gets them to stay isn't always what you'd think.
- You can make a big difference by making little improvements to the right things.
- You can spend time, toil, and treasure on things that don't matter if you don't learn from your constituents first.

Recently, DonorVoice worked with an international relief charity on an analysis like this. It found that if the organization could improve their engagement communications with their donors by one point on a ten-point scale, it could improve the lifetime value of their donors by almost one Euro.

DonorVoice also discovered if the organization could improve their fundraising communications with their donors by one point, it could improve the lifetime value of their donors by almost 70 Euros.

Their engagement communications – e-newsletter, member magazine, website, blog posts – made almost no impact on their donors' retention and value. What mattered to donors – mattered greater than 70 times more – was feeling like their donation was having a positive impact, feeling valued as a supporter, understanding how their donation was used, and having it put toward the charitable activity that mattered to that donor (their identity-based reason for giving).

These were fixable experiences, repaired and improved with a fraction of the resources that were going toward all the "nice" engagement communications that weren't making a difference. For

---

* People other than me, that is. Personally, I've cultivated my soft, pale, unattractive physique so no one is interested in creating a connection with me at the gym. It's as close as I will get to the superpower of invisibility.

them, the engagement communications were their shiny elliptical machines and pristine yoga studios: expensive, shiny, and just about worthless.

For you and your organization, it will likely be different: a touchpoint that doesn't touch hearts, a newsletter that serves so many internal masters it has no point, a discussion of branding that is entering its 27th month.

This sounds like bad news. A significant part of what you and I do is worthless.

Ick.

But the good news is that with organized donor feedback and analysis, you can cut out what doesn't work and fix what's broken with the time and money you got back.

An example of a "fix" was one organization that measured satisfaction post-donation online. Their form had 50-60% of people saying it was "very difficult" to use. Text analysis of the free responses that people had named a few culprits:

- Their email and web confirmation pages were four pages long to print.
- Their form wasn't mobile friendly.
- They had a huge image on the top of the page that made it load slowly.
- Instead of simple $50 buttons, you had to read multiplier copy that read "$50.00 to send $10,500 of X."
- They hadn't incorporated PayPal.

Over a month, it fixed all these issues. Conversion went from 12% to 32% and the people who said the form was "very difficult" went from 50-60% to less than 1%. I've yet to see an organization that hasn't been able to improve with feedback.

You can also model and predict based on a few variables (commitment, satisfaction, and identity) who is going to stay with your organization and who is going to defect. This advance warning gives you a huge advantage when it comes to retention.

Amnesty Belgium brought all these feedback tools to bear on retaining their face-to-face donors. It's no secret that face-to-face donor retention is extremely challenging. On the street, your fundraisers aren't meeting cultivated lists of people -- they are meeting random folks.* Amnesty experienced this randomness in action. Despite years of acquiring new donors through face-to-face canvassing, their number of total sustainers on file remained static. It took a significant investment each year to keep running in place on the treadmill.

Something had to be done. It asked these donors for their commitment, satisfaction, and identity right at point of acquisition. These were the most predictive variables in their modeling, so collecting these data was like buying a crystal ball.

When it measured experience, and matched that with a model using commitment, four groups presented four different donor journeys:

1. High commitment, high satisfaction: This is what you love to have. Keep them and upgrade them.
2. Low commitment, low satisfaction: I'm surprised you could sign these people up. They don't particularly like you or the experience they had with you. These people are unlikely to be good long-term donors.
3. Low commitment, high satisfaction: They liked your canvasser, but don't know that much about you. These are the "persuadables," ready to hear your messaging and be convinced.
4. High commitment, low satisfaction: Red alert! These are people who love you but didn't have a great experience. These are the donors most likely to forgive and become productive long-term donors with a bit of apology. Amnesty Belgium focused on

* OK, not totally random -- they are placed in areas to maximize their potential success and screen people based on what they look to be. After these screens, however, it's largely random.

> these folks instantly, often with a phone call to see what went wrong. In this case, a $4 phone call can save a donor who cost $250 to $500 to acquire.

They found that people who complained and had their complaints immediately resolved retained even better than people who enjoyed their initial experience. The Rolling Stones were wrong: you can get some satisfaction. It requires you to measure your donors' satisfaction with all their experiences and fix the things that are broken both for that donor and globally.

This example is particularly instructive because commitment and satisfaction became the most predictive variables in their modeling. This means it had a better idea of who would lapse with just these questions. (It got even better when incorporating traditional F2F data like age and amount of first gift. But if you could only have self-reported data or transactional data, you'd want the self-reported data every day of the week.)

Moreover, Amnesty Belgium could reward those canvassers who were bringing in the best quality donors instead of those bringing in the largest quantity of donors. Those who brought in large numbers of dissatisfied and uncommitted donors would have been gold to the canvassing agency. After all, these organizations get paid by the donor and pay their canvasser by the hour. Thus, any canvasser with above average donors per shift is a success.

Amnesty Belgium has different objectives from that canvasser. Their goal isn't quantity of donors, but quantity of donors who retain. Having commitment and satisfaction data allowed them to refocus their program on their goals rather than their canvasser's goals. It could reward the solicitors and solicitation tactics that brought in the most committed donors, not the most donors. This greatly diminished high-pressure tactics that may boost acquisition response rates but leave coffers dry in the long term.

The whole process increased Amnesty Belgium's six-month retention from 60% to 80%. Or, put another way, it was able to cut their attrition in half. This meant an additional 24 Euros per year per donor.* Considering the cost of obtaining any donor, this is a great breakthrough.

What could you do with half the attrition you currently face?

This technique works for any means of acquisition. Different canvassers had different levels of success in getting donors who stay. Replace "canvassers" with "mail pieces," "lead generation campaigns," "DRTV spots," or "channels" and it still works. As do the tactics. Regardless of channel, it always works to:

1. Measure donor quality at point of acquisition.
2. Fix the experience for those who need it.
3. Improve your means of acquisition using retention as a goal.

Moreover, you gain the data necessary to become a preferred organization for your donors. You know what donors want in the beginning and you fix things. You know what they want for the long haul and give it to them. Your donor journeys fit the roads the donors want to travel, making them more likely to travel them with you.

But how do you get these donors to begin with? That's our next section – building an audience, then a donor base.

---

* For Americans, European F2F recruitment often starts at much lower ask levels than in the United States, with the goal of bringing donors into the organization, then upselling them; your gain on retention would likely be higher.

The media organization nonprofit: Building an audience

The tragedy of the commons, part 2

> *"All companies have customers. Lucky companies have fans. But the most fortunate companies have audiences. An audience can be your secret weapon. A lot of companies still spend big bucks to reach people. Every time they want to say something, they dip in to their budget, pull out a huge wad of cash, and place some ads. But this approach is both expensive and unreliable... Today's smartest companies know better. Instead of going out to reach people, you want people to come to you. An audience returns often on its own to see what you have to say. This is the most receptive group of customers and potential customers you'll ever have."*[118]
>
> –Jason Fried and David Heinemeier Hansson

You have a rod and reel. Tonight, you will eat the fish you catch today. If you catch nothing, you eat nothing.

So you head toward the nearest body of water. Many other anglers are plying their trade. Most fish are on the west side; you follow them. You find them using similar bait; you ape them. As you pull up your third fish, you congratulate yourself on your wise choices. You will return to this spot while the fish keep biting. Soon, you will be the person that new anglers follow, watching you for cues on location, bait, and technique.

Consider this now from the perspective of the fish. Two schools of thought exist.* One has short memories (the Dories) and believes the

* Get it? Fish? *Schools* of thought? I crack me up.

western part of the water is a good place to get tasty morsels. The other believes the western part of the water is a trap (the Ackbars).

After several fish generations, the balance of power shifts decidedly to the Ackbars, who have a tendency not to be hoisted skyward. If too many Dories and too few Ackbars were swimming around at the beginning, the entire fish population might be at risk.

So it is with donor acquisition. (Here I speak mostly of direct mail acquisition, as it is the most popular and the one with the most liberal ethos about list sharing.) We fish from the same pool of donors as other organizations. We self-select to the techniques (aka bait) we will use, seeking out premium-based donor pools and lists if we use premiums to acquire and non-premium-based donor pools if we do not. Or we use a mix of techniques, matching our tactics to the type of donor we wish to acquire.

We get ever more efficient about where we fish, using models and the best fit lists to hone our selection of territory. List cooperatives will even tell us about the best spots for fishing, using data to determine where you will find the best donors.

But the real best donors are ones that organizations keep for themselves: monthly, major, planned giving, and so on. On average, a donor will lose 10-15% of their lifetime value to your organization once swapped.[119] Organizations see what happens when the "best" fishing spots get overcrowded – the fishers keep going, but the fish don't.

And overcrowded those spots will be. We are too often in denial about this simple fact. I once asked a panel of list cooperative leaders when they see diminishing marginal results. To how many organizations does a person have to give to be less likely to give to the next one than they were the last? If someone gives to 25 organizations, are they as likely to give to the 26th?

The representative from the co-op said no such point existed: everyone who gives to another organization is always ever more likely to give to the next one.

This is mathematically impossible.

Somewhere on that co-op's file is the person who gives to the most nonprofits – let's say it's 86. Since they have never seen anyone give to

87, that would have to be the point of diminishing marginal returns. It's probably before then, but there (by definition) is a point.

In other words, the co-op's answer is like saying people get healthier and healthier and healthier until the moment they die, when they are at the peak of their health. (And they will be even healthier postmortem.)

In reality, those who we would count as our supporters feel they have to defend themselves from us, using piles and lists and feedback missives to hold us in check. They may not know their dopamine does this, their oxytocin does that, and their ACTH does the other thing, but they know and guard against the implications.

Our current mail acquisition strategies are the tragedy of the commons writ large. We are poisoning the minds of those who would support us.

Yet, it is in everyone's best interests to mail people who have given to other charities. After all, they meet a basic criterion: they are willing to give a charitable gift. It is an article of faith for many that it's easier to get someone who donates to one organization to donate to another.

The truth is, though, that the ol' fishing pond is shrinking. Stocking it isn't just the economically right thing to do; it's also the actual right thing to do. If the price of donating to one is being solicited by all, to sort one's mail into "maybe" and "no" piles, we risk overfishing our waters without restocking, driving people out of giving.

That is a pity: giving is a good thing. It's possibly the best thing.

Yes, people do it for their own happiness or they seek a tax break or they want to look good or a myriad of self-serving reasons.

But we are all on this mostly blue orb together. And to act like it – to serve another – is one of the great beauties of being human. This is a joy we can and should spread beyond those who currently feel it.

Thus, we must add a tool to our toolbox. We've spent most of our time getting people who give to care about us; now, we must get people who care about you to give.

It's a heavy burden to create the next generation of charitable donors. Someone must do it. But how?

We become attention merchants. We create content that demands to be consumed and interacted with. We build an audience and trust with that audience first. Then, and only then, we engage with people the way they want to engage: with their wallets, their labors, and/or their voice. This audience and our relationship to them is our asset, our growth formula, our store of food for the winter.

We can't count on anyone else to do this for us. You may not remember the name Aylan Kurdi. Yet you likely remember his photo. He was a five-year-old Syrian boy lying dead face-down on a beach in Turkey. For a moment, his photo focused people on the humanitarian catastrophe in Syria and the plight of the refugee.

For a moment.

Researchers looked at this specific case, tracking Google search trends for Syria, refugees, and Aylan. Within one month, they were all back to baseline or near baseline. Similarly, donations to the Swedish Red Cross working in Syria returned to baseline within six weeks. The study's authors said:

> "[t]his form of empathy quickly faded and donations subsided, even though the number of Syrian refuges seeking asylum in Sweden was relatively high and consistent throughout the period that we sampled (36,000–40,000 per month)."[120]

The suffering didn't go away. Attention did.

Earned news media can get you attention for an issue. It is incapable of sustaining focus on your issue. That's why it's called news – it literally originated as the plural of "new." It also focuses disproportionately on the sensational. It takes 280 deaths from storms, 1,696 deaths from droughts, or 38,920 deaths from famine to get as much media attention as one death from a volcano or two deaths from an earthquake. If you can see it on the Universal Studios tour, it's going to get more media play. Worse, if your newsworthy moment happens at the same time as another newsworthy issue – say, the Olympic Games – you will be crowded out and get less funding for your issue. [121]

You can get sustained focus on your issue three, and only three, ways:

1. Create attention among people who care about your issue frequently and deeply, building your own spotlight for when the large ones are focused elsewhere.
2. Harness the spotlight while you have it, whether it is news attention or the fleeting micromoment a person spends with a search engine.
3. Both #1 and #2.

And the gold standard is to be able to take people acquired by #2 and convince them to become the people in #1.

We can't count on others to own the audience. They won't get our message out; when they do, it will be the Cliff's Notes version, unable to satisfy those hungry for substance. Thus, we must create our own media audience. The only difference is traditional media audiences get sold brown sugar water and things for ~~four~~ three easy payments. Yours will be able to make a positive mark on the world.

As I write this, the current foreign policy debate is over whether the United States should pre-emptively strike a country with nuclear weapons.[*] The current domestic policy debate is whether the United States should have a domestic policy. And mass media is, well "mass" – looking for the largest number of clicks and eyeballs. It's nigh impossible to get sustained attention for ongoing clean-up in Puerto Rico or SNAP eligibility criteria or Veterans Administration mental health resources in the media tools of yore.

But the people who have your identities and want to be a part of something bigger than themselves as a part of their identities want to hear from you. They want your news. For the people you help and for the people who make your mission possible, those issues are vital. They want to hear about them from someone. Ideally it would be someone they trust. You know… someone like you. If you aren't going to fill

---

[*] As I edit this section, I think how outdated this is – the current debate is whether we should strike a different country with conventional (for now) weapons.

that void, something else will – another issue, another organization, another way to spend time and treasure.

Being the media organization for your supporters holds great value. At the top of the conversion funnel, we are running out of people who give and who want to give to new issues and organizations (at least running out of them versus the number of entreaties they get to take on new organizations). This is challenging, but thankfully part of this answer, like the Scarecrow's brains, Dumbo's not-feather, and the True Meaning of Christmas*, has been in us the whole time. We can test the effectiveness of bringing in new constituents to the organization by looking at those already in the middle of the conversion funnel (e.g., newsletter subscribers, advocacy participants, content consumers, and those served like alumni) and the ones who give at a distance (event participants, emergency donors, P2P donors giving to their friend more than the organization).

At the middle of the funnel, someone who gets their news on an issue from you will trust you more than any other. People who trust you are more likely to donate. And, if they are donating to one of your news stories, you also know the types of content and interactions they are more likely to react to in the future.

Once someone has donated, providing media still has great value. Look at the NRA. Not the politics of the NRA, but rather their construction of identity.

Theoretically, the impact of the NRA should be small. Gun owners are a minority of the US population (up to 86 million owners, depending on the study[122]). Of those, about five million are NRA members, according to the NRA. Even of those members, 74% say they favor background checks for private gun sales[123] (which the NRA opposes).

Or put another way, a minority of a minority of a minority opposes background checks for private gun sales; 84% of Americans support them[124]. But they aren't mandated in the United States. The NRA has done an outstanding job of unifying and activating its membership.

* Spoilers: it's caring, God, and/or family.

Recent research[125] by Matthew Lacombe talks about how this happened. He analyzed the editorials in the NRA's American Rifleman magazine and found:

> "The editorials show that for decades, the NRA has cultivated an image of gun owners as having a particular set of positive characteristics: They are reputable, law-abiding, honest, patriotic citizens who are self-sufficient and love freedom. And gun owners are presented as different from several distinct out-groups, especially politicians, the media and lawyers.
>
> Over this period, nearly three-quarters of NRA editorials framed gun regulation as attacking gun owners' identities. Rather than using technical, evidence-based appeals to argue that gun control won't reduce crime, the NRA argues that gun control disarms law-abiding citizens so that they're unable to defend themselves and their country."

This consistent message shapes the viewpoints of the NRA membership. Lacombe also looked at letters to the editor about gun control over the same period and found:

> "Pro-gun letters consistently mimic the NRA's political appeals. Nearly two-thirds of the letters use identity language that speaks proudly of "us gun owners," describing them as patriotic, courageous and so on, in contrast to "those anti-gunners," described as radicals, elitists and the like. Most of these letters talk about how gun control would hurt gun owners' lifestyles and values. The mimicry remains consistent over the decades; as the NRA's editorials change, the pro-gun letters change, as well, echoing the contemporary themes and descriptions of both gun owners and gun-regulation advocates."

How about those who support gun control? He found that fewer than half of anti-gun letters used identity language. When they did, it was usually casting the NRA as a villain; fewer than a quarter of letters talked about their authors' identity. This isn't just an organization that has found its tribe; it shaped what that tribe thinks about the NRA and about themselves.

Nonprofits have three frequent objections to this out-of-the-box way of thinking: 1) it's not our business; 2) it's too expensive; and 3) it's too hard.

To the first, remember we aren't in the railroad business; we're in the transportation business. Or, more literally, we are in the business of creating the desire for action, then converting that desire into action itself. That we can do this by building what would have been a media organization is irrelevant.

To the second, the costs of operating a media organization have never been lower. You could run one entirely online with owned assets and little-to-no marginal costs. Audiovisual equipment can be as cheap as the phone in your pocket. There is no need to buy ink by the barrel, at least to start. You already have the raw materials. You have stories: stories of heartache and hope, terror and triumph.

Which leaves us with "it's too hard." To this, I'd agree. It's easy to do what you've always done. But if you do what you've always done, you are going to get what you've always got.

Co-opting the new competitors: Google and Facebook

> *"Senator, we run ads."*
>
> – Mark Zuckerberg explaining the Facebook business model to Sen. Orrin Hatch.

In 2018, Americans watched our elected representatives struggle with understanding Facebook's business model the way I struggle to break into modern plastic packaging. Come to think of it, maybe the senators would have been better able to grasp an advertising model if they'd used a pair of scissors or their teeth.

How Facebook makes money is easy: ads. (They could monetize it a score of other ways; they are all likely coming.)

The tricky bit is how it got in a position to make that money. To make money from ads, you need eyeballs; to make real money from ads, you need both eyeballs and data.

Facebook got organizations to <u>give</u> them eyeballs and data. Facebook didn't run ads that said "Like us on Facebook." Your local car dealer did. Your school district did. Your nonprofit is probably advertising Facebook right now.

Somehow, Facebook got organizations to give them their audience, their audience's eyeballs, and their audience's data. Every time you send someone to Facebook to like you, Facebook gets that person[*], their attention, and the fact that they like you. Those are all things Facebook can leverage to sell ads; it does.

This isn't a new idea; a newspaper ad is little more than the advertising trying to capture the newspaper's audience. Heck, our mail acquisition packages are attempts to try to get some other nonprofit's audience. The new part is that, with Facebook, we did it for free.

It's brilliant. It's also the way we need to think about acquisition. We aren't trying to attract donors; we are trying to attract an audience. This audience is looking for some quid for their quo.

But Facebook and Google are also ahead of us, trying to get our donor data, and our donations, *before* we can. Facebook used to have a five percent transaction fee; now it doesn't. It's easy to donate through the site; if you want to donate through non-Facebook functionality, you must click a pop-up box to leave. And it's growing by leaps and bounds – it doubled Giving Tuesday donations in 2017, then almost tripled them in 2018.[126]

---

[*] Although by now, Facebook likely already had them.

Google also has created Google Search Donations, so a donate button shows up next to your organization when it is searched for. This donation goes to their donor-advised fund, which is then dispersed to you.

On the one hand, these are super convenient. We work to minimize the steps necessary to donate; these have zero steps. Donors don't have to come to your site. And it's free.

But this isn't a panacea. It isn't any sort of acea, because:

You don't own the donor. In its terms of service for donations, Facebook says it will provide the nonprofit with first name, last name, and email address (if they specifically opted in).[127] Notable in their absence are physical address and opting into different channels of communications, meaning that you have no effective way to contact this donor if they gave no email.

This is still better than Google. In its FAQ, Google says:

> "Will I receive donor contact information? No. At this time, Google does not share user contact information with Google for Nonprofits organizations. We recognize that this is an important component of the relationship between nonprofits and donors, and are considering how to strengthen this in the future."[128]

At press time here, Instagram was creating a donation platform as well and, suh-prise, suh-prise:

> "The company said it was too early to talk about how the donor data that Instagram collects through this feature will be shared with participating charities."[129]

These are donors who are unlikely to keep giving if only because you can't take steps to retain them. The lifetime value of a $20 donor acquired any other way is more than $20 because you have a chance to turn this person into a long-time donor. The lifetime value of a $20 donor acquired through donations in Facebook or Google Search

Donations (or potentially Instagram) is $20. They aren't the only ones not to give up this information – witness cause-related marketing or text-to-donate efforts – but this does not make it any less pernicious.

You don't own the donor relationship. Congratulations! You have a great welcome series, online and offline, that thanks donors appropriately, starting with a warm thank-you letter, followed by a series of communications that learns more about donors so you can communicate with them in the way they'd like.

You can't send it.

Even if you have the email address, Facebook declares it, not you, is sending a payment receipt to donors, including your name, logo, mission statement, and EIN. Ditto Google.

As you might guess, this receipt fills in the blanks and checks the boxes. It does not, however, tell a donor what their gift did or anything about the organization, resulting in an acknowledgment that is about as personalized as a McNugget.

It's deceptive. People think they are donating to you – they are not. They are donating to donor-advised funds that act as a pass-through. This is disclosed to the donor the same way the undercoating fee is disclosed to you on a used car: under duress only.

So let's say a donor calls you up at the end of the year and says they need a new receipt for their $100 donation. You don't see it in your database. You tell them they didn't make any such donation to you. You will be right. That fact will not do you one bit of good for your justifiably irate donor.

Other nonprofits can target your donors. Let's say you work for Operation Smile. A list of Smile Train donors would be golden for you. That's why in the direct mail world, you have a list exchange and rental arrangement that you will not rent to competing organizations lest they poach your donors and vice versa.

However, Facebook allows you to advertise to people who are interested in Operation Smile and Smile Train. This means if you work at one, you can advertise to fans of the other. Could you target your advertising beyond just fans? Could you target donors of the other organization? While no such targeting currently exists, Facebook has also made no promises to keep that donor information secret. And since, up until September 2017, they allowed advertisers to target a category called "Jew Haters,"[130] I am personally not betting on moral rectitude winning out over revenue.

They are potentially playing a long game to replace you. It is as shocking to think that for-profit companies want to benefit from their philanthropic activities as to believe that there is gambling going on in Rick's Café Americain. Right now, for-profits partner with nonprofits in affinity programs and other cause-related marketing efforts where donations are conditioned on purchase of a product. These are effective ways to turn a nonprofit's constituents into a for-profit's customers, often at a cost to the for-profit of a couponing or discounting scheme. These are often beneficial to company, nonprofit, and donor, so we're not arguing to avoid these win-win-wins.

For-profits are also giving their products and services directly to what would traditionally have been philanthropic recipients. For example, aiming to wire the world is often product specific:

- Amazon's Kindle Reading Fund aims to increase the distribution of Kindle readers and eBooks through the world. Some of this is through the nonprofit Worldreader (which had previously been platform-agnostic), but Amazon is also making direct donations to libraries, hospitals, schools, etc.[131]
- Facebook's Free Basics program has brought a free, limited version of the Internet to 42 countries and 25 million people. It was, however, kicked out of India for violating their net neutrality standards; the Free Basics program has an alleged pro-Facebook bias.[132] In fact, Facebook's Internet.org efforts to wire the world are part of their business development group, which is both truth in advertising and a remarkable bit of business realpolitik.[133]
- While Google's Free Zone efforts to provide free Internet appear to be defunct, its Loon program now aims to wire the world sans wires through high-altitude balloons.[134]

When Google has worked on other social good issues, it has also flowed through their tools. Its efforts to fight infectious diseases, for example, have come from mapping through Google Earth to create Google Flu Trends.[135]

For-profit companies have solid business reasons for acting on their own behalf in the traditionally non-profit space of philanthropy. And it would be easy enough to do. It is one small step from accepting donations to privileging those causes that accept donations through your platform. It is another small step from privileging causes to starting your own associated cause when you perceive a gap, or weakness, in the nonprofit market. Then it's another small step to privileging the house brand over the external one.

We can use history as our guide, as the pattern is a simple one and oft repeated. Google and Facebook link to outside resources and make them more valuable through search and social connection, respectively. Then, these services incorporate that outside information into their offering. For Google, this has played out with shopping, air travel, mapping, and structured snippets; Facebook has started their own proprietary news sources, gaming apps, and in-site lead generation tools for businesses. The trend is consistently toward these sites incorporating more functionality to minimize the time and effort you spend anywhere else.

One might argue this isn't a goal of these services – donations are not a massive profit center. But they are a source of good will. More than that, donations are often an expression of a core identity. Thus, knowing all donations gives these services extremely valuable data. It's great to charge an enterprising attorney beaucoup bucks for mesothelioma search terms. It's even better to target in perpetuity those people who have made an honor/memorial donation to a mesothelioma charity. And if that charity does not exist, these services can logically create it. Think how much could be charged by these services for information about your ACLU or Judicial Watch membership to the left or right. If those organizations won't give up that data, it can be taken by creating the competition.

This could just be paranoia. Google and Facebook may not be trying to replace you. They may just be taking in donations in your name, monetizing this by adding to the store of data they use for themselves and/or sell to others, and depriving you of the most important part of the transaction – the ability to build a relationship with the donor.*

Facebook and Google donations may be good at helping you get transactional donations. But it will take more information sharing, privacy negotiations, and abilities to do donor stewardship in place before donors through these platforms are ready to become organizational donors.

Until that point, they are your competitors. You want to build an audience; they are trying to take it from you.

Let's flip the script. Let's take their audience from them and build our own. Yes, we will have to pay them for the privilege. But we will also create a group of people who we can talk to, and learn about, without the toll-charging intermediaries.

We've talked about how key *who* you talk to is. Let's add a layer to this and talk about *when* to talk to people.

The power of a micromoment

> *"Do I dare*
> *Disturb the universe?*
> *In a minute there is time*
> *For decisions and revisions which a minute will reverse.*
>
> *For I have known them all already, known them all:*
> *Have known the evenings, mornings, afternoons,*
> *I have measured out my life with coffee spoons;"*[136]

* This isn't unique – it's basically the cause-related marketing model, which is why you should press any partners in this space to share purchaser information. They likely won't, but best you know from where they are coming.

– T.S. Eliot

There are the moments that matter for all of us. Depending on our ages, we remember where we were when the Twin Towers were hit, OJ led the police chase, man landed on the moon, or JFK was shot.* Similarly, there are the charitable events that touch and inspire many givers – disasters like hurricanes, tsunamis, or the Trump presidency.† You may not remember where you were, but many of us went out en masse to donate to relief efforts. Whether you can plan for these or not, they are large-scale events.

Then there is the moment that is deeply personal. You feel a lump. You turn to the Internet, looking for information, help, and hope. This (hopefully) is not a moment you remember a year later or, if you do, it's part of a happy story. In that moment, however, it was everything.

From a nonprofit perspective, these are entirely dissimilar. Fundraising and/or constituent building campaigns go out for the former; the latter is unknown.

To the individual, however, they are the same thing – an emotional impact needing resolution. I remember 9/11, searching British and Australian news sites for information because 1) American news sites were flooded and crashing and 2) I'm not bilingual. I've never used

---

* Actually, we don't. Memory researchers tell us that people who are asked to write down where they were at the time of the incident will change their recollections significantly, to the point they will then *doubt their own handwritten statements*. One year after, only 63% of people recalled where they had been and only 40% recalled the emotions they said they'd felt. (See, for example, https://www.scientificamerican.com/article/911-memory-accuracy/) This seems like a microcosm of the human condition: often in err, rarely in doubt. But we think we remember these things vividly, which is enough for our purposes here.

† For my #MAGA colleagues, I'm talking here about the functional impact as being like a disaster. Many organizations report spikes in giving post-election as a way of resisting the Trump agenda. Many of these donors function like disaster givers in that they join for an event. It's up to the organization to retain them for the long-term. Thus, they fit in this list of people who behave like disaster donors.

some of these sites again; some no longer exist. In that moment, however, that news was my world.

I also vividly remember Googling how to give CPR to a dog. I'd never needed that information before. I hope never to again. In that moment, however, that question was my world.

These are *micromoments*. And they need not be as earth-shattering as these. When was the last time you wondered who that actress is and what movie you knew her from?[*] When that happened, were you content to just not know?

No. Not knowing is so 1990s.

So are not comparison shopping, not buying, not getting what you buy for weeks, not hearing about your donation, not being able to reach the person you want to reach, and not hearing back.

"Instantly" has gone from impossible to luxury to boooooooooring. As a result, these micromoments come and go so quickly.

As organizations, we are the sum of these moments to those we wish to reach for donations and support. The organizations that address people's needs and wants in these moments win trust and loyalty.

This type of expressed intent – whether it's searching for something, going to a web site to learn, opening that piece of mail, etc. – eats demographics for dinner. You might think, for example, that the people searching for video games are 18-34-year-old males. Only 31% of them are.[137] So by targeting people who are looking for video game content, rather than a demographic segment, you can get the people that advertising on *Family Guy* won't get you.[†]

We are not just targeting a group of people. We are targeting a behavior. And we are using that behavior to turn their audience into our audience by being useful to people in their time of need or want.

---

[*] When in doubt, guess a Law and Order episode. Everyone has been in a Law and Order episode. Except me. I tried out for Shifty-Looking Accountant. I must not have been shifty looking enough, because I look a lot like an accountant.

[†] Is this still what 18-34-year-old males watch?

Our new potential audience members

First responders: Reactive giving is not new. Here in the United States, the Johnstown flood of 1889 killed 2,208 people[138] and caused about $500 million in damage in today's dollars. Red Cross president Clara Barton came to the United States to lead disaster recovery efforts. She also raised funds for same, garnering $96 million in today's dollars from Americans and 18 foreign countries.[139]

Now, disaster giving follows a predictable cadence. Blackbaud data show that online giving peaks three days after a disaster. This pattern holds for the spikes after Hurricanes Katrina, Sandy, Matthew, and Harvey/Irma, earthquakes in Haiti, Japan, and Nepal, and Typhoon Haiyan.[140] Within two days of the Notre Dame fire, $1 billion had been pledged.[141] The news goes out that help is needed; first responders respond.

Recently, however, reactive giving has surged to disasters of the human-created kind. In 2017, 21 percent of United States donors said they gave at least once because current political events threatened something they held dear. These donors were twice as likely to be first-time donors to any organization; most gave to causes they'd never given to before.[142] In full disclosure, my wife and I fall into this latter category, adding the Southern Poverty Law Center to our charities after Charlottesville. For the left, giving goes to those institutions that it feels are under threat; for the right, increased security in the economy increases giving to traditional groups like religious and veterans' organizations.[143]

When it was revealed that Donald Trump had told Stormy Daniels that "I would never donate to any charity that helps sharks. I hope all the sharks die,"* the Atlantic White Shark Conservancy and Sea

---

* Is this still a thing that we have to say "allegedly" for? Let's stick in a footnote with an "allegedly" in it, just in case. He **allegedly** told Stormy Daniels this about sharks, which just happens to line up with his anti-shark tweets. Those anti-shark tweets could have just been because Trump was on the side of the Jets in West Side Story.

Shepherd Conservation Society reported a spike in donations. Captain Paul Watson, founder of the latter, said that they'd received "quite a few" donations from first-time donors who mentioned the president's comments. "Anything that focuses attention on the plight of sharks worldwide is valuable, so I guess in that way the president did a good service," said he.[144] I'll go one step further: I believe this is the first time any president's comments to a porn actress had a positive conservation impact.*

Similarly, a Facebook fundraiser…

RED ALERT RED ALERT RED ALERT: RUNNING A FUNDRAISER EXCLUSIVELY ON FACEBOOK WITHOUT A PLAN TO GET DONOR INFORMATION OR COMMUNICATE WITH THE FUNDRAISER IS A BAD IDEA. IF YOU ARE CONSIDERING THIS, PLEASE REPEAT THE SECTION ON HOW FACEBOOK MAY BE TRYING TO REPLACE YOU AND AT LEAST COME TO PEACE WITH THE FACT THAT YOU ARE GETTING DOLLARS, NOT DONORS. WE RETURN YOU TO YOUR REGULARLY SCHEDULED DISCUSSION OF REACTIVE GIVING.

Similarly, a Facebook fundraiser to help parents reunite with children who had been forcibly separated at the US-Mexico border and caged by the United States government raised $20 million from 500,000 people in four days.[145]

Disasters are particularly valuable to us as fundraisers because of the *availability heuristic*: if you can recall an example of something, it must be as or more important than something that you can't easily recall.

A classic example of this from the literature is people overestimate the number of words that begin with the letter R or K.[146] They also underestimate the number of words where R or K is the third letter. People can easily recall things that begin with R or K: that's how they are stored in our brain. Because people can more easily get to them, they think it happens more often.

---

* We all know Warren G. Harding would've if he could've, but that was before talkies.

This can affect how our causes are seen by the public. Crime, for example, is frequently reported on the news. (Lack of crime makes for lousy visuals). As a result, more than half of Americans believed that crime was going up every year (so far) that begins with a two. In fact, crime fell in every one of those years (except for a tiny increase in 2001).[147]

Shark attacks kill fewer people than failing airline parts, but as the news adage goes "if it bleeds, it leads." And shark attacks bleed, meaning that people (including as mentioned earlier, President Trump) systematically overestimate the danger of shark attacks.[148]

If your issue is on the news, then, you have the availability heuristic working for you. It could be, and probably is, the case that systemic poverty harms many more people in Haiti than hurricanes. However, it is when a hurricane hits that donors rush to give aid. They are our shark attacks.

Are these events likely to attract donors and supporters unlikely to stay with you, motivated as they are by a moment, not a mission? Not necessarily so.

To learn why, we need to delve for a moment into donor psychology. It's an article of faith that causes need to make you feel something. In fact, you will hear some professionals bemoan they lack puppies or kids as imagery and thus are disadvantaged in the battle for heart strings.

This make-them-feel, get-a-gift linear relationship is incomplete. Looking at 2017's "rage givers," you found they were not, in fact, giving because of rage. Rather, the most common emotions cited for reactive gifts were hope (61 percent) and empowerment (58 percent). Anger fueled only a quarter (26 percent) of gifts.[149]

Most people aren't citing, then, the emotions they had from the news. They are citing the emotion they sought from their gift.

Now, people are notoriously bad at knowing their own underlying reason for doing something. Emotional reactions happen 3000 times faster than rational thought[150], so most often our rational brain is stuck justifying the decisions we've already made. As a result, people don't know why they do things. Consider a study that asked people to rank their top 16 motivations. Sex was rated #14; money was rated number

#16. Then it measured people's actual subconscious motivations. Money was #5; sex was #1.[151] This should not surprise people who have met other people. It was a surprise, however, to people thinking about themselves. They thought themselves chaste and incorruptible, but really they dreamed of having a very special moment in Scrooge McDuck's vault.

So maybe people said they were giving because of the emotion they wanted (hope) but really were giving because of the emotion they had (rage). Let's test that. Let's use our magic mood-freezing pill.

Spoiler alert: magic mood-freezing pills don't exist. The placebo effect, however, does exist. That is where people believe they have or will have an impact from a medicine regardless of whether the active ingredient is present. Researchers got test subjects to be happy, sad or neutral (by asking them to think about happy/sad/neutral things). Then they told half of each of these subgroups that they were going to take a magic mood-freezing pill – their mood would not change for the near future.[152] These subjects were all then asked to help.

If people help because they have a negative emotion, you would expect that sad people would be most likely to help regardless of whether they took the pill.

What really happened, however, is that sad people helped when they could change their mood. However, when they thought their mood could not change, they didn't help. This clearly supports the idea that it's not about the emotion the donor feels before they make a gift; it's about the emotion they anticipate they will feel after they make a gift. If you can't feel better, why change?

In fact, you may be able to increase giving by calling out the emotional outcome. Catholic Relief Services tested adding the line "Did you know that helping others can make us feel proud too?" to the postscript of an email. Giving increased 81 percent.[153] Similarly, when you tell environmental supporters they'll feel proud as the result of a green action, they are more likely to take it.[154]

This is good news for our reactive givers: you don't have to replicate the exact emotional circumstances that led to a gift to get another gift.

Rather, you must promise the donor you will take them to the same or similar emotional place with their continued support.

As Pam Loeb said about their study on reactive givers:

> "In being "donor centric," organizations need to be strategic about channel preferences and targeted messaging. These data suggest that organizations should also be alert to the emotional triggers and real-life trajectory of donors. Going forward, the most successful organizations will offer the right combination of urgency with hope and progress to keep these donors invested and feel as if their efforts make a difference."[155]

So far, though, it seems like attracting these donors is rather like trying to attract lightning. One never knows when or where a disaster – natural or unnatural – will happen. After all, President Trump is unlikely to declare war on sharks.*

It is still worthwhile to prepare for your moment, even if you aren't a traditional disaster relief organization. The Humane Society of the United States has an Animal Rescue Team that mobilizes for those animals who don't know what's going on, have no voice, and can't choose whether or when to evacuate. During Hurricanes Harvey, Irma, and Maria in 2017, they provided tens of thousands of pounds of supplies for human and non-human animals, thanks in part to their 62,000 new donors to the organization specifically for disaster relief. The American Kidney Fund raised $490,000 during the hurricanes (and distributed even more than that) to help dialysis patients impacted by the storm.[156]

Both knew that the value in these gifts, however, wasn't primarily the gift itself; it was the promise of a potential long-term donation relationship. The Humane Society had an aggressive call-to-thank (not ask) program and robust reporting on the impact of the gift. They also

---

* I really should not make predictions like this lest I give folks ideas.

asked these donors for a second gift (specifically, trying to get a monthly gift conversion) only after learning a bit about them and creating ads customized to the desires of these donors.

The key to this type of disaster or news-based marketing is to build your ark before the rain starts, engaging on social media outside of news and disaster times. A study of nonprofits engaged in fundraising after the Fukushima nuclear plant disaster of 2011 found that organizations that engaged on social media before and after the disaster were significantly more likely to raise larger amounts than those who tried to engage solely after the disaster.[157]

Preparation pays dividends. The Human Rights Campaign raised $277,000 around the Obergefell marriage equality decision, as well as gaining 61,000 new constituents who opted in for emails and 35,000 who opted in for texts.[158] This was the result of a two-year planning process and a five-month communication stream about the decision that included 18 emails, 10 texts, daily social posts, live events, and a social media campaign. The communications were only possible because of the preparation – it had to be ready for a spectrum of decisions from sweeping change to crushing disappointment and all permutations in between. In the end, despite having prepared numerous messaging permutations, it ended up having to take a bit from a few different potential communications when the decision came out.

The first responder supporter and donor can be valuable and can be retained (albeit usually at a lower rate than the average donor). These donors may not look like the donors we are used to getting. Someone who rage-donates because of the tweet that broke the camel's back has a different reason for donating, connection to the organization, and personal identity than someone who has donated to you for 20 years despite, not because of, your ideological inclinations. And treating one like the other will lose that one at best and both at worst.

That's why it's important to both act on a micromoment plan reflecting a different future for them beyond the moment of acquisition. The same often holds true for our advocacy supporters, whom we'll talk about next.

Advocates: You might think of advocates as the politically minded little sibling of the first responder, as these donors don't necessarily give – they get their emotional fix by advocating for different policies. However, I hope to convince you these are also constituents worth having.

Some organizations do not do advocacy work. And you may be involved with those. But I'm guessing most know that a change in government policy could make life on their issue better or worse.

The fact is our nonprofits exist to fill gaps. We live for the day that we are no longer needed – one of perfect justice, health, opportunity, and equity, sans want or deprivation. On that great day, we soldiers for causes can take up golf. I've heard it is good exercise.

Until that great day, though, we have work to do. Public policy can be a headwind or a tailwind depending on the direction we can get the winds to blow. Make no mistake: if we don't try to change the winds, someone else will.

Can we advocate? Absolutely, but only in small doses, because the IRS Web site says:

> In general, no organization may qualify for section 501(c)(3) status if a substantial part of its activities is attempting to influence legislation (commonly known as lobbying). A 501(c)(3) organization may engage in some lobbying, but too much lobbying activity risks loss of tax-exempt status.[159]

So what does "substantial part" mean? One way to look at it is a Justice Potter Stewart-esque* "the IRS knows it when it sees it" type test. The other one is as a percentage of revenues.[160]

---

* In Jacobellis v. Ohio, Justice Potter Stewart said that he would not and perhaps could not define hard-core pornography, but "I know it when I see it." For many years thereafter, the Court would send potentially pornographic materials to Justice Stewart's office for review. This role is now filled by Justice Clarence Thomas.

Note this applies to expenditures. If you set up an online petition about a specific bill and allow constituents to email their representatives, you incur no marginal costs. The only costs are for the platform that allows for this type of advocacy and your time working on the alert, both of which don't increase as the number of people who take the action increases. This is part of why online advocacy is so popular among nonprofits.

Advocacy also works as a strategy because some of our constituents (and our donors) are advocates. They will email their representatives every time you ask them and sometimes when you don't. They will ask for action on issues you haven't yet covered. They will push you and your issues on social media; some of them will be as educated as you on your issues or more so.

It's incumbent upon us to acquire these advocates when we can, using the moment – whether their moment, our organizations' moment, or the zeitgeist's moment – to draw them in to our mission and make them part of our audience.

First, though, let's consider an oft-leveled charge – that so-called "slacktivists" are looking to feel good about themselves while doing very little.

This can be true, sadly. When it is, it is oft the fault of the campaign, not the campaigner. People who sign a petition are more likely to donate to a related nonprofit afterward. [161] In fact, one study found that online campaigns can double response when the donation ask is coupled with an advocacy action. The study also found advocates are seven times more likely than non-advocates to give financially.[162] One of the best non-holiday fundraising emails I've sent wasn't a fundraising email. It was an advocacy email. The organization only asked for money after someone completed the action alert. The donation ask was specific to the issue on which the person had acted. There's gold in them thar hills for the right message.

The concern – and it is legitimate – is the signaling of virtue with advocacy, but no donation may be enough to accomplish what the potential constituent wants to accomplish. This virtual signaling has been found in the lab. Researchers had three groups: one who was given a poppy to wear in honor of veterans, one who was given that same poppy in an envelope so it would be for private support, and one who was given nothing. At the end of the hallway, the groups were asked to donate. Those who showed private support (poppy in the envelope) gave an average of $.86, public supporters gave $.34, and the control gave $.15. They further refined this study in other ways and found that people who give private support are more likely to support in the future; people who give public support are either no more likely or less likely to support the cause than those who did nothing.[163]

This has been echoed in an online advocacy context. Researchers looked at pledges for donations made through an online social media/donation facilitation platform. People who broadcast their pledges on social media were more likely to delete and not fulfill their pledge donations versus those who did not broadcast.[164] This fits the thesis of people publicly pledging to look good, not necessarily to do good.

We see this in all areas of our lives. It's called *moral licensing* – doing one good thing, or appearing to, gives you moral license to do something bad. In looking at shopping carts, for example, selecting a virtuous product makes one more likely to subsequently pick a "bad" product. Other studies have shown that people who have eaten something indulgent are more likely to do good deeds – compensation in both directions. [165]

How can both be true? How can donors want to be consistent and more likely to donate when they've pledged, but be morally licensed and less likely to donate when they've pledged?

This can be reconciled. In another study, people were sorted into three groups. One group was asked to write about good deeds they had done. A second group was asked to write about bad things they had done. And, not surprisingly, the third group was asked to write about neutral things. Then they were asked whether they would like to donate a part of their fee for participating in the study to charity.

Significantly more people donated, and donated more, from the people who were asked to think of good deeds than either bad deeds or neutral actions.[166]

This is consistent with the idea that people who think of themselves as good people are more likely to do good things. People act in relation to their self-conception. But how does this explain moral licensing?

The study found moral licensing happens not when people see themselves as good or bad, but when *others* see them as good or bad. For example, in the study of shopping carts discussed above, the person would be judged by the person checking us out. If you think this doesn't happen, you have never worked at a grocery store.*

This fits with our study on slacktivism: people who did good things to help people are more likely to donate; people who did good things to get recognition as a good person are less likely to donate.

Think of the old saw "I'm not a racist – I have plenty of friends who are [name of target group] – but …" The person is working to establish positive external conception before saying whatever is going to follow. That's why in the history of humankind not a single thing that came after the phrase "I'm not a racist, but…" has ever been good.

So, in short, an advocacy campaign can work to acquire people who will want to take additional actions with you if and only if it is private. Public petitions appear to satisfy a person's desire to manage their reputation, so they were less willing to take other actions. Remember the poppy in the envelope!

When treated properly, advocates will convert to donors at a greater rate than most audience members. Thus, you want them.

Reciprocal exchanges: Organizations vary widely in their ability to get donations from those we have served in some way. On one end of the spectrum, you have higher education. Here, service recipients are the majority of individual funders: alumni represent 26.1% of total giving to universities, compared with 18% for non-alumni individuals.[167] This may not seem like a huge difference, but remember the largest U.S. university living alumni network is Penn State's 673,000[168] in a nation of over 300 million. That means that American universities are raising

---

* I have. We do.

more from the .2% (or less) who are alumni than from the 99.8% who are not.*

Hospitals and disease charities also have built-in advantages to get donation from those they have served. Poverty relief organizations, on the other hand, give assistance to those unlikely to have the near-term means to donate.

This, however, uses a narrow definition of what it is to serve. Reciprocal exchange is hardwired into our psyche; the desire to give back can be triggered by far more minor services like information.

When I worked for Mothers Against Drunk Driving, we were initially puzzled: why was web traffic down by about a third in the summer? We knew that summer tended to be associated with slightly lower response rates. As people vacation, they aren't frequently checking their mail, whether snail, electronic, or voice. However, drunk driving crashes increase over the summer[169] with the intersection of more driving and more drinking.

We looked at the content these visitors were consuming and found our answer. Statistics and information pages were popular every part of the year except summer, when usage plummeted. Summer meant no school. No school meant students aren't writing reports on and researching drunk driving and underage drinking.

This audience was a significant part of MADD's web traffic, a clear and distinct audience. While this audience isn't ripe for conversion to donors, they will be in the long-term. In the meantime, this audience is critical for volunteer support and programmatic outreach; teens and young adults who choose to focus on MADD's issues were wonderfully active and activist about demanding an end to drunk driving.

Every organization has people (or should have people) who are looking to learn about their issues. Some have an interest in the issue for a school report or because they heard a news report. But others are deeply personal.

---

* Base rates matter.

When our daughter wasn't speaking at age two, our (now former) pediatrician told us everything was fine. After all, he said, Einstein didn't talk until he was four.* Even as first-time parents, my wife and I could see our daughter was different from other children. So we consulted the internet and found that her behavior lined up exactly with autism.

Among the great many resources we consulted for diagnosis was Autism Speaks. As we then educated ourselves about autism, we kept coming back to the Autism Speaks site. We ordered their free 100-Day Kit for what to do in the 100 days post-diagnosis.

It helped find a doctor who could diagnose and help. It helped us advocate for our kids in the school system, find medicines that have helped, and learn more about how our kids' brains work. When we thought our world was ending, those materials and that organization was there for us.

From that day to this, we've been donors. We're one of those committed donors we've talked about. This relationship happened because of a match of identity and because of reciprocity – we received, so we should give. As Oprah said "Life is a reciprocal exchange. To move forward, you have to give back."[170]

This type of help-seeking behavior isn't just limited to disease charities. When we lost Benny, our Chihuahua who predated our marriage, we wanted another dog after an appropriate mourning period. We had some very particular criteria: good with our kids, good with loud noises or surprises (because of the kids), a puppy (so the kids could see him/her grow up), and from a shelter.

Thus began my wife's search for a dog. My role was limited to reminding her that, no, we could not bring home all the dogs.

Fortunately, our local shelters have dogs adopted quickly and happily. This was, however, unfortunate for Meg's search. She'd daily

* If your doctor says this to you, get a new doctor. Generalizing from a sample size of one – e.g., "well, I smoked when I was a kid and I (hack, hack, hack, choke, spit) turned out just fine" – is not good medical practice.

comb their web site, falling in love with every single dog along the way, only to drive to the shelter and find that dog had been adopted or that s/he didn't respond well to kids. Long story short, she brought Emma home and she's the perfect dog.[*]

The process made Meg attuned to how and whether the other dogs that she'd met would be adopted. She continued, and continues, to peruse the shelter's web site, making sure that every dog she met found a home (they did) and finding new dogs with pictures to die for. This is the stickiest of sticky content.

These types of micromoments have macroimpact. When people are looking for help, it's often because they are receptive to a change in their life; they are more likely to engage with new brands and organizations if they've experienced a life event. Richard Shotton and Laura Weston asked customers which life events they'd experienced and whether they'd changed brands. Across ten different types of products and six different life events, customers were far more likely (21% versus 8%) to change brands if they'd recently undergone a life event.[171]

When life events disrupt our existing patterns, we're willing to change our shoe brand. More importantly for nonprofits, many life events shift our priorities. If a loved one is diagnosed with cancer, you are more likely to donate to a cancer charity. If you move to a new town, you'll likely switch from donating books from your old library to your new one. People who have kids shift their giving from animal charities to education charities.

So when a person is searching for information or help, they may be telling you "I am experiencing a life event. I am willing to learn and engage anew." When you bring up this new information, it's important that it aims for a positive emotional outcome. People choose to avoid information if it will make them feel bad. In one case, people were willing to pay $10 to avoid finding out if they had herpes because that diagnosis would make them feel anxious.[172] Just as we donate for the

[*] To us, she's better than your dog, but I'm sure your dog is also a very good dog. I give your dog 14/10.

emotion we seek to feel as a result, we seek information to change our emotional state.

Empowering or hopeful information, then, is a valuable lead generator. As an experiment, DonorVoice put up Facebook ads for the American Diabetes Association encouraging people to take a quiz to assess their risk for Type 2 diabetes. This was framed as something you could do to reduce stress about diabetes – if the screening was high-risk, you were automatically given tools you could use to help manage your condition and to learn more. By making the state of uncertainty scary and knowledge an anti-anxiety power, this framing was able to attract the curious and the nervous to their screening tool. Since healthy living and getting folks screened is part of the mission of the ADA, this outreach fit perfectly with their mission. It has the side benefit of attracting visitors to the site and building their reservoir of gratitude for this helpful tool.

Anyone at the right moment. Scratch that. Many of these "right moments" for the charity are the wrong moments for the potential constituent or donor. We're asking you to reach out to people when the world or for the individual are imperiled, when rage or hope or grief or fear peak and overwhelm. These are not the moments for which one would wish. Let's try that again.

If a person has an identity that makes them more likely to support or be interested in you, there is no wrong time to approach them. Your goal is to take their identity and provide the connective tissue between that and your cause. Once you know who you wish to attract and when you want to attract them, it's great to create campaigns that work on that intersection. That said, campaigns aimed at just the "who" or the "when" can also be highly effective.

How to seize the moment

> *"You can't just trod out Ephesians, which he blew, by the way, it has nothing with husbands and wives, it's all of us. Saint Paul begins the passage: "Be subject to one another*

*out of reverence to Christ." "**Be subject to one another**." In this day and age of 24-hour cable crap, devoted to feeding the voyeuristic gluttony of the American public, hooked on a bad soap opera that's passing itself off as important, don't you think you might be able to find some relevance in verse 21? How to end the cycle? Be subject to one another!"*[173]

– Martin Sheen as President Jed Bartlet

Except in rare cases like our reactive donors, people don't search for your website to donate. The Norwegian Cancer Society asked people coming to their site "which five tasks are most important to you?" Of the possible 79 tasks, six tasks got 25% of the votes:

- Treatment of cancer
- Symptoms of cancer
- Preventing cancer
- Types of cancer
- Latest research
- Choosing a hospital

Dwelling in the cellar were:

- Donating
- Volunteering
- Making a memorial gift
- Making a gift in your will

By redesigning around what their users would be doing on the site and ruthlessly paring their forms to only what was needed, it increased one-time donations by 198% and monthly donors by 288%.[174]

We've been told to begin with the end in mind. The challenge is many of us think with *our* end, not *our constituents*' end, in mind first.

We want to get subscribers, donors, volunteers, advocates, etc. Thus, we make the donate button red, huge, and on every page. We shadowbox* the site for every possible occasion like, for example, Wednesday.

This type of optimization has its place. That place is second, not first. The Norwegian Cancer Society example is interesting, because their ask came after, and only after, it had met their constituents needs and wants. A user looking for the latest research would get a topical article about how nanoparticles and microbubbles are able to target cancer drugs to the cancer, turning a shotgun into a rifle. At the bottom of this article, well below any perceived "fold," came the ask:

> "There is a real and ever stronger hope that the nano-technologists can give us a better cancer treatment. Can we count on your support in the future? Give a gift today – every krone helps in the fight against cancer."[175]

The National Catholic Register tried a similar approach. After their news content, it put a donation call-to-action asking readers to donate to keep the content free. Their conversion rate jumped to .02%. That doesn't sound like a lot, but the conversion rate was previously .0025%. That call to action was worth an 800% increase in conversions, which meant a five-figure revenue increase for them.[176]

Interventions before leaving the site can also be effective. National Catholic Register tested an exit-intent shadowbox on their site and increased name acquisition conversion by 48%. It also increased sign-up 39-fold when it tested a slide-out banner for mobile devices.[177] Similarly, Care Net put an inline form for a petition on their home page (instead of having to click through to a separate petition) and increased conversion 32%.[178]

Maybe a donation is the right post-content ask. Maybe it's signing up for a newsletter to get more medical updates on cancer treatments.

---

* Or letterbox or interstitial or whatever we're calling pop-up ads today.

Maybe it's advocating for government funding for cancer treatment. The goal is to have one – and only one – call to action in your content. This eliminates two types of content that don't convert:

- Content with zero calls to action. This is the church-and-state approach where content is content and donation asks are asks and never the twain shall meet. They are on your site because people thought constituents would like the information. Or so you can discuss your programs. Or whatever. It's time to think of this as less church-and-state and more peanut-butter-and-jelly; when the ratios are right, they make both better. Everything you create should have a point of driving a conversation forward, even if it is but a bit.
- Content with various calls to action. Let's assume you have helped solve someone's problem. They are ready for their social mandated moment of reciprocity. And you give them "You can donate. Or you can volunteer. And we have action alerts. And you can join us on FacebookTwitterInstagramPinterestMySpace TinderGooglePlusYouTube." To ask for everything is to get nothing. You want to tell a user what the next logical step is for them to make a difference.

One clear call to action means you can spend time in the piece setting it up. If you are educating the reader about how to see what autism treatments their insurance covers, it is a natural segue to ask the person to email their legislator about insurance parity regulation for autism therapies. You've solved the problem; now you can give them a solution that adds to the solution that they wanted when they came to the site.

The conversation must begin with "what does the user want to do/learn/be?" then progress to "what does the user want to do after that, based on what they've already done?". How do we be subject to each other?

Creating this process breaks into three steps: getting people to come to your content, creating the content itself, and finding where you want users to go next. You might note this doesn't always end in direct donations, however, so let's start with the zeroth step: justifying this approach to the people who write your organization's checks.

The financials of lead generation

> *"Content marketing is a strategic marketing approach focused on creating and distributing valuable, relevant, and consistent content to attract and retain a clearly-defined audience – and, ultimately, to drive profitable customer action."*[179]
>
> – Content Marketing Institute's definition of content marketing

I know. It probably scares you to not be asking for money. But one of the underrated aspects of donorcentricity is starting off with the idea of "how do I solve this person's problem?". A traditional fundraising approach of donation asks at every turn is interruption marketing. It is mistakenly taking people away from what they want to do, attempting to force them to do what you want them to do, resulting in them doing neither.

People who come to your site with the intent of donating will donate. For the majority that come with some other intent, what is their mindset and how can you help them achieve it?

Let's take the person who wants to do something about your issue. That something is, to them, to email their legislator about a piece of legislation you are working on. If we facilitate what they want to do, ask them for additional information about themselves, then ask with knowledge of why they might which to give, we are more likely to achieve the first step at least, building our audience. And this lead generation (followed by conversion) model can make financial sense. Studies have shown that asking people to take a petition first, then donate, donate more than those simply asked for money.[180]

How much money can we get? The 2018 M+R Benchmarking Report estimates that the average nonprofit gets $.91 of value from the average visitor to their website.[181] We'll talk in a bit about an identity-based campaign for the American Headache Society* that urged users to take a quiz. That campaign attracted visitors to the site at $.31.

So, $.91 in value for a cost of $.31 – a win by all measures. Add in the fact that none of the 31 cents were fundraising costs (this was programmatic outreach) and the campaign looks even better.

This adds up. The Democratic Congressional Campaign Committee (DCCC) spent $2.6 million to grow its list in early 2017, through a mix of Facebook lead generation ads, display, and paid petitions. Those new supporters gave $11.5 million in the 2018 election cycle, more than quadrupling the DCCC's investment.[182] On the other side of the budget spectrum, Kennedy Center bought $1,979 of ads that brought in 757 email addresses that raised $6,105.[183]

You will, of course, want to do your own math for your own organization and content. Ideally, you will look at:

- The percent of people engaging with a piece of content who will become a constituent; multiplied by…
- The percent of those people who donate multiplied by…
- The lifetime value of those donors (or, failing that, the value of donations of the average donor over a reasonable payback period).

This will give you a figure for how valuable it is to attract people to that piece of content. If you can attract donors for less than that number, go for it. If you can't, either don't make the investment or first invest in improving the conversion, donation, and retention rates of people coming to that page.

* I had originally anonymized this to American Hangnail Society, but a British colleague advised me that isn't a thing overseas.

Need something quicker and dirtier? Pull a list of everyone who came into your online database via the activity you want to quantify. Pull a list of the donations these people made online over the past year. Average the sum of the donations by the number of people in your database via advocacy action to find the one-year value of an advocate.

That's it.

I can hear purists screaming: "what about future year revenues from an advocate?", "what about the value these constituents have in recruiting other constituents?", "what about the gifts made in other channels?", etc.

I agree this is not the best way to calculate an average advocate's lifetime value. It is, however, a quick one. And it sets a baseline: if you know the average advocate is going to pay for themselves in 12 months, their other activities will be gravy. If you work this equation and it says the average advocate on your file gave you $3 last year, you know that acquiring an advocate for up to three dollars is valuable. If your advocacy page converts at 10%, you know that you can pay up to $.30 per click. You can experiment with online petition sites, which charge $1.50* per advocate. And you can value your online communications that bring in new advocates versus those that bring in new donors.

So this dart throw, primitive though it may be, can help you determine your communications mix and investment. Not bad for something you can do in a spreadsheet in 15 minutes.

Beyond the financials, remember that these content items are also part of your mission. As Kivi Leroux Miller reports in her excellent *Content Marketing for Nonprofits*, Dana-Farber created content for information seekers who weren't in their target audience, with content about cancer prevention written in common language. They are working to help fight cancer before cancer starts, with the additional benefit that

---

* Plus or minus.

they work to create awareness of Dana-Farber as the best choice if you do need a cancer center.[184][*]

Getting people to come to your content

Field of Dreams lied to us. A generation of people was told that if you build it, people will come. A total, utter lie.[†] And don't get me started on the better mousetrap zealots.

This is not to say that quality doesn't matter. That's too cynical even for me. But quality content with marketing will beat quality content without marketing just as surely as a Smith and Wesson beats four aces.

Virality is another pernicious marketing myth. Woe be unto you if you get that question from your executive board member about why you spend so much on marketing when you could just make something that will go viral instead. Derek Thompson's excellent book *Hit Makers*[185] dedicates an entire chapter to why virality doesn't exist, showing things often perceived as "going viral" start because of a large broadcast audience or pick-up by opinion leaders or those with large audiences. In one study he reports on Twitter messages, only about one percent of Twitter messages are shared more than seven times. Even among those shared messages, the overwhelming majority – 95% – of the messages you see on Twitter are from the original source or from someone only one degree away from the source.

We see these examples in our own field. People talk about the Ice Bucket Challenge going viral, when the largest portion of its reach came from influencers like *The Today Show*, *The Tonight Show*[‡], Presidents Obama, Bush 41, and Clinton, LeBron James, Justin Bieber, Oprah Winfrey, Bill Gates, Mark Zuckerberg, Martha Stewart, etc, etc. The

---

[*] This is one of the great things about nonprofits – actively trying to make themselves unnecessary. Imagine Apple's new ad campaign "we have $1000 phones available; here's how not to need one" and you can see how odd and special this is.

[†] Also, Iowa, while very nice, is theologically not near heaven.

[‡] These two shows cover all possible times.

same thing for the Kony 2012 "viral" video. Most of the people who were interacting with these campaigns came from these traditionally broadcast influences, not from a peer-to-peer groundswell. In short, it came from people who had an audience. Rather than showing the irrelevance of having a built-in audience, it shows the value of having one and working with those who also have one.

We'll talk more about the Ice Bucket Challenge later, as it teaches additional lessons. But creating content then hoping for viral lightning to strike is not one of them. Rather, it's a call to action to invest in building an audience you can interact with when you need to and when they want you to.

Let's start with the free solutions. I know you are a nonprofit. When forced to choose two of three from the cheap, fast, or easy triptych, you are forced to choose cheap twice.

You can get some results from free efforts. Hopefully, you have your Google Grant already. A quick guide:

- If you don't have an account, get one.
- If you have an account, maximize your spend.
- If your spend is maximized, optimize your spend.
- If your spend is maximized and optimized, you are at a large enough non-profit that you should be able to get a budget for paid ads if you are justifying it well.

If you would like more detail – and who wouldn't? – I recommend Josh Barsch and Steve Isaacs's book *The Google Ad Grants Playbook.*[186*]

* There is a point at which this book will serve mainly as a recommendation for other books. I'm OK with this; Francis Ford Coppola said he put a scene of someone cooking in each Godfather movie so, in case someone didn't like the movie, at least they'd have a recipe. I hope you like the movie, but just in case, these references to other books are my recipes.

While it's harder to stay compliant with Google than it once was, advocacy pages will often have high click-through rates and can help you stay above their 5% click-through threshold with your ads. It's usually a safe bet that the person searching for "email congress seal clubbing" wants to email their elected officials about seal clubbing. And if they click through on your ad, they are probably on the side of those opposed to clubbing. The same is true for quality informational content that answers the question that a searcher has. Donation asks are more problematic; not only is the click-through rate prohibitively poor, but you are not the first nonprofit to want to get your ad shown anytime someone searches "donate."

Frequency is also your friend. Every time you log into Google Ads, it will have recommendations for you to have a sentence in the first half of your ad to increase clicks or split your ad groups up or add keywords or create a dynamic ad or what-have-you. Follow the recommendations and continually refine.

You also can make your own assessment. List out your ads and see which have the lowest interactions. Re-write the ads and test the new ads against the old. Also, list out your ad groups, see which URLs have the lowest conversion rates and work on the conversion side of things on your Web site.

This is a highly iterative process. Every improvement you make in your base click-through rate allows you to go deeper into search terms and get more constituents the same way a more effective acquisition mail piece or ad campaign allows you to get more people on the same budget. Your model should be the survivalists on *Naked and Afraid* who, while sitting in their makeshift shelters, are weaving many fish traps.* It's a numbers game, one that rewards the patient, diligent practitioner.

---

* At least the good ones do.

Another free[*] effort to attract constituents is search engine optimization. If you write your content and then sit down to do your search engine marketing, you've already lost. From your Google Grants and other research, you need to know for what people are searching. Then weave those terms and phrases into your content. In fact, this should be a driver for that type of content you aim to create, making content that people want to view.

Now, you have a platform from which to further optimize. Make sure your partners are linking to your content, as link popularity is still a key indicator of quality. Similarly, go to other people's content that is related and complementary to your own and comment on the piece, complementing their content and linking to your own. Always practice good etiquette when doing this: you want to make sure you are doing as much to promote the person you are commenting on as you are getting, including linking to them from your own content. Additionally, on social media, what little remains of organic reach can be a laboratory as to what content your most fervent supporters[†] want.

But these are baby steps that will get you only so far. The main goal of free efforts is to maximize them, then use them to prove out your case for additional investment. Who knows? Maybe that's why services like Google Grants exist – to show you the value you can get with incremental investment.[‡]

Speaking of incremental investment, most of my focus on attracting an audience will be done online. This is because the economics are best online for acquiring constituents, then converting them to donors; it is more often too darned expensive to use face-to-face or mail or phone or DRTV or the like just to get an audience. That said, some organizations build a non-donor audience offline. The Royal Society for the Protection of Birds in the UK uses a multichannel effort to get people to

---

[*] Yes, it costs your time and thus is not truly free. But so often nonprofits are willing to spend time instead of money.

[†] Or that social media platform's more avid users.

[‡] Narrator: That is absolutely why.

call, write, or submit an online form to participate in the Big Garden Bird Watch, a crowdsourced census of bird life. From those who request a kit, it recruits future members; the effort pays for itself over the long term.

I focus on channels here and specific tactics here with some trepidation. Had I been writing this a decade ago, I'd include tips on maximizing your MySpace presence or the advantages of location-based services like FourSquare. Even in those channels where succcss is possible, it isn't sustainable at its early levels – see The Law of Shitty Clickthroughs discussed earlier.

Eventually, novelty wears off. Tactics are forbidden. Con men are banned. And the fast gives way to the effective.

We seem to be at that inflection point with Facebook. In 2012, Facebook had fewer than one million advertisers; today it has over six million. Those advertisers are facing an environment where Facebook has focused on organic content (not for brands, but for people), so inventory wanes. Ad inventory on the main Facebook ad peaked in 2017.[187] And what happens when more demand meets less inventory? Prices go up. For the first quarter 2018, CPM and CPC (cost per thousand ad impressions and cost per click, respectively) were up 91% and 92%.[188]

Now, let's look at the audience. North American daily active users are flat; European DAUs are down.[189] So you can't count on new people expanding the audience.* And clickthrough rates (CTR) are flat.

So advertisers are getting less for their money. This is especially true when it matters most. At the end of 2018, M+R Strategic Services reports the amount spent by nonprofits on Facebook went up 25%. The number of clicks? Down 2%.[190]

This is neither to praise nor bury Facebook. If you consider that Facebook may become just another channel, or even a subset of the

---

* Assuming you are in one of these markets. Facebook global usage is still expanding, but not in the markets where it (currently) makes most of its revenue.

larger digital advertising ecosystem, that's still huge. We aren't at the end of Facebook, just at the end of the beginning.

In Andrew Chen's original post, he says that the answer to the law of shitty clickthroughs is to invest more time to find the next gold rush. In the US, for example, some major cities have no discernable face-to-face presence, while every British city with a population of 50,000 and above is targeted. But this is also a reminder that no hot thing remains hot forever. Eventually, we here in America will be saturated as well.

The idea of donor identities to attract and train transcends channel, as does creating one's own media company to attract and retain donors. Knowing your donor and showing your donors that you know them works on every platform in every channel.

Plus it is not as if the "old" channels go away. In the first quarter of 2018, American adults spent 666[*] minutes every day connected to media (that Nielsen can measure – thank you for reading a book, a non-measurable medium when in dead-tree form). Of those, 250 minutes were spent on boring ol' TV and another 36 minutes on time-shifted TV. Another 106 minutes were spent on radio. Yes, radio: the same thing on which your grandpappy listened to *You Bet Your Life* or *The Milton Berle Show* or the Deeply Shocked Hindenburg Announcer guy. Radio was third in time spent (behind TV and smartphones). This diminishes somewhat among 18-34-year-olds, but even they still spend 42% of their media consumption time on TV and radio.[191]

Yes, the technologies to connect to media change. Remember, the first *Fast and Furious* movie was about a heist of combo DVD/VCR players.[†*] But storytelling, in video, audio, and print will always be fresh.

---

[*] No conspiracy theories, please – the patterns hold true for Q4 2017 when it was 647 minutes. It will be a different number in Q2 2018. It is unlikely that Satan used the Q1 2018 Nielsen report as a mark.

[†] See, there used to be these things called videocassettes that you would buy or rent (from a store, not a kiosk) that kept video and audio on a roll of VHS tape that you would have to wind forward or backward (aka rewinding) to get to the spot you wanted. You played them on a VCR, which stands for VideoCassette Recorder. You

So please look at these examples as just that – examples of what is possible. New whizbangs will always emerge. Old reliables will always persist. What we seek is a mindset that will work after the specific tactics and channels enumerated here are no longer relevant. Most of the attraction of an audience will be digital, as it covers the media where acquiring leads then converting to donors is cost-effective. That should not exclude other media in the cultivation and conversion process, as long as those media fit with the prospective donor's preferences.

One place to start is with Google and Facebook. Why, given that I've called Google and Facebook your future competitors, would we advertise with them?

Scope.

Right now, these two networks (I'm grouping Instagram in with Facebook because Facebook owns Instagram) own 68-75% of the market, and 90% of the growth, in online advertising.[192]

So, for the near term, you have three major places in online advertising: Google, Facebook, and Hope. Hope is hoping for the telegram, fax machine, or carrier pigeons to make a comeback. Or

---

could also "tape" – that is, record to this videocassette tape medium – live television to these tapes on the VCR. When DVDs (Digital Versatile Discs) came out, which digitally encode and stamp media onto a circular silver disc, people wanted to get this new technology, but they also wanted to watch all the movies they'd accumulated on VHS tapes. Thus there was a time, albeit a brief one, where a combination DVD/VCR player was a valuable thing because you could watch your old movies and get new ones on the new DVD format. There's no nonprofit marketing value in this footnote at all; just thought you might need a reminder that the Fast and Furious franchise began with small-time heists and street racing given that the characters are now all basically superheroes who violate the laws of physics as often as the laws of traffic.

* What's a VHS tape from the previous footnote? It stands for Vertical Helical Scan for the technique it used to scan the tape and create a video signal, but quickly got changed to Video Home System in the minds of consumers, because we only think of "helical" as something to do with DNA. VHS was once one of two major videocassette recording technologies, the other being BetaMax. VHS won the format wars, in part because it was more willing to allow sellers of more adult entertainment to use their technology. In case you were starting to think that people's motivations were always pure.

Yahoo!, which seems equally likely. While it's likely that Amazon and Snapchat will eat into this over time, Google and Facebook will still be worthwhile if they have "only" 60% of the market.

Yes, this is scary. Facebook and Google are large. You, relatively speaking, are not. You, for example, could not swing a US presidential election if you tried, much less accidentally. Your advertising budget is a rounding error on the rounding error of their rounding errors.

Despite challenges and changes, these sites are effective. One NextAfter test evaluated Facebook versus three list rentals. It found Facebook produced 193% more leads at 44% lower cost, producing 285% more donors. This meant an 81% lower cost to acquire than its nearest list rival.[193]

These sites are even better at this when paired with identity. Let's take the example of a disease-focused charity: the American Headache Society (AHS).* Their identities are: direct (I have headaches), indirect (someone I care about has headaches), and no connection to the cause. When DonorVoice looked at their file, only three percent of their file were people who had no connection to severe headaches. A bit over a third (35%) only had indirect connections to severe headaches. And 62% of their donors had headaches themselves (despite severe headaches impacting only about nine percent of the general population).

With that one finding, it stopped trying to differentiate among direct connection, indirect connection, and no connection. Instead it concentrated on attracting, retaining, and differentiating between those with direct and indirect connections.

It created a tool that asked a few basic questions. Those questions screened for the prospects' likelihood of getting severe headaches. The prospects also signed up to receive more information about how to lower their risk, manage their condition, and/or generally live a headache-free existence. They also were asked to support AHS in those

---

* Yes, this is anonymized. But I can already see the DRTV spot for this organization with Sarah MacLaughlin singing very, very softly.

communications and the organization identified people who had headaches, one of their core identities.

It is an excellent tool, but the strategy around it had *Field of Dreams* thinking; just because AHS built it didn't mean people would come.

So AHS started with Facebook ads, asking people to learn their risk of severe headaches in just one minute. Because Facebook is soooooooooooooooooooooooooooooooooooooooooooooooooo oo dedicated to privacy, it wouldn't allow them to target ads to those most susceptible to headaches, so the targeting was super broad. We were worried that CTR and ad relevance would suffer.

Relevance certainly did suffer – we had to advertise to a lot of people who weren't likely to get severe headaches. Nonetheless, the CTR was 5% and the cost-per-click was $.31. It turned out that the right people were worried and clicked on ads regarding headaches. The demographics of participants matched nicely with those who should be worried. (This is why, even though third-party data is often embarrassingly bad, it can still be used to attract people, as long as you work to get real first-party data thereafter.)

Using identity to get low-cost leads isn't just for disease organizations. Consider an experiment DonorVoice did for Make-a-Wish, an organization that grants wishes to children with severe illness in the hopes of both bringing them joy and helping their medical outcomes. Thus, it seems natural that medical professionals who worked with children in a position to have wishes granted may have a different reason for giving than a layperson. It was just a matter of priming that identity as a reason for support.

Thus, we put up Facebook ads with identical images and calls-to-action, but with different descriptions:

- No identity: When you donate and help grant a wish, you help her fight her illness.
- Soft identity: You know the heartache of a child diagnosed with a critical illness. When you donate and help grant a wish, you help her fight her illness.

- Hard identity: As a medical professional, you know the heartache of a child diagnosed with a critical illness. When you donate and help grant a wish, you help her fight her illness.

Note the only difference between soft and hard identity are the four words "As a medical professional."

We advertised this to Facebook groups for medical professionals who would be working with critical illnesses.* The heavy identity had 74 clicks on 4300 impressions, for a click-through rate of 1.72%. The soft and no identity conditions had 59 clicks on 4824 impressions, for a click-through rate of 1.22%. A 42% increase.†

This is a blunt, simplistic way of priming medical professionals. One assumes we might have had better results featuring a medical professional in the advertisement itself.‡ Even with this blunt instrument, we got positive results.

You can also advertise to your existing or lapsed donors. On Facebook, start with Facebook Custom Audiences. You upload a list of your donors (and/or constituents) with that identity. You can then market to that list with advertisements targeted to that identity – no more monolithic message to the masses. Google has a very similar process. This is a good way of getting additional donations from your current donors (hint: run people who have donated recently as a suppression file or as an audience to upgrade to monthly giving).

You can also use this as a conversion audience – if you have event attendees who fit your valuable donor identity but haven't yet donated

---

* Groups like emergency medicine physician, emergency room nurse, oncology RN, pediatric nurse practitioner, pediatric nursing, pediatrics, and registered nurse.

† Why did the heavy identity have almost as many impressions as the other two conditions combined? After all, that's no way to run a test! Answer: The Facebook algorithm was already optimizing for click-through rate and refused to show the soft and no identity ads as often. As a result, we were also able to get the hard identity clicks more cheaply than the soft and no identity clicks.

‡ Although the image of a tiny child ballerina dancing with three professional ballerinas used in the test was, scientifically speaking, super cute and compelling.

directly, you can advertise to them. We've also seen examples where targeting a custom audience who are receiving a mail or email solicitation can lift the response rate to that more traditional communication.

Retargeting is also effective. This involves putting a pixel on your website and marketing to those who go to that part of your site. The trick to using this to target an identity is to target only on specific parts of your website. It's a dirty non-secret: not everyone who comes to your site is valuable. You want to avoid advertising to the kid who comes to your site looking for information for their school report, for example.

So, if your most valuable donors are those who have the disease your organization works on, having the pixel as part of the patient resource section will give you the best prospects. You can also use this to try to convert people to donors after they have interacted with specific content (e.g., an advocacy alert).

This match of content to the retargeted user is vital. Months ago, seeking information, I visited the site of a disease charity that will remain nameless. I am still retargeted for donations, which would be fine (although they may be better off starting further up the funnel, given that I was seeking information). The real sin is that it is targeting me for honor and memorial donations. The drumbeat was so intense that I felt I needed to reach out to my parents to verify their status and to see if this organization knew something I didn't. Thankfully, I was not in the market for a memorial gift.

You can also target interests and behaviors. I recently did this for a start-up nonprofit. It had no donor file and no web traffic, so everything above was moot. I was targeting people who were interested in policy debate (the organization funds debate programs where funds have been cut), so I asked Google and Facebook for the intersection of people who give charitable donations and those who are interested in policy debate. Most their initial web traffic came from these efforts.

Depending on your target donor identities, lookalike audiences can also be very helpful. In a pre-identity world, you would take your best donors, upload them to Google, Facebook, and other platforms and ask these purveyors of pixels to find people who look like this audience.

But you know this is likely to get a lukewarm response at best, since your best donors probably cross different donor identities, give for different reasons, and thus are quite different people. (If you don't know this, please drop me a line to let me know where my identity section went awry.)

So you, smart donor identity user that you are, load your constituents by identity, trying to find people who look like those donors.

Now is when I circle back to explain why I said "depending on your target donor identities." Like the NSA, it's possible for Google and Facebook to know vast amounts of information, yet to have people overestimate the amount they really know. If you have a donor identity of "parent" or "cat people" or "medical professional," these services should give you a lookalike audience that looks very much like your current best audiences.

However, if your donor identity is "prostate cancer sufferers" or "parents who involve their kids in their philanthropy" or "crime victims," Google and Facebook will give you people who they think look like those people. But, since they are basing this on their searches and catalog purchases and whether they like Jimmy Buffett[*†], the results will be slightly more accurate than feeding the audience into a Ouija board.

So getting people who don't look like your donors is one potential peril of lookalike ads. The other is getting people who only look like your donors.

Huh? Why is that bad?

Lookalike audiences won't just look like your donors on an identity basis. Google and Facebook are aiming for all types of similarities. Thus, if you are missing donors you could be appealing to, whether by

---

[*] They do: crime victims are huge Jimmy Buffett fans, with a .86 r-squared correlation between victimization and Parrotheadednesss.

[†] The above footnote is entirely fictional; it exists only to satirize the difficulty in tying demographic and interest variables to some focused donor identities.

donor identity or demographic variable, a lookalike audience won't help you get them; rather, it will focus on the way your donors look now.

Even the mighty techs fall victim to past-based myopia. Amazon recently scrapped a machine-learning based recruiting tool. Its sin was discriminating against women. Why would a machine pick up this very human bias? The machine learned by looking at resumes submitted to Amazon over the previous decade. Since the tech sector skews male, especially for technical roles, the machine learned that male CVs were preferable[194] (not in the sense that they were actually preferable; instead, they saw that the humans had picked largely male engineers and it replicated that bias).

While the AI was forbidden from taking gender into account, it got around this by:

- Penalizing resumes that included "women's" (as in "women's chess club captain").
- Dinging at least two all-female schools.
- Favoring verbs more commonly found on male engineers' resumes like "executed" or "captured."

If it comes as a surprise that our myopia can be institutionalized, baking our biases into our black box algorithms, I strongly encourage Cathy O'Neil's *Weapons of Math Destruction* or *Technically Wrong* by Sara Wachter-Boettcher. Both discuss how this type of discrimination enters our algorithms for loans, health insurance, criminal justice sentencing, voting, etc., and other ways algorithms institutionalize inequity.

The way these companies create a lookalike audience is functionally the same as how Amazon assembled their machine learning for hiring: putting in success stories and asking for a lookalike audience.

Thus, if you have a database full of cat people and you run a lookalike audience/modeled list approach, it will give you an audience full of cat people. Yay! But it won't tell you what would happen if you tried a dog appeal to dog people. It can't imagine that counterfactual.

And if you have mostly Siamese cat people, the model will skew towards more Siamese cat people and away from Persians, tabbies, calico, etc.

This limits your options. Imagine an organization that uses premiums all the time in both acquisition and cultivation. You probably know an organization like this; you may work for one or donate to one. It wants to test out of this or at least test into a two-track program where only the people who need premiums get them.

But the results say it can't. It tests non-premium pieces to an acquisition audience. The anti-premium donors it acquires don't do well in the donor program, because it's all premiums.

It tests non-premium pieces to their donor audience; their pro-premium donors trash the appeal after failing to find their tchotchkes. All because it has a well-worn path that it follows for all but this deviation.

Replace "premiums" in the above paragraph with "matches" or "multipliers" or "appeals to a specific donor identity" and it works just as well. Replace "premiums" with "men" and you have Amazon's former algorithm. Say what you want about the challenges of nonprofits setting up data-driven marketing, but we can apparently set up self-reinforcing systems with the best of them.

This is not to say you should not do lookalike audiences. In fact, do them. But they should be a part of an overall acquisition strategy that searches by identity and interests that cut across demographic categories. You should also be continually brainstorming for identities to which you appeal. Looking on your file to see who is staying with your organization despite not being part of your current target identities is a good start. They are giving because they love you *despite*, not *because of* your marketing.

This is only possible, however, if you know your donor. Wading online to advertise to people who want to do good things is like trying to boil the ocean. And may the powers that be have mercy on your soul if you try to attack it with just demographics and a dream. But if you start with a strong knowledge of your donor and his/her identity, you can make online audiences work for you.

You can also investigate pay-for-play options. These are solutions that will deliver an audience to you, already opted in and ready to receive your message. I'd recommend starting everywhere else first. You will need to have a strong, distilled message to keep these folks and a planned content diet for them upon acquisition. It's better to build those muscles first than to hear the starting gun and only then realize you are in a race for which you haven't trained.

But if you are humming on all cylinders except scale, this is a way to scale. As mentioned previously, organic traffic is challenging and nonorganic traffic can get expensive. So pay-per-constituent is refreshing in its directness. The most prominent of these are online petition sites focused on that advocate identity. For (approximately) $1.50 per lead – the cost varies based on the level of targeting and volume – you get all new leads, all workable email address, and both postal and email addresses.

If you do go down this road and want to then try to convert these constituents to donors, consider these tips from Care2, one of the vendors in this space:

- You must quickly respond to an acquired lead. World Animal Protection, for example, got 4.7% and 6.9% donor conversion from two telemarketing campaigns following up on leads.[195] While more expensive than email or mail, this type of outreach is immediate and thus likely had a significant impact.
- The more related to the initial outreach is to the petition, the better. If you sign a wolf hunting petition, a monetary ask to help stop wolf hunting fits very closely to your expressed preferences and goal.
- Be yourself. The greater emotional connection to the organization, the better. Some organizations who don't do a lot of advocacy activities start with advocacy petitions that aren't hyperpartisan (e.g., sign a petition for clean water). This attracts the types of leads that are likely to fit with the organization long-

term. Conversely, if you have a strong advocacy bent, lean into it.
- Be mobile friendly. You are mobile friendly, right?

Most importantly, you need a customized post-petition/pledge journey. Too often, these campaigns fail because the communication stream for your advocates looks exactly like your communication stream for everyone else. The next logical action for such a person is doing more advocacy actions or supporting more advocacy efforts. It is not mailing in a check to support your annual fund, taking a call from a telemarketer who doesn't know anything about the constituent, or joining your walk coming up in 42 short days.

Unfortunately, that's too often the next action many organizations request. It's as though their goal is to expose people to as many different aspects their organization as possible.

They might as well put up a banner proclaiming:

This organization doesn't know who you are
or what you care about,
but we do want your money.

A singularly unappealing message.

You may think this is trading an overfished donor pool for an overfished advocate pool. After all, the people who take many, many petitions will be overrepresented in the leads you get. That said, those constituents have opted in to hear from you and care, at least a little, about your issue. It's now up to you to convert them and make them your audience.

Beware the "where"

> *"All the weapons of influence discussed in this book work better under some conditions than under others. If we are to defend ourselves adequately against any such*

> *weapon, it is vital that we know its optimal operating conditions in order to recognize when we are most vulnerable to its influence."*[196]
>
> – Robert Cialdini, *Influence: The Psychology of Persuasion*

On a scale of 0 ("no") to 100 ("yes"; with "possibly" in thc middle at 50), men said they were, on average:

- A 20 to the question "would you keep trying to have sex after your date says 'no'?"
- An 88 to the question "would you use a condom even if you were afraid that a woman might change her mind while you went to get it?"

Or at least that's what they said when they were not aroused.

Researchers then got the men aroused[197] and asked the same questions. Their answers changed significantly. On whether they would pressure after consent had been withdrawn, they went from 20 to 45 (a.k.a. "probably not" to "maybe"). And they went from 88 to 60 (a.k.a. "almost certainly" to "probably") to condom use when that use could allow for a change of mind. These were just two of many different changes men in the study underwent while aroused; they also found many things more attractive and increased their willingness to blur and cross ethical lines to have sex.

Context matters.* In the heat of the moment – whether the moment is arousal or intoxication or a group of people – inhibitions (including positive inhibitions like legality or morality) are diminished.

People like to think of themselves as consistently the same person throughout their lives. They are not. They are willing to say things at a

---

* That's one possible conclusion. The other is that men are scum. These are not mutually exclusive explanations.

football game that they would not say in front of a child or parent. They treat their boss differently than the person whose boss they are. They behave better dressed to the nines than in stained sweatpants; people treat them differently too. Every waking moment, people are some combination of core self and environment.

Thus, *where* your message is received affects *how* your message is received. If someone likes the context in which an ad appears, they are more likely to like[198][199] and remember[200][201] the ad. If someone trusts the source, they are more likely to trust the headline, even if it's the same headline with the sources randomized.[202]

Much programmatic advertising doesn't acknowledge this, with a goal of turning each person into an eyeball, one no more valuable than the next. But it does matter. Benignly, imagine what you'd think if you saw a luxury brand in a discount bin or a dollar store.

Or, don't imagine. Think of the violinist who played for almost an hour at DC's L'Enfant Plaza subway entrance at the height of morning rush hour. He cleared $32.17. This wouldn't be remarkable except that the violinist was Joshua Bell, one of the great classical masters who can normally command up to $1000 a minute for his playing. He was playing on a $3.5 million-dollar Stradivarius. Only seven of the thousand people passing him even paused in their daily grind.[203] Context matters.

More malignantly, witness the campaign of Sleeping Giants against most-racist-website-you've-heard-of Breitbart.[*] Sleeping Giants (staffed by only two part-time volunteers) worked on the (correct) assumption most brands didn't know where their digital ads were running. They would then publicize the ads on Twitter, tagging the advertiser to ask if the advertising decision was conscious. Advertisers were shocked to see their ads next to stories like "Gay Rights Have Made Us Dumber, It's Time to Get Back in the Closet"[†][*] and "Birth Control Makes Women

---

[*] If this descriptor isn't true, I hope it's because you haven't heard of Breitbart.

[†] They did use a comma here, not a semi-colon, perhaps because of how stupid gay rights had made them.

Unattractive and Crazy."[204][205] This type of publicity also caused AT&T, Johnson & Johnson, Coke, Pepsi, and Walmart to pull marketing from YouTube and Google when their ads ran next to offensive materials.[206][207]

Who matters. *When* matters. *Where* matters as well. We need to choose media that are part of the message. Only then will we get people as part of our audience who trust and respect us from the beginning. That location isn't at the bottom of a random webpage next to the bikini pictures, the You'll Never Believe What Happened Next, and the Number Eight Will Blow Your Minds.

A cancer research organization wanted to see how this type of native advertising would work for them.[208] They tested two brand ads and one aimed at audience growth. The audience growth ad was an article for loved ones to offer support during challenging times, asking visitors to download a PDF by giving their email address – exactly the type of identity-based appeal to someone in their time of need that should work.

With a $2,000 test budget, the campaign reached over three million people. This is in theory, of course; banner blindness means that most users simply looked past the ad.

At $.83 cost per click, the campaign got about 2400 clicks. The participants said engagement was low on the site. This is because of the context of the sites plus the lack of targeting of the ads. After all, some native advertising sellers say they reach 90% of US Web users. Picture targeting[†] your advertising about cancer care to ten people picked at random from the web. Then discard the worst one. You still have a very high haystack-to-needle ratio in trying to find an audience that will engage with your advertising. As the testers put it: "In our case, ads were likely shown to audiences well beyond the users who were already looking for helpful cancer-related content that we hoped to pay for."[209]

---

[*] No, there's not a citation here. One of the major factors in search engine listings is link popularity, so that's a hard pass.

[†] We are using the term "targeting" loosely here.

Thus, native ads and pure programmatic advertising doesn't look like a fit for the nonprofit looking to bring in a more valuable constituent and go deep, not wide, with outreach.

That said, online advertising for content is still in its infancy. One doesn't look at a baby, say "Can't feed itself, can't walk, and aromas are horrible." and give up.[210] The rest of the Internet has yet to catch up to search engines' abilities to match advertising with immediate intent. It will catch up. We should be ready when it does.

Meanwhile, I don't recommend the current generation of commodified native advertising and programmatic outreach to generate leads. But I heartily endorse the next generation or the one after that. Eventually, those who produce quality content will demand both advertising of the same quality and the prices to match. At the same time, you as the nonprofit will be willing to pay significantly more for the ad, knowing you can match the identity of the incoming constituent to a high-value constituent in a positive context.

Matt Ipcar calls a variant of this world "native advocacy," where a publication and an organization work in harmony on sponsored content.[211] Let's take for example the issue of the day in the United States as I write this: whether children should be forcibly removed from their parents and put in cages with insufficient guarantees that they will ever be reunited with their parents. Imagine if you can marry that op-ed against caging children with advertising from RAICES or ACLU next to it instead of sunglasses, credit card offers, and "Where Are They Now" stories about C-list 80s TV stars.* We should be able to match the content to the context.

---

* In case you think I'm exaggerating, here are the native advertising headlines on a major news organization's major news story as I write this:

- Glasses-Wearers Are Going Crazy Over This Website
- Forget Paying For Antivirus (Do This Instead!)
- If You Can Qualify for Any Credit Card, These Are the Top 6
- These Are The Best Flats You Can Buy – Here's Why
- [Pics] Man Turned Boeing 727 Into His Home – Wait Till You See The Pics

People are already making the donation leap in small quantities without the advertising. In perusing feedback from donors across organizations, you can see from comments when a particularly touching piece has been written or a trusted author has recommended a gift to the nonprofit. Donors will say "I saw you in X." where X is a media source of interest and influence.

Some media outlets have already picked up the marriage of their mission and a nonprofit mission. The Food Network and The Cooking Channel have both made Share our Strength | No Kid Hungry a cause that fits in to their advertising and their programmatic content. Velocity works with Mothers Against Drunk Driving. Even less targeted media will put up a URL and text-to-give number when there is a disaster. You could even see channels setting up their own causes just as I warned tech companies might do. After all, if it makes sense for nonprofits to become media companies, it also makes sense for media companies to become nonprofits.

This also works in reverse. I was going to say it's my dream to see a nonprofit evolve into a traditional media company instead of vice versa. But it's already happened. The National Geographic Society has a TV channel* and a magazine. The highest circulation magazine in the United States is AARP Magazine, from a nonprofit. Number two is AARP Bulletin. Scouting, Smithsonian, and NRA's American Rifleman and American Hunter are also in the top 100.[212] Religious cable channels are so common that there is a National Religious Broadcasters association.

You need not dream of having (Your Nonprofit Here) News Network. The important point is the need to create your own audience so you can promote yourself with your own content.

What content?

---

* Technically, they are a minority partner with the Walt Disney Company for the TV channel – you need not do all the heavy lifting yourself.

"A-B-C. A-always, B-be, C-closing. Always be closing! Always be closing! A-I-D-A. Attention, interest, decision, action."[213]

– Alec Baldwin as Blake

All this marketing to get leads is nothing if the content you are selling does not convert visitors into constituents. You are looking for gateway content – a door by which someone enters your organization and becomes part of your audience.

That's why as you work to satisfy the needs of people coming to your site, you must also keep the other eye on the end of conversion. You can approach it either with the end in mind ("I want people to email their legislators through our advocacy system; what would make them want to do that?") or from what is in the content ("I have this white paper here on the dangers of bovine flatulence; what would be a logical thing to do as a result of this?"). Either way works if you then work toward the other goal.

You are looking for two types of content (for both your current and your prospective audience): permanent and ephemeral. Permanent is a bit of an exaggeration, as you will have to update some "permanent" content, either on a routine basis (e.g., yearly for new statistical releases) or as new learnings become available (e.g., you want your "what to do when you are diagnosed" guide to have the most recent treatments). This is Ron Popeil content: set it and forget it until the timer dings.

Ephemeral content is created for the moment. It's the advocacy action on a new issue, the blog post about a disaster, the attempt to turn news coverage to you and the work you do. This sounds daunting and resource intensive. It really requires the same things as the permanent content: knowing for whom you are creating, knowing why you would create content, and streamlining ways of getting stories and turning them into content.

Content creation requires two initial steps. The first is determining what people want and will listen to. Keyword research isn't just for search engine marketing; it can drive what content you create. Check out what people are looking for around your issues and see if you have content to match that has logical calls to action that would come from it.

Also, search for some of these terms yourself. You will likely see some search terms where the person who searched for that item probably didn't find what they were looking for. You can be what they were looking for. Conversely, you'll find that some of the content is good. If you can't improve on it, don't tackle it in the same format. But if you see that good blog posts, but no videos, on the topic, then a video it is.

Similarly, in your Google Analytics or equivalent, you can see how people came to your site and what they searched for. This can be illuminating. I worked with one nonprofit that went through this analysis and found that most people who found them through search were looking for one of their tertiary services – one that they rarely talked about or promoted. What's more, their content on it was scattered incoherently throughout their site.

Working together, we centralized their content into one coherent page that then linked out to the various locations where this service could be found, making it much easier to find. We also increased the fee for this fee-for-service part of their mission, figuring that good marketing could increase participation. That was, in fact, the case; that part of their mission now accounts for a more substantial part of their revenues.

I've done this in my own writing. When I did my first blog, I had written a couple hundred blog posts (a number that now seems quaint). Two of my first blog posts – *The Science of Ask Strings* and *Anchoring, Ask Strings, and the Psychology of First Impressions* – were responsible for more than 10% of the traffic to the site. At that time, ask strings were Gladys Knight; every other topic I wrote about was a Pip.* It's no accident that my first white paper was about the science of ask strings

* For those a bit younger, ask strings were Justin Timberlake and other blog posts were the other NSYNC band members. For even younger folks saying "Justin Timberlake was in a band?!", yes, he was – that's my point.

and I continue to learn about the topic (to the extent you can in an area that is so audience-specific).

Likewise, look at what people are clicking on in your newsletters and in social media. While this won't get you outside of the types of posts you've already been doing, it will help you find some guaranteed crowd pleasers.

The other step is a content audit: collecting all your assets and determining their use. One of the principal challenges to content marketing efforts is empty-page-itis. But, in the words of Steve Jobs "Real artists ship." Looking through old emails, blog posts, internal documents, photo libraries, etc., can give you not only inspiration, but content that requires just a dusting off and some polish:

- Three blog posts = an enewsletter.
- Nine blog posts = white paper.
- One white paper = one slideshow.
- One slideshow slide + verbosity = blog post.
- Your boss who loves to talk about her favorite program + camera = video.
- Your blog + editing = donor newsletter.

Heck, this book is in part blog posts stitched together. You can assess for yourself how well or poorly that's turning out.

You should also embrace what I call content fractals. You should be able to zoom in a level on any paragraph – even every sentence if you have powerful sentences – of a blog post, add a level of detail, and get another blog post out of it. Likewise, you should be able to go big picture and make a blog post one paragraph (or a sentence) of a more general blog post. Consider this Matryoshka doll of content:

1. What a cure for cancer would mean
2. What research is necessary for a cure to cancer
3. How cancer research is funded
4. What policies are best to fund cancer research
5. What policies are being debated about cancer research now

6. How you can advocate on those policies
7. How you can advocate for S. 1234, which increases cancer research funding
8. A phone script for calling your senators about S. 1234

Notice that #1-4 are permanent content; #5-6 are semi-permanent content that would have to be updated periodically; #7-8 are ephemeral. As such, the media for each changed: more immediate media like podcasts, emails, social media posts demand content like those about S. 1234; #1-4 are permanent enough you could get a book out of them.

The demands on you also change. Permanent content has time to leisurely meander through a review process and have each word polished to a mirror shine. Ephemeral content demands rapid response. Ideally, you've done prep work for what you are going to do when news arises, perhaps even writing potential briefs in advance. And, as with Human Rights Campaign on the Obergefell marriage equity Supreme Court case, you will need rapid response to meet the unexpected.

Notice these content topics are interlinking. Your discussion of how you can advocate for cancer research policies will link up the chain to what policies are best and what are best right now. It will also link down to how you can advocate for S. 1234. This gives diehards the opportunity to delve deeply into issues, newbies the ability to get more content, and you better search engine listings, as linking between related quality content transfers some halo effect from one to the next.

When you create this content, it must be at the level of your constituent. Bill numbers are about as geeky as you want to get in policy speak. I have had the pleasure of working on the US highway bill. When writing about this, it's tempting to use the language policymakers use for the bill: e.g., "we don't want another continuing resolution. We need to get the authorization through the conference committee, so we can then appropriate the money to the program and distribute the Section 402 funds to the states."

If you say this, most of your constituents will hear the muted trombone of Charlie Brown's teacher going "wah wah WAH wah

WAHWAH wah." If they didn't talk about it on Schoolhouse Rock, it isn't going to fly with a mass audience.

Similarly, we nonprofits can also (but should not) use our own inside baseball speak. DonorVoice did some testing for a nonprofit working to feed children. It found it would reduce how much people liked a message by about a quarter if it used the phrase "nutrition hubs." Inside the organization, this was a useful phrase – it wanted to create places in communities where kids could always go to get fed whether school was in or out. Noble cause. Useful concept. *Death* for fundraising. It was too complex. Explaining the concept works for them – people just don't like the jargon.

The same thing for acronyms: you talk about your KPIs or LMICs; donors say WTF and STFU. We can also use language intended to soften a blow when we mean for a blow to land. How many appeals do you see or hear with underserved people? One gets the idea that the person is a goal thermometer and with just a little bit more of the nonprofit's program, they can be filled all the way up to whatever the correct level of service is. Or, worse, one sees "underserved" and reads "undeserved" – a significant difference that can be conflated when skimming.

Most times, underserved people are poor. People with food security issues are hungry. People who have been impacted by violent crime are victims (if they choose to so classify). Stakeholders and beneficiaries are "the people your donation helps." We can tell the story plainly and evocatively.

Likewise, the problems of the underserved aren't challenging. They aren't suboptimal. They are bad. They are hard. If you are talking to the right audience, they might even suck.*

We don't *effectuate* things. We don't *create an intervention*. We don't *empower* things to get done. We don't *help* do things. We <u>do</u> things, thanks to the generous support of our donors. Or better yet, you and supporters like you do things.

---

* Rare. Depends greatly on your brand voice and your target audience.

Easy things make brains happy.[214] Happy brains do the things people ask them to[215] (like donate). The easier something is, the more it convinces.[216] Simply named stocks go up more[217]; simply named people get more jobs[218]. And simple gets more donations.

This simplicity also goes into the types of content you create. You shouldn't shy away from having more challenging fare. But challenging fare is for your committed folks; it isn't gateway content. You attract people with simplicity. Few people will be retweeting the American Constitution Society's "32 Ways the Taney Court changed the Constitution"* or downloading it to build the ACS's list.

But a "Which Founding Father are You?" quiz† could be a way of building interest, then lists. Traditional media companies do this as well. The New York Times' most read content of 2013‡ wasn't about the Boston Marathon bombing (stories #2, #3, #7) or pieces by elites (Angelina Jolie at #4 and Vladmir Putin at #5). It was a piece called "How Y'All, Youse, and You Guys Talk" with a quiz that placed you in the United States based on your word choices.[219]

If people are acting toward a goal, that goal should also be appropriately concrete and attainable. Researchers looked at concretely framed positive goals like "make someone smile" or "increase recycling" versus "make someone happy" or "save the environment." Across several test cases, the people who pursued a concrete goal were happier, because hitting the goal met their expectations, and thus more likely to do good in the future. Oddly enough, that's not what test subjects thought would happen, making this a stealthy effective tool.[220]

Fighting for simple isn't simple. Complexity is a tricky bastard. He will plead "it's just one more" for every field in a form, every message in a communication, every step in a process, and every snowflake in an

---

* #1: Slaves are totally cool to have and not people at all!

† I'm totally a John Adams: single-minded to the point of annoying, effective, good orator, necessary, incompetent fighter, a bit arrogant, married at or above himself, and not nearly cool enough to get anything more than a mention in hip-hop musical.

‡ Alas, more recent versions have focused more on politics.

avalanche. And he will tell you it is easier, faster, and/or cheaper to do things his way. And he will be right. But easier, faster, and cheaper aren't always better.

Simplicity doesn't mean forgoing details and evocative language. In one study[221], witnesses were asked how fast two cars were going when they crashed. Except instead of crashed, the authors tended a few different verbs; here are the results:

- Smashed: 40.5 MPH
- Collided: 39.3 MPH
- Bumped: 38.1 MPH
- Hit: 34.0 MPH
- Contacted: 31.8 MPH

Let me stress this: they watched *the same crash*. But you could make that crash faster or slower by 30% with your word choice.

In the classic *Made to Stick*[222], which I strongly recommend, the Heath brothers relay the study that stuck in my mind as "the Darth Vader toothbrush study." Simulated juries were given eight facts for and eight facts against a parent retaining custody. Thc stories differed only in detail. Half received irrelevant details for the good side: e.g., instead of just "Mrs. Johnson sees to it that her child washes and brushes his teeth before bedtime," they added "He uses a Star Wars toothbrush that looks like Darth Vader."

The other half received irrelevant details for the dark side: e.g., in addition to "The child went to school with a badly scraped arm which Mrs. Johnson had not cleaned or attended to. The school nurse had to clean the scrape," they mentioned that the school nurse spilled the treatment, staining her uniform red.

Jurors who heard vivid details for the good things judged Mrs. Johnson to be a more suitable parent than jurors who heard the unfavorable arguments with vivid details.

These details come into play especially when you are telling ephemeral stories at the lowest fractal levels. OK, since I just talked about simplicity, let's try that again…

These details come into play especially when you are telling timely, urgent stories about individual people or events. They make the difference between sticky and forgettable. So in these types of stories, find your Darth Vader toothbrush.

This must be put in the service of giving the potential constituent something of value. Sometimes it's informational. Sometimes it's tangible – a window cling, a pocket constitution, a bumper sticker (although a word of warning that this will tend to attract people who like stuff and thus may require stuff to donate; we've already discussed why that is bad). Sometimes it's something that's also of value to you: they sign a petition and feel better about themselves, having made a difference; you get an additional petition signer. But it always fits their identity and the need they had when they came to the site: to respond, to advocate, to get information, to honor a loved one, to feel differently from how they do now.

We are hardwired for reciprocity: giving to those who give to us. In a simple experiment, psychologist Dennis Regan found that a small gift of a can of Coke resulted in selling twice as many raffle tickets as when he gave no Coke. This result held whether the purchasers liked the person giving the Coke or not – the norm of reciprocity is so strong they acted regardless.[223]

So, in short, your content should be designed to:

- Meet the burning need of a specific constituent identity or identities.
- Give something of value to the visitor.
- Get something of value from the visitor (usually getting them to sign up) in exchange, with the promise of being able to deliver more value to them.
- Clear out everything else extraneous.

And if you are thinking that this is also a good time to put a permission-based marketing system in place, where people signing up have control over their communications, congratulations! You are seeing how these strategies can build on each other.

Where do you go from here?

> *"The psychological transformation from paying attention to giving money is the process of integrating that cause from the external world into one's most inner sense of who they are."*
>
> – Jen Shang[224]

The first few days after which you get a person's information are a critical courting period. However, we have precious little time to act after content is consumed. Gratitude decays. Researchers find that the person receiving a favor values it more than the favor-doer at first. Over time, however, the favor-recipient's value of the favor goes down and the favor-doer's value of the favor goes up.[225] This is neatly summarized by the saying "What have you done for me lately?"

And the half-life is shorter than you might think. A university hospital mailed 18,000 requests to former patients. It batched these and sent them (approximately) quarterly. This meant that some patients received them right after their procedure; some received them months later.

Researchers found that every 30 days delay in sending the letter after a patient's last visit cut response rate in half. This decay was even greater among those with the most serious conditions and the best outcomes (presumably because they had more gratitude to decay). As the researchers concluded:

> "Organizations that provide a service or otherwise interact with potential donors may be able to dramatically

> increase donation rates and fundraising revenue by decreasing the delay between an interaction with a prospective donor and a donation request."[226]

Even though you are not performing life-saving surgery on a constituent with your content, the idea applies to pet adopters, museum/park/library visitors, event attendees (for a good event), content consumers, etc. If you are providing value to your constituent, you will get gratitude. Speed gets people while they remember you and remember you fondly. We need to use this precious time to get what we need.

"What we need" is usually considered to be a donation. You want to claim those clams, loot that lucre, and seize that scratch.*

But that's not the only thing. Nor it is the first thing. After all, you've acquired someone in theory, but not in practice.

I know; it should be simple. You do acquisition/lead generation; you get a constituent on your data file. It's not complicated. It's an assembly line, but instead of putting in steel and getting out a GMC Acadia, you put in money and get an audience.

But let's consider this in reverse. You go to a new restaurant. It's so horrid you imagine Gordon Ramsay calling people [redacted] donuts in the kitchen. You pay your bill and vow never to return.

Are you a patron of that restaurant?

After all, they've given you food; you've given them money. They've acquired you!

Viewed through this lens, our definition of acquisition and lead generation could use some work. This is especially true when fully three-quarters of one-time donors will not give again.

I would propose we have a constituent when we have at least one of these:

---

* Apologies to my international readers but queue up for that quid doesn't quite have the same ring. Just talking about getting money in the door.

- Permission to contact them again (and not just implied permission).
- Information that allows you to better to communicate with them (not "talk to them" – this should be a two-way street).
- Either a first gift after cultivation or a second gift if it was a gift that initiated the relationship (after all, if they began as a donor but don't return, you might be the Gordon Ramsey-ed kitchen; be prepared to have your grease traps checked and the resultant reside shoved in your face).

Constituent onboarding often focuses on the gift to the exclusion of permission or information. This seems to be backwards, as getting permission and/or information makes getting a gift so much easier. Each bit of information makes for a different, and better, constituent journey. An effective report and appeal to the donor – including a good first or second gift ask – should incorporate information you've learned about the donor.

And you should seek this information as soon as is possible – at or near the point of acquisition. In telemarketing, one (anonymized) UK animal organization asked people who called in if they considered themselves cat people or dog people. They tested three versions of the script: one for cat, one for dog, and one for both/neither/declined. This simple change resulted in a 15% increase in response rate and a ten-pound increase in average annual gift. It's tempting to think of this as a neat one-time direct marketing response raiser. And it is. But this approach also informs every interaction this organization has with these donors with similar increases in response.

Acknowledgments and onboarding mailings and emails are the best time for learning more about the donor. If it is in the acknowledgment, it must be done with some care. In fact, Penelope Burk admonishes against this in *Donor Centered Fundraising*, saying "[t]o avoid leaving the impression that you are already gathering information that will help you plan the next solicitation, it is preferable to leave space between a thank you and any other request."[227]

This is true, so best not to ask questions aimed at planning the next solicitation. Rather– especially for new constituents– you can ask about their wants, needs, and preferences and then honor those needs and preferences. After all, this is respectful – we appreciate your support and want to make sure we honor who you are and why you support us.

But the second-best time is right now. That's right: even your multiyear stalwarts can benefit from your learning more about them. Pamela Grow gives an example, saying it was the smartest thing she ever did. She took a file and program in decline and asked some of the best donors what their motivations for giving were. The results?

> "Eighteen responded. Several sent in checks, although I hadn't asked for money. Three eventually became major donors.
>
> Their responses were illuminating. They were poignant and sometimes humorous. They shaped my strategy going forward and many of their comments played a permanent role in the agency's marketing materials."[228]

So, good news! It's never too early – and it's never too late – to learn more about your audience. Specifically, you want to know:

Identity: You probably guessed that by now, but perhaps not how important is it. Consider the ASPCA's "Tell us about yourself!" page that asks for identity and topic preference. From this information, it customized emails and subject lines to fit the cat versus dog preference of the donor. The response rates increased 230 percent as a result. Now, that was in 2007, so donors are probably more accustomed to customized emails. But that's also part of the point: people are now used to customized emails. If you aren't sending them, you are well behind the times.

Satisfaction with their experience: When you reach out to constituents based on only transactional information, you are assuming they are happy with their experience. Not everyone is.

I had a fitness watch to monitor my lack of fitness. For the sake of anonymity, I'll call it a FitGit. I was embroiled in a technological fight to get this to work as advertised for months. Part of the challenge was getting emails back from customer service about this product. Simultaneously, yet in a different universe, I got an aggressive number of emails asking that I order another FitGit.

I haven't. I won't.

The fact that I bought doesn't make me more likely to buy again. Likewise, the fact that a donor donated doesn't necessarily make her likely to donate again; the fact that someone engaged your content doesn't mean they liked it. A dissatisfied constituent – shocker – is less likely to donate.

By assessing experience data immediately, you cannot only better predict whether they will donate; you can also fix the issue, both for this person and for the others.

But, oddly, many organizations don't ask for this information. If they do, it's often only after the "Share on social media" acknowledgment. Can we agree it would be better to find out if someone has good things to say before asking them to say things?

Commitment: Knowing donors' commitment levels creates effective models and remediation plans. But knowing donors' commitment has benefits that go beyond knowing whether they will give or not. Donors who are highly committed are (far) more likely to become your monthly donors, multiple year donors, major donors, bequest donors, etc. In short, your committed donors are not only the donors who will retain; they are the ones you want to retain.

Preferences: If you are asking for channel preferences as part of your onboarding, you are no longer limited to welcoming someone through their channel of origin. Welcoming them in all their preferred communication channels increases the likelihood they will engage with you in all of them. Then you get all those great multichannel donors you've seen conference PowerPoint slides about*, increasing retention, but you are also cutting waste out of your program. You can also ask donors what topics and what frequency they desire.

These can all be collected in short order and all at once. In 1986, Botton Village started sending new supporters a preference form that asks about frequency, channel, and topic preferences. The form also captures information for bequest giving. A modern version would probably ask about email and phone capture.

Results? Ken Burnett reports that they have nearly 10,000 Christmas-only donors who respond at 61% with an average gift of 64 pounds. Their average donor gives for nine years.[229]

Asking for information is the primary role of this courtship phase of your relationship. You'd be remiss, however, if you didn't also let the person know why they were so smart to start a relationship with you.

Roger Craver's classic *Retention Fundraising*[230] points the way here. He posits seven drivers of donor retention:

- Are you effective at your mission?
- Does the donor know what to expect from interactions with you?
- Are your thank-yous timely?
- Do you listen?
- Does the donor feel s/he is a part of something important?
- Does the donor feel appreciated?
- Does the donor receive information about who is being helped?

* That confuses correlation with causation. Often, the reason someone will give you multiple channels in which to communicate is that they like you. Thus, it's not necessarily that multichannel donors are more valuable; it may be that more valuable donors are more likely to seek multiple channels.

I would extend this to non-donor constituents. You want your early communications to communicate these same things, where knowing more about your constituents is part of making them feel appreciated.

Thus, in this courting period, you should be looking to give them as much information as they want about your organization, but no more. If someone wants a sip of water, they do not want it from a fire hose.

As an adopted Tennessean, I think of when the Nashville Predators first came to town. Hockey should not have taken root in this southern soil. This is not the midwestern and northeastern hotspots where people strap on skates immediately after their first steps.

That's why one of the Predators' early moves was to create Predators University and Hockey 101. These educational activities run before games when broadcasters walk fans through the rules and strategies of the game (basic questions, like how many games are in a season).[231] Brochures covered information like who gets credit for an assist. [232] TV broadcasts also feature players demonstrating tactics and skills for the watching audience. Newer fans are also provided headsets in the arena to listen to the broadcast and get insights into what's occurring on the ice.

Educating the fan base is so important, it's viewed as the responsibility of everyone in the organization. Team president Jack Diller explained "We believe strongly in the education process, so we invest heavily in Predators University, Hockey 101, and similar kinds of programs. We reach out to our audience to explain the finer points of the game."[233]

In 2017, the Predators were in the Stanley Cup finals and *The New York Times* reflected on the phenomenon:

> "Harden [the senior VP for ticket sales and youth hockey, who started selling tickets at a mall food court] reflected on Nashville's evolution during a recent drive with his wife, Paige. He flipped on the satellite radio to the NHL Network, where a caller from Alabama, in an accent thicker than Harden's Texas twang, wanted to talk not

> about Rinne or Forsberg, Ryan Johansen or P. K. Subban, but about the team's third defensive pairing.
>
> Years ago, Harden worried that Paige would lose confidence in him and break off their engagement given his struggles at the kiosk, but she had faith – in him, in the Predators. And now, as he listened to a man in a different state, in the middle of football country, discuss Nashville's blue line, he turned to Paige and laughed."

The great thing here is that the Predators, like us in donor onboarding, know that new people are always coming with enthusiasm, but no knowledge. Their crowd has people who cheer when the Predators sustain time in the offensive zone* and those who wonder why that's a good thing. That's the challenge that faces them, and us, in onboarding.

Not everyone needs a larger number or depth of communications in onboarding. For Nashville, many auto workers had moved from Detroit to Nashville, bringing their hockey love with them. So too with us nonprofits. An international relief organization used commitment to test the effectiveness of its "welcome" communications, randomizing donors to receive zero or six introductory communications. It found those donors who were highly committed to the organization had their retention go **down** by nine percentage points when they got additional communications. They said things like, "Stop convincing me; I'm already convinced." More knowledgeable donors are less likely to donate to awareness activities and more likely to donate to mission activities[234], another way of segmenting.

But for low-commitment donors, the six additional communications corresponded to a 12-point **increase** in retention. They said things like,

---

* Sustain time in the offensive zone = have the puck near the opponent's goal. Even if you don't score, it's a good sign because better things happen when the puck is near your opponent's goal than when it's near yours.

"I believe you do important work, but I actually don't know you well." Those who don't know as much about you need to get more introductory communications; those who are passionate about you need fewer. This sounds counterintuitive in a direct marketing world where conventional wisdom preaches greater volume to those who love us and more tentative efforts with those on the fence. However, the data bear this out.

If you try one-size-fits-all welcome communications, you will either fail to retain (or convert) those constituents trying you out or pay for the privilege of dissuading your best potential donors.

These data are also helpful in predicting who will become a donor. Environmental Action found that opening an email from their welcome series increased the opener's likelihood of opening an email over the next six months by 20%. Further, it increased their likelihood of opening all emails over the next six months by 1-3%.[235]

As you are acquiring constituents in micromoments, you will likely be acquiring more low commitment donors. This isn't to say they will not be valuable to your organization, but rather than they don't know that much about you. They signed up because of the disaster (global or personal) or the quality information you provided rather than deep seated personal ties. It's your job to familiarize them with your organization and your cause.

This process is made much easier if you know which touchpoints add to commitment. Surveying your donors properly, as with a DonorVoice Commitment Study*, can find which communications were important and worked (keep), which were important but didn't work (change), and which weren't important (drop).

---

* For example, see Catholic Relief Services experience with this at http://www.theagitator.net/wp-content/uploads/Why-do-donors-give-Answers-from-Science.pdf. It's vital that you ask donors things they can answer like what they think of a touchpoint, and not ones they cannot, like how important a factor is. We lack metacognition – we don't know why we think what we think.

For example, if you are like most organizations, you have an email newsletter. Is that an effective tool for increasing your donors' and potential donors' commitment and lifetime value? Is it telling the right types of stories? Asking for the right types of engagement?

If you don't know the answers to those questions, think about all the time and treasure that goes into creating and sending that newsletter, not to mention the effort to acquire people to read it.

We have a natural tendency to think of a communication as a "conversion email for advocacy participants" and look at its success or failure to convert in a vacuum. In reality, conversion and retention begin at the point of acquisition (whether donor acquisition or general constituent acquisition). Every communication to and fro builds or detracts from a well of goodwill and commitment.

Thus, saying "this was a bad conversion email" may be like saying "I'm a bad driver" because my car is out of gas – it may or may not be true because problems loom upstream.

OK, you've educated the constituent (if they want or need it) and asked them for additional information to drive (and predict) their future giving. Can we ask them for money already?

Yes, **after the person has completed what they came to do**. This can be:

- At the end of the content experience, as we saw in the Norwegian Cancer Society example.
- On the confirmation page. If someone downloaded a white paper, it could be "this white paper was made possible by the generous support of people like you" or, perhaps even better, "now that you know about the plight of the Brown Bar-ba-loots, can you email your legislator to add them to the list of protected species?"
- In a lightbox. In addition to coming up after a page opens, you can also launch them as they are about to close. This type of ask can serve up your best reason or pitch to complete the action they came to the page to do.

- As a follow-up email. The test here can be what is the appropriate action to ask for. If you have someone who has taken an action alert, what do they want to do next? And what is of most value to you?

Whether you have additional information from them or not (ideally you do), you can be very specific in your ask. That is, if someone took your Brown Bar-ba-loots action alert, your donation ask can be a Bar-ba-loot specific campaign, which can and should be reflected on your donation page, confirmation page, lightbox, and email follow-up. (And follow-up mail campaign or telemarketing campaign – whatever communications means you and they agree upon).

What if you have a new constituent (Great!), you've sent them the appropriate welcome series (Perfect!), but they didn't donate and they didn't tell you more about themselves (Boo. Hiss.)?

First, we should lower our expectations: someone who doesn't give you more information is far less likely to retain. In a study of DonorsChoose donors, researchers found that those who gave additional information were 150-200% more likely to make another donation.[236] Failure to answer is itself an answer of sorts.

After we rightsize our expectations, should we drop them into the communication channel of origin and hope for the best? As our Direct Marketing Master Yoda[*] would say: "No. No. No. Quicker, easier, more seductive."

But in this case, not ideal. It's not ideal for the constituent and it's not ideal for learning more about what this person wants – you may be freezing what this person "is" before you've had a chance to find out.

The person has already told you that they are responsive to three things:

---

[*] Don't believe me? Check out Yoda's donor newsletter at http://agentsofgood.org/2014/01/how-to-newsletters-101/ .

- Medium: If they respond to a mail piece, for example, they do not hate mail pieces. It may not be their only, or even their favorite means of communication, but it is one to which they respond.
- Message: Your mission probably entails multiple things. Your goal may be wetlands preservation. You work to accomplish this through education, research, and direct conservation. If someone downloaded your white paper on the current state of wetlands research and your additional research goals, you know that they are responsive to that research message. It may not be their only or favorite message, but they respond.
- Action: If someone donates, they are willing to donate. If they sign a petition, they are willing to petition.

You are trying to chart the middle ground 'twixt sending the same thing repeatedly and bombarding people with different, alien messages, media, and asks.

Thus, I would recommend what I'd call the bowling alley approach in honor of Geoffrey Moore, who advocated for a similar approach to entering new markets in his for-profit entrepreneurial classic *Crossing the Chasm.*

The idea in the for-profit world is that you enter one market with one product. Once you have a foothold, you try to introduce into that same market a different product; and in a different market you introduce your original product, in the same way that hitting a front bowling pin works to knock down the two behind it.

In our nonprofit work, we play three-dimensional bowling.* The idea behind the non-profit bowling alley, or "change one," approach is that you should change only one aspect at a time of your medium, message, and action.

---

* In sci-fi, you see people playing three-dimensional chess, but never three-dimensional bowling. Discuss.

Let's take our hypothetic wetlands organization as an example – they work to educate, research, and conserve. They have people who download white papers and informational packets, people who take advocacy actions, and donors. And their means of communication are mail, phone, and online.

Let's further take a person who downloads a white paper on research, providing her email address. The usual temptation would be to drop her into the regular email newsletter, append her mail address, and drop her into the warm lead acquisition mail stream.

But this would not be the best approach: you would be taking someone who, for all you know, is interested only in one medium, message, and action and asking them for something completely different.

Rather, it would be better if at first you probe other areas of interest. Ideally, you would ask her:

- Online for downloading additional information about research (same medium, message, and action).
- Online for advocacy actions and donations related to research (same medium and message; different action).
- Online for downloading information about education and conservation (same medium and action; different message). Note that most organizations will have several dimensions along with message can vary; try to vary only one at a time.

And if you absolutely must append her mail address, you would make her ask specific to "we need your help to help make our research resources available not just to you, but to policymakers across the country" – tying it as directly as possible to where their known area of interest.

Over time, you should get a strong picture of this person. Maybe she is willing to do anything for your organization by any means if focused on your research initiatives. Maybe she is willing to engage with you about anything, but only online. And maybe she likes research and conservation, but not education; online and mail, but not phone; and getting information and donating, but not engaging their representatives. Be willing to learn. More importantly, be willing to give up when her disinterest makes it clear that a venue is no longer worth pursuing.

This last point is vitally important. A colleague recently got a donation ask from an organization. He last interacted with them (giving a small gift from their gift catalog) seven years ago. In the intervening time, he has returned no mail piece, answered no phone call, opened no email, and made no gift.

Sending this request should been cost-prohibitive, regardless of their segmentation. My colleague would say his commitment to the organization is low. He does not fit their donor identity. His behaviour* shows no interest to the organization. The mail piece doesn't fit his original interest (straight ask versus gift catalog).

If you are making money from your 84-month lapsed, low commitment, identity-mismatched, non-engaged donors, we should switch roles: I desperately want to read *your* book.

At some point, you must put down the boombox, turn off the Peter Gabriel, and drive away.†

Taking your relationship one step at a time helps you learn your constituent's desires over time, even when those desires aren't to continue a relationship. Moreover, you can learn without culture shock. If someone downloads a white paper and you ask them to take an advocacy action on that same issue online, they may not be interested, but they likely see the through line to the action they took. If they download a white paper and get a phone call for an unrelated action, they likely will not. It's the difference between a donor response of "I can see why you'd think that, but no thanks" and "what the hell?"

---

* I've added the "u" because this colleague is British.

† This is from an 80's movie Say Anything, where John Cusack used this technique to woo back a lost love. Like many wooing techniques from many 80's movies, do not try it lest you be justifiably arrested.

(followed by the constituent equivalent of getting a drink thrown in your face).

It's also why I recommend going back to the original communication mechanism for lapsed donors. In that case, it may be literally the one and only thing you know that works.

You may say that you don't have the resources to do five different versions of each mail piece or telephone script. But you can do this inexpensively if you are varying your mail messages throughout the year. For a warm lead acquisition strategy, simply make sure the advocacy people get the advocacy mail piece and not the others for now. If you find out some of them are responsive to a mail donation ask, you can ramp up cadence later, but for now, your slower cultivation and learning strategy can pay dividends.

The content journey does not end with acquisition. Constituents who consumed your content to enter your organization will likely want to get similar content in the future. Going back to them with similar content offers, and expanded offerings once their preferences are better known, keeps these constituents engaged and builds their ties to the organization.

This content can be integral to the donors' value proposition. Donors can be enlisted to help sustain and create valuable content as we've seen with *National Catholic Register*. The content can also be part of a membership or supporter offer. For example, supporters of the U.S. Olympic and Paralympic Foundation are generally (and not shockingly) fans of the Olympic Games. One of their more popular benefits for supporters is a viewing guide for the various sports. The organization is now branching out into providing resources to help donors learn about and engage with preliminary events and to see Team USA athletes in non-Olympic/Paralympic competition.

You can see both approaches in combination in the marketing for public television and radio stations. A donor is asked to support programming creation and dissemination and often receives content-based premiums and content itself for their support. In fact, WETA looked at their donors who came in and are retained by their content (the WETA Passport program that gives access to content for members).

These donors seemed to be lower value, because at $60 per year ($5 per month), they lagged $120-210 per year TV and radio pledgers in initial revenue. However, these donors had extremely low acquisition costs and better retention rates (55% over 12-month versus 37% for TV pledgers). As a result, these donors have a high lifetime value.* Because these donors are more plentiful, these content-based members will be responsible for more revenue than traditional pledges, mail, online, or face-to-face over the next five years.[237]

Likewise, cultural institutions like museums and libraries have also found the value in asking for content creation support as well as specialized content for donors like symposia and tours. This approach need not be restricted to these types of nonprofits. The Southern Poverty Law Center sends educational resources like their Teaching Tolerance tools for educators and their Hate Map to donors to build their understanding of SPLC's efforts against hate groups. Donors are then asked to support these media.

These content-based strategies tie directly to your donor's identity. If a donor comes into the organization because of a screening test they took, other materials for learning and lessening risks could be of great value. If they came in because they or a loved one had been diagnosed, a different content offer for that identity would have similar (if not better) value. This is the value of being a media organization – these materials create loyalty and commitment at the same time as they create their own justification for funding.

In short, our media organization will seize on the right time and/or audience to bring new constituents into the organization with quality content that gets the person to sign up for more. They will then work to learn more about that person to make ever more customized, personalized requests for the person to take additional actions like, and especially, donating. They will then continue to create content for these ideal identities, deepening the relationship with the donor and building the value proposition for them to donate.

---

* Lower than online and pledgers, but higher than mail or canvassing.

Once you have a content base, you continue to create, refine, and optimize. One of the simplest ways to judge your content's performance is to look at a classic consultant's 2×2 matrix:

- High usage of the content; high conversion to your end goals. These are the things that make you happy. For example, if action alert usage is the highest activity on your site and advocates are among your most likely people to donate, you are doing your job well.
- Low usage of the content; low conversion to your end goals. You can ignore these things for now; they'll require a lot of work to get into shape. You have lower hanging fruit to pick right now.
- High usage of the content; low conversion to your end goals. This is one form of an opportunity – you want to work to optimize the path from the microconversion to your end goal. Let's say many people are downloading your white paper, but few of them are donating. You might find that your communications are largely around different topics from the white paper and your asks aren't related – these are all fixable things.
- Low usage of the content; high conversion to your end goals. If almost no one comes to your content, but almost everyone who comes becomes a constituent, you should be working to get as many people as possible to come (if only to see whether this is correlation or causation).

Also, if you are getting fancy, you can compute the value of a piece of content by looking at the donation history of people who take the action. I'd advise you to get fancy, but the matrix is a good start.

Hopefully, I've given you enough justification for creating your own non-profit media organization. But in case everything else didn't land, here's one more: it's scalable. A white paper that brings ten people into your constituent file takes as long to write as one that brings in 10,000.

Most fundraising efforts can't do this. Your gala will hold only so many people. Your major gift officer can handle a portfolio of 150 people, no more. Same for your foundation and corporate relations folks. Only so many grants exist in the world. And while outbound mail can amortize stories over larger audiences, the larger costs – paper, postage, names – are all variable.

Content marketing is a flywheel. Pushing it is slow at first. But it acquires a momentum all its own.

Being a media organization is a rare way you can scale your revenues without similarly scaling your costs. That is why we write, create, record, and draw people to our materials. Hopefully, this vision of the future can push you through the fear of the blank page and help you get to a future where you aren't dependent on rented names, but rather are creating your own sustaining audience.

The donor-directed nonprofit: Giving your donors some control

The competition

> *"We're dead alright. We're just not broke. And you know the surest way to go broke? Keep getting an increasing share of a shrinking market. Down the tubes. Slow but sure. You know, at one time there must've been dozens of companies making buggy whips. And I'll bet the last company around was the one that made the best goddamn buggy whip you ever saw. Now how would you have liked to have been a stockholder in that company? You invested in a business and this business is dead. Let's have the intelligence, let's have the decency to sign the death certificate, collect the insurance, and invest in something with a future."*[238]
>
> – Danny DeVito as Larry Garfield

Imagine with me that you are listening to the radio and they mentioned a horrific famine affecting four countries in Africa. This should not be too hard to imagine; in 2018, famines in Nigeria, Somalia, South Sudan, and Yemen have been called the greatest humanitarian crisis since World War II.

You want to do something about this. Back when you used to travel for business, you went to Nigeria a few times. You have colleagues there and have an affinity for the country.

So you want to help out. Not necessarily to end all famine – you know better than to try to boil the ocean with a $50 gift – but to help the people of Nigeria somehow.

You search online and see two options. One is an international nonprofit that you know and respect. They have several pages and copious information on their site about the famine in Nigeria and what they are doing to alleviate the plight of Nigerians. You click donate, but the donate page says nothing about Nigeria or the famine. You fear your donation will go into an undifferentiated pot of money.

So you try the other site. You can see the name of the person to whom you are donating, where in Nigeria they live, and what they want to use the money for – some force-multiplying activity that you think will help them and those around them. Even better, the donation is a loan, so when the small business you are funding makes back its money, so do you. You can then reinvest that money in another enterprise and another and another. You pick a picture and a story and donate.

It's time to view these and efforts like them as serious disruptors to the nonprofit status quo. Donors are looking to fund an impact and a cause, not necessarily an organization. Why should they pay what they perceive to be (but aren't) high overhead rates when they can do a microloan with Kiva, or directly fund a school through DonorsChoose, or find a person in need through GoFundMe?

These organizations are growing in impact. From 2011 to 2018, Kiva went from $89 million deployed in loans to $158 million. They went from 458,000 lenders to 640,000 in that same time period.[239][240] DonorsChoose went from 471,000 donors in the '15-'16 school year to 767,000 donors in '17-'18.[241][242] Remember, this is at the same time as the broader sector was (and is) bleeding donors.

Established nonprofit brands are engaging this fight based largely on the trust they have justifiably built over generations. Like IBM in the early computer market, this works for a time. People used to say "no one ever got fired for buying IBM" for a reason. No one still says this about personal computers. It was true until it wasn't.

This trust is fragile because it is predicated on low-engagement donations. If our example person listening to the radio about the famine in Africa had just a generic sense of wanting to do good and no tie to Nigeria, the first donation page of the respected international nonprofit works well enough. But the donor who wants to do something specific – to dig a bit deeper – finds the connection with this trusted organization lacking.

It is certainly true that most donations are low-engagement donations where the donor will not comparison shop. Perhaps a nonprofit could rely on trust as their differentiator and still maintain for the long term. This leaves aside important implications of losing high-engagement donations:

- High engagement donors tend to be larger donors. They tend to be the donors that retain over the long-term. They tend to be the ones who evolve towards higher-value types of giving like monthly, major, and bequest giving. Since only four percent of donors give 76% of donations and the top third of donors giving 96% of revenues according to the Fundraising Effectiveness Project[243], discerning donors are exactly the donors you would want were you choosing. Remember, you don't want to be loved – you want to be preferred.
- The donors to crowdfunding sites also tend to be younger than the average nonprofit's donors. This means they neither have the same legacy trust of longer-standing nonprofits nor (more importantly) will they develop it in the long-term without a change.
- Markets generally tend toward what higher-involvement individuals are doing. When air bags first came out, they were only on luxury vehicles; now carmakers compete to see how many they can cram in. I worked in the produce department of a grocery store in 1996 when the store got its first organic section. It sounded a bit granola hippie to me, which is why I didn't see the organic food movement coming. This lack of foresight is one of the many reasons I do not own my own island. What was a luxury becomes commonplace.
- How many donors can you afford to lose? When Hurricane Harvey hit, the American Red Cross used its 136-year-old brand to raise and deploy $312 million in the first three months.[244] GoFundMe used its seven-year-old brand to raise and deploy $27 million in the first 30 days.[245] Some of GoFundMe's donations

probably made the pie bigger – donations that would not have been made without directed philanthropy. But some of this came from donations that would have originally gone to the Red Cross.

The other challenge of relying on the "trust us; we know what we are doing" model is it's a bit like being the best gunfighter in the West: you must win definitively every time. Your competitors only need to win once to crack the façade.

The customized one-on-one experiences of giving to a specific person (and low overhead rates – more than the failure of those as a yardstick later) are often used as a proxy for effectiveness. This is unfortunate because, while crowdfunding sites can be very effective distributors of philanthropy, they are not (currently) engines for systemic change. A crowdfunding site can raise funds for a needed surgery; it does not address why the surgery was so expensive or why insurance did not cover it. It can help get new textbooks for an underprivileged classroom; it can't address fundamental funding disparities between the richest and poorest school districts. It can help raise money for a victim/survivor of a drunk driving crash; it can't prevent drunk driving.

Philanthropy should help individuals, but organizations should also strive to fix problems upstream. Or, as Dr. Martin Luther King, Jr., put it, "Philanthropy is commendable, but it must not cause the philanthropists to overlook the circumstances of economic injustice that make philanthropy necessary." Consider a site like GoFundMe, which is often used to pay for United States health care costs – costs that are higher than in other countries and often externally funded in those same countries. You pay for a surgery without making future surgeries more likely.

Crowdfunding can also sometimes reinforce structural iniquities. Researchers looked at direct philanthropy on Kiva, asking assistants to rate photos of people requesting microloans by, among other things, attractiveness, physique, and skin color.[246] The study found that, all other measured things being equal, those people who were one standard deviation:

- More attractive had an 11% shorter time to get full funding.
- Heavier had a 12% longer time to get full funding.
- Darker in skin color had an 8% longer time to get full funding.

For perspective, asking for 10% more money increased the amount of time to complete the loan by 13%. So, being more attractive and skinnier than the average was the equivalent of getting almost 20% more money.

This isn't unique to crowdfunding. Nonblack hosts on Airbnb get 12% more (right in the same ballpark as the Kiva premium on whiteness) than black hosts for similar rentals.[247] Nor is this a problem with Kiva. I can't reasonably blame the crowdfunding sites for this any more than I reasonably can blame my mirror for what it shows me in the morning.[*]

The challenge is humans are more inclined to whom they are socially close. That, unfortunately, means supporting "us" more than "them." This is replicated on sites like Kiva, where people are more likely to give closer to home. On Kiva, because most supporters are from North America, a philanthropic venture in Asia has a 95% lower chance of being funded than a North American one.[248]

None of this means you shouldn't give through these sites. Helping one community, school, or person at a time is noble in and of itself, especially when it helps solve larger issues like who has access to the multiplicative powers of finance, like Kiva, or allows teachers to break out a top-down dictation of the resources others think they need, like DonorsChoose.

But philanthropy should also fund a traditional nonprofit's roles of pushing for systemic solutions and focusing its solutions based on need. It shows the limits of donorcentricity, with a desire to drive our nonprofits with our donors, not giving them the keys.

Unfortunately, these are usually tough sells. For years, we have talked about the systemic problems through the story of the one. It's the

---

[*] I can't *reasonably* blame my mirror, but I *do* blame my mirror.

one that touches the heart. Emotion is far better than education in low-dollar appeals[249] (and since you attract people as low-dollar donors, that hurts acquisition as well). If someone can see a person's plight and fix it instead of chipping away at an underlying problem, easy usually trumps thorough.

The advantages of trust and systemic, studied solutions are not going to be enough. Thus, these crowdfunding competitors look like classic disruptors, forcing traditional nonprofits to adapt or die. This can be a good thing – a purging fire that clears out the inefficient and ineffective. It does, however, mean that the efficient and effective need new factors on which to compete –showing donors that you are 1) using their gift wisely 2) for the ends they desire 3) where they desire.

Using their gift wisely

> *"The next time you're looking at a charity, don't ask about the rate of their overhead; ask about the scale of their dreams – their Apple-, Google-, Amazon-scale dreams – how they measure their progress toward those dreams, and what resources they need to make them come true, regardless of what the overhead is."*[250]
>
> – Dan Pallotta

Let me start with the obvious point: judging nonprofits by their overhead rating sucks.

It's important that nonprofits:

- Answer the phone.
- Balance the books.
- Create contracts.
- Defend their trademarks.
- Enforce their employee policies.
- Fundraise.

- Get rid of bad employees.
- Hire quality employees.
- Identify donor prospects.
- Join amicus briefs on issues of importance to the nonprofit sector.
- Keep their web site secure.
- List open positions.
- Manage employee salary and benefits.
- Nab embezzlers.
- Operate an office.
- Produce financial statements.
- Query potential donors.
- Run a modern technical infrastructure (or, at least, a semi-modern one).
- Set strategy.
- Train staff and volunteers.
- Use a database.
- Venerate their donors with thank-you notes.
- Wire their offices and provide running water.
- X-amine legal documents.
- Yield to regulations.
- Zone out during board meetings.

OK, the zoning out may not be important. But the board meeting is.

All these activities and more are lumped into overhead. Donors, when given a choice, will generally choose not to fund overhead. [251] When someone says they want to fund a mission or a cause but not the overhead that goes along with it, they often think they mean that they want to make sure nonprofit executives don't fly to Gstaad on their private Gulfstream G650s.

What they mean, whether they know it or not, is that they don't want nonprofits to pay salaries and benefits that are (often barely) competitive with for-profit companies and thus remain competitive for quality talent.

And in a fit of irony, many anti-overhead people also will say they want nonprofits to function more like businesses, while starving the legal, HR, IT, financial, management, and revenue-producing structures that allow nonprofits to maintain professionalism.

Overhead ratios are not just a suboptimal way of evaluating charities. If that were the case, you could tolerate them being part of the mix as people evaluate nonprofits. In reality, they are **actively negative** ways of evaluating nonprofits. The nonprofits that do the "worst" on overhead are often better and more effective organizations.

So when a rating system or a person says the nonprofit that spends 91.2% of its funds on programs is better than the one that spends 90.9%, it is creating a race to the bottom. Lest you think I'm exaggerating or merely waxing poetic, Ann Goggins Gregory and Don Howard looked at the impact of overhead fixation in their 2009 article *The Nonprofit Starvation Cycle*[252]:

> "Our research reveals that a vicious cycle fuels the persistent underfunding of overhead. The first step in the cycle is funders' unrealistic expectations about how much it costs to run a nonprofit. At the second step, nonprofits feel pressure to conform to funders' unrealistic expectations. At the third step, nonprofits respond to this pressure in two ways: They spend too little on overhead, and they underreport their expenditures on tax forms and in fundraising materials. This underspending and underreporting in turn perpetuates funders' unrealistic expectations. Over time, funders expect grantees to do more and more with less and less—a cycle that slowly starves nonprofits."

Of course, this article was from 2009. Since then, nonprofits have discovered the immutable truth that robust infrastructure – investing in their employees and their systems – makes all organizations, including nonprofits, more likely to succeed. Thus, they have drastically increased their investments.

These investments were delivered to nonprofits by a magical elf riding a beautiful and gentle unicorn as wood nymphs, leprechauns, and Bigfoots* backed them up with song and evocative dance.

Back in the real world, nonprofits generally have lean and mean in their rearview mirror and now are emaciated and pissed off. The best that can be said about the overhead myth is that people talk about it as a myth. Most actions, however, still follow it. Charity Navigator, to pick an example purely at random†, has decried the overhead myth *and* still bases four of its seven financial rating criteria on this ratio under different guises.

So why do people look at overhead rates? Because they are an easy proxy for a **legitimate** concern: "is my donation making the difference I want it to make?".

Easy, but not good.

Caviola et al[253] called this the *evaluability bias*: people look for and want one easy number that tells them how good something is. They found that when people are presented with a charity, they look for a low overhead rate and value it for its own sake. However, when presented with two charities and both overhead and effectiveness ratings, they valued effectiveness over overhead ratios.

This means that people care more about whether a charity is effective than overhead rate, but overhead is a cheap and easy proxy when effectiveness isn't or can't be explained.

One is reminded of the man who is looking for his car keys under a streetlight. A policeman comes over and asks what the man is doing. After the explanation, they both look under the streetlight together. After a few minutes, the policeman asks if he is sure he lost them here, and the guy replies "No, I lost them in the park."

"So why are you searching here?"

"Because this is where the light is."

---

* Bigfeet?

† Sarcasm: this is not at all random; I've chosen them specifically.

So, in summary, overhead percentages are misleading and counterproductive, but donors take them seriously unless you can give them a real discussion of impact. They take them especially seriously if they compare you to the direct donation organizations that largely exist as a pass-through of your donation to an individual or project.

So how do you best position your overhead?

The UK Charity Commission had prospective donors look at four different versions of an ad for a fictional charity:

- A fundraising statement about how your donation is needed.
- A logo for the Charity Commission.
- A statement of impact for that charity.
- A pie chart about how funds are used.

The most effective framing of overhead was the humble pie chart*, followed by the organization-specific statement of impact. Both were effective at raising trust and donation intention, likely by educating donors that not as much is spent on overhead as they think.[254]

But why test four treatments when you can test 6,656 treatments? That's what the Data and Marketing Association Nonprofit Foundation (DMANF)† and DonorVoice did in a test with nonprofit donors. Using the DonorVoice Pre-Test Tool, they found four solutions among a variety of techniques that can help you better position yourself against low-overhead, targeting-giving competition:

1. Presenting things other than overhead well. Since you've read this far, you almost certainly guessed that properly presented donor identity made a difference. You are correct; testing found that:

- **Donors preferred an identity statement that matched their own experience**. If you personally knew what it is like to have

---

* Pie chart nuances often befuddle both presenter and audience, but the overhead pie chart is usually very simple: "good" part big, "bad" part little.

† Now part of the Association of National Advertisers.

cancer or care for someone with cancer, that statement spoke to you.

- **Getting an identity wrong was worse than not having an identity statement at all.** For example, the statement "you haven't experienced cancer in your life but you can imagine what it is like for those who have" polled worse than leaving this section blank. This is because most people in the sample had a personal experience with cancer, whether direct or indirect, so this mismatching hurt results.
- **Overall results masked these differences by identity**. That is, if you look at the overall results, it looks like identity hardly mattered. But when you looked just at people who held an identity (e.g., a direct connection) getting that identity right mattered very much. So too may it be with your results. A test communication could look to have the same results as a control overall but have a substantial positive impact with one identity and a negative one for another. That's why it's important to test different messages with different identities.

Additionally, the test found that having external validators improved results. In fact, any of the four external validators – the Charity Navigator four-star seal, a DMA certification seal, a GuideStar Platinum seal, and a star rating and testimonial from a donor (think Yelp, but for nonprofits) – worked better than no validator. Even the lowest performing trust indicator (in this case, the testimonial and rating) substantially overperforms not showing a trust indicator at all.

Of the ones presented, the Charity Navigator rating performed best, followed by GuideStar and DMA certification, which were virtually tied.

Now would be a good time to mention DMA did not actually have a DMA certification. In other words, a totally bogus seal still helped increase trust. Please don't tell Russian hackers – they've messed with our trust enough.

So even if you don't have a four-star Charity Navigator rating, you can bolster your credentials with a BBB rating, GuideStar seal, or even donor testimonials. The trick, however, is this was done with a fake charity. It had no brand name or credentialing and thus was uniquely reliant on validation. What would happen if this had been done with a real charity?

Turns out researchers have done this. A researcher looked at Charity Navigator ratings specifically. He found that a one-star increase in the charity rating led to a 19.5% increase in charitable contributions.

But wait! That was only the result for relatively smaller and unknown charities. For larger charities, the researcher found the third-party ratings had an insignificant impact on donations.[255] As stated previously, people will look at efficiency measures, but only in the absence of other information about a charity (specifically, their personal preferences and identity). Thus, these external validators may be more important as you are introducing yourself to donors (i.e., acquisition) than to those who already love you.

You may think it is not fair that poor Charity Navigator ratings are hardest on growing nonprofits who should be investing most in overhead to grow their programs and services. You would be right.

2. Presenting overhead well. Like the UK Charity Commission, we found that the pie chart worked well: the second-best treatment of overhead. Transparency on what percent of a gift went to mission is a strong builder of trust.

Two other treatments – educating donors that the cost of a mailing is small and asking donors to cover overhead as part of their gift – did no better or worse than not mentioning overhead at all. The idea behind noting that fundraising costs are very low was to give transparency into the actual costs of fundraising, which donors seem not to know. This test seems to indicate it's something they don't care to know. Asking for an additional donation to cover overhead has come into vogue recently for online donations (to cover processing costs). The bad news is it doesn't help; the good news is it doesn't hurt either. So, if you are getting additional donations this way, go for it.

But I mentioned that the pie chart only did second-best. What was best for that attribute?

3. Eliminating overhead. It turns out donors don't care how you spend *your* money. They care how you spend *their* money.

It sounds like a semantic difference – after all, if donors are donors, then their money becomes your money.

But it makes all the difference in the world. Think how the new breed of donation platforms and intermediaries work: they do not have high overhead costs *for your gift*. Kiva, for example, had $3.9 million in fundraising and administrative costs out of their total expenses of $17.7 million in 2017.[256] But they and their supporters created $152 million in loans because of that infrastructure.[257] If you gave a microloan on Kiva, you don't see the overhead – your loan is going directly to a person in need, giving you the correct perspective of low overhead.

This fits the reality: people value the overhead of their gift over the overhead of the organization. Remember the study that showed donors have an aversion to overhead? That study also showed that even if charity: water's overhead rate was 50%, donors would give functionally at the same rate to it as if charity: water had no overhead at all if that donor's personal donation was overhead-free. [258] Again, it didn't matter what the organization's overhead was; it mattered what the donor's overhead was.

The researchers went even farther, testing a campaign that looked at whether having a lead donor, matching donor, or lead donor covering overhead influenced donation rates to increase. Here were the conditions:

- Control: "Our goal in this campaign is to raise money for the projects. Implementing each project costs $20,000. Your tax-deductible gift makes a difference. Enclosed is…"
- Seed money: "A private donor who believes in the importance of the project has given this campaign seed money in the amount of $10,000. Your tax-deductible gift makes a difference. Enclosed is…"

- Matching gift: "A private donor who believes in the importance of the project has given this campaign a matching grant in the amount of $10,000. The matching grant will match every dollar given by donors like you with a dollar, up to a total of $20,000…"
- Seed money to cover overhead: "A private donor who believes in the importance of the project has given this campaign a grant in the amount of $10,000 to cover all the overhead costs associated with raising the needed donations…"

Here were the results, in response rate and revenue per piece:

- Control: 3.36% with $.80 revenue per piece
- Seed: 4.75% with $1.32 revenue per piece
- Match: 4.41% with $1.22 revenue per piece
- **Seed covering overhead: 8.85% with $2.31 revenue per piece**

This seed funding covering the overhead means that a person's gift goes 100% to the mission. As such, it's a very effective way to get people to give.

It's also easy to do in the short term, but hard to do in the long term. For the short term, many organizations run matching gift campaigns supported by a corporate or major donor. It's relatively simple (hopefully) to explain the science of lead gifts covering overhead to that funding and asking their permission for this frame of their gift.

For the long-term, though, it requires an organizational commitment and business-model-level thinking. An organization that has done this thinking is charity: water. Their 100% model means they keep two bank accounts that are audited independently. The one covering overhead is funded by a small group of private donors and corporate partners who buy in to funding the expenses that help the organization grow.[259]

That sounds radical. And it is. It is how (or at least part of how) charity: water has grown from $1.7 million in donations in 2007[260] to $33 million in 2012[261] to $50 million in 2017.[262] Despite its effectiveness as a model, few organizations have followed it. But it is simple compared to going to the next level: a donor-directed enterprise.

For the ends they desire

> *"Restricted giving misses a fundamental point: to make the greatest impact on society requires first and foremost a great organization, not a single great program."*[263]
>
> – Jim Collins

Allowing donors to restrict their gifts was the most popular option in our test using the Pre-Test Tool.

As one who has tried to get restricted funds allowed at an organization, the main argument against this is the headache that would come from having multiple restricted funds (which can be mitigated by a strong caging vendor and clear online giving forms and databases). But often the folks who will have to work harder because of restricted giving, knowing that this rationale won't carry the day, say "what if everyone restricted their gift?". Or, more to the point, what if people restricted their gifts in a way that changed the way an organization's budget is shaped?

It won't. It just won't.

In one test of restricted giving, only two percent of donors decided to restrict their gifts, yet allowing someone the choice to restrict their gift raised an extra $40,000, far more than the amount restricted.[264] In another, allowing a restricted gift option increased average donations by 54%, but fewer than 40% of participants designated their gift.[265] Even organizations like Heifer International, which have massive online and offline gift catalogs with similarly massive numbers of options, find every year that their most popular, can't-miss option is "where needed most."

People want to be asked if they want their gift to be restricted. Most don't care once that option has been given. You've already signaled you can be trusted and you care about their opinion by letting them restrict it if they'd wanted.

So offering a restricted gift option will bring in more money and won't tie your hands financially. Also, it's better for the donor. Telling someone that their $10 goes to buy a bed net to stop malaria increases both giving and donor happiness versus that $10 going to a general child health fund.[266] As we've seen with direct giving websites, because donors will bias their gifts toward the whiter, skinnier, and more attractive*, you will have to compensate by biasing your help the other way, but hopefully you are doing an accounting trick in both cases for taking from one pocket and putting it in another.

Your finance department, however, won't do it. You've tried. At some point you realized you could explain the science to your CFO for the rest of your natural life† or you could do your job. And you chose to do your job. That's a wise choice – the better part of valor.

How about something almost as good as restricting gifts without having to go 15 rounds with your finance department?

In our Pre-Test Tool study with DMANF, the restricted gift option won ("I want my gift to go towards:"), whether with a "where needed most" option or not. That was only barely better than the next option: asking for the donor's preference ("From your areas of work, my highest priority is:"). The former is clearly binding; the latter clearly not binding. But on a 100-point scale, restricting your gift was an 80; expressing preference was a 72. Close enough, as they say, for government work.

Does this work in the real world? In fact, the American Diabetes Association tested this in mail acquisition. Their control package had no ability to express a preference and their test version allowed someone to share their highest priority among:

---

* To be clear, these are three separate attributes.

† And some of your unnatural life, rattling the chains you forged in life as a warning for the marketers who would follow.

- Finding a cure.
- Helping patients and families.
- Providing access to care for diabetes.
- Supporting medical professionals.

This test version had a $3.40 increase in average gift and an 11.6% increase in overall revenue.[267] Another anonymous organization tested it similarly and found substantial increases in their acquisition response, but decreases when tried on the donor side (presumably because the organization already should have known their preferences).

Ah, but will it work online? After all, we are taught to purge online form fields like we are Stalin circa 1937. The commandment comes down from the online fundraising heavens: Let there be as little friction as possible between you and your donor's sweet sixteen credit card digits.[*] The test results supported this purge: fewer fields mean higher revenues.

But maybe donor preferences are the exception. Maybe, as we've argued, people want to tell you about themselves and about their reason for giving.

The Heritage Foundation tested this online. Like what the DonorVoice Pre-Test Tool recommended in the DMANF test, they asked donors "Where should Heritage focus its efforts?" rather than asking them to specifically designate their gifts. This was done online with a drop-down box of priorities.

The results? A (statistically significant) 21.7% increase in conversion overall with a 29.1% total increase in donations when they asked for preferences.[268] Three years later, they redesigned their donation form and retested. They found an (also statistically significant) 33.9% increase in conversion overall with preferences.[269]

People want to be consulted. Being able to share their viewpoint on what an organization should focus on is *almost* as valuable as being able

[*] Or fifteen for AmEx, but it doesn't really roll off the tongue.

to specific direct their donation. Plus, knowing what this person wants to support should also make future appeals a bit easier and more compelling, no?

Direct funders like Kiva and DonorsChoose allow us to sponsor/loan to the person/classroom/situation we want to and get a customized experience from that donation. All is not lost, however, for traditional nonprofits. By setting up our business models so that we are overhead-free and donor-directed, we can increase our donations and focus our enterprises. But even if you are not ready for that revolution, you can use lead gifts to pay overhead expenses and using donor preferences to guide you.

Where they desire

Organizations like Kiva or DonorsChoose can also outmaneuver the nonprofit unwilling to allow their donations to be restricted by getting more local. As we saw, North American Kiva donors were far more likely to give to North America.[270] Within the continent, DonorsChoose donors have a higher retention rate when they are giving close to home, best within a few miles.[271*] Donors consistently ask for a gift to go to a place where a disaster has happened or next door to help their neighbors.

In the digital age, people have identities that transcend our physical space. That hasn't eliminated, however, our tribal nature. People give to those who are close to them on social distance – those who look like them, think like them, and act like them. Part of this is also tied to physical distance. People are more willing to give when the gift can impact locally.

But your finance department won't let you do this restriction, even though this is literally the easiest type of restriction to do. All you must do is make sure the amount you spend in a location is greater than the amount restricted to that location. And, yes, you've explained that most people don't restrict their gifts; they just give more when they have the

---

[*] Or very far away – there is a sag in the middle (much like myself).

option to do so. You can always to try to get a better finance department, but for the time being, you don't live in that world.

Fortunately for you, as with restricting gifts to a mission area, you can get most of the way there. One way is to localize asks other than donations. An environmental organization tested two petition-focused Facebook ads to Floridians: one to ban fracking throughout the United States, the other to ban fracking in Florida. Only the location changed in the copy yet click-through on the Florida-specific ad increased 27%.

Another way around restrictions is localization of copy without localization of gift. The Red Cross tested localization to see what the relevant tribe size is. People received solicitations for one of four efforts: the annual drive, the state drive, the winter drive, and the city drive (with the name of their state and city filled in). Customizing this down to the city level significantly helped response rate:

- City: 5.51%
- State: 4.12%
- Annual: 4.01%
- Winter: 3.82% – proof that people hate winter

Those who received the city mailing also had a 4.8% higher average gift.[272]

The authors went a step further and looked at community size. Sure enough, people from smaller communities were even more influenced by having the drive be about their city than people from larger ones. After all, it's easier to have community pride for Greendale, WI, than the entirety of Chicago, IL. In part because Greendale is awesome, but mostly because of size. The tighter knit the group you identify with, the more likely you are to act.

You may already do this level of customization in the mail, where it's been part of the standard agency annual fund playbook for decades. Oddly, it is infrequently deployed in online missives, likely because of the difficulty in getting your online CRM to send out an email with the right location in it and to customize the resultant donation form similarly. For those who do it, a 20%ish boost likely awaits.

Location can also be baked into social nudges. When telethon callers were told someone from their same community and of their same gender made a larger donation right before their call, they gave almost 25 percent more than when they were told that same person made a smaller donation or when the person who gave the larger gift wasn't from their same community and/or gender.[273] Similarly, experiences with circling an ask string value and telling donors (when accurate) that people in their community give that amount on average show this generally increases average gift. We want to keep up with the Joneses of our like identities and tribes.

You can take passive localization further than either of these. I found this out by being an idiot.* While at MADD, seven states volunteered for a localized version of a conversion mail piece, trying to get non-donor constituents in their state to become donors. Each state used their own story of a victim of drunk driving, which I inserted into a larger direct mail piece. I wanted each story to be authentic, so I didn't change one jot, tittle, or comma in the narratives. When we got back results, three states had response rates 50% higher (or more) than three other states (with one in the middle). So I dug into them to find if there was method to the madness.†

You may already know what I discovered. If so, I hope you are having a good ol' laugh at my expense. The three states that had the significantly higher response rates included the name of the state or a prominent city in the state in the copy. The three states that had the significantly lower response rates told the same types of compelling stories but didn't mention the state in which they occurred. In my zeal

---

* I highly recommend this method; it is far easier than knowing things.

† Or MADDness.

not to change people's stories, I'd customized to the state but didn't show my work by stating as such.*

I'd blindly stumbled into a great experiment: it showed that using a localized story *and labeling it as such* substantially increased response rate. It's not accidentally discovering penicillin, but I also didn't have to deal with mold.

If you talk about domestic impact, you likely have accidentally done this same test. One nonprofit told a story of impact from Florida in their October mail piece; the pieces before and after had no identified state of impact. I should mention their October mail piece performed much better than those than surrounded it. The 49 non-Florida states had their revenue per piece increase 66% in October versus the combination of September and November.

In any other mail test, a 66% improvement would be the story. In this test, however, Floridians had their revenue increase over 150%. **A localized story had more impact than a substantially better performing mail piece**.

As with MADD, this wasn't a test we'd planned for. We were able to backtest to get the results. My guess is you might be able to do this as well with your own file.

Would it be laborious to collect and write 50 different stories for each mailing and email that you plan? Absolutely. Donor focus has its limits. But when you run the numbers, using a 50% increase in response or your own backtested results, my guess is you will find that it's worth it to customize to some of your largest geographic centers, whether those are cities, states/provinces/counties, or countries where the critical masses of your donors live.

So:

---

* What was the state in the middle, you ask? That story mentioned the name of the interstate on which the crash occurred, but no other identifying information to the state. The interstate is a prominent road in that state but, true to its name, goes through multiple states. Thus the reader may have an identification from driving on that interstate, but not have the state-based identification other readers had.

- Crawl is customizing your appeals with location names.
- Walk is using social nudges, telling people what people like them do to increase giving.
- Jog is telling stories from their area so they emphasize more deeply and know they can have an impact where they likely most want to.
- Run is allowing them to restrict their gift to a location.

While donor direction is the platinum standard – the transformative way is to allow donors to have the impact they want to have – not all organizations are ready to make the leap. Done is better than perfect. When these first steps prove out, you'll hopefully be able to build the reams of data and mountains of spreadsheets that turn you into the irresistible data force to your finance department's immoveable object.

A caveat

When you give, give unrestricted funds.

Just because you should offer restricted giving as a technique to raise more money for your mission doesn't mean you should give that way.

You do not restrict the chef at your restaurant by saying you won't pay for salt. You do not limit your mechanic to only metric wrenches. You do not say "the defibrillator paddles look so cool on TV; use them to treat my lower back pain." Such things are recipes for having bland (and probably spit-in) food, leaking cars, and heart attacks.

So too with nonprofits. Even as a nonprofit professional, you should assume that the people in the organization to which you are giving know its ins and outs better than you. If you doubt this, think of all the people outside of your organization who think they know your job better than you. Do you want to be one of those people? No. No, you do not.

As Vu Le, Executive Director of Rainier Valley Corps and writer of the Nonprofit AF blog, put it:

> "General operating funds allow us nonprofits to be most effective at helping people, including saving lives. By restricting funds you are impeding our work; therefore, your philosophies and policies are causing people to get hurt and die. And that is unethical."[274]

If you don't think an organization will use your donation wisely, don't give to them. But if you think they will, give joyously and know that a quality organization will maximize the impact of your gift and do the good you want to do in the world.

The starfish nonprofit: Distributing power and story

"Starfish have an incredible quality to them. If you cut an arm off, most of these animals grow a new arm. And with some varieties, such as the Linckia, or long-armed starfish, the animal can replicate this magical regeneration because in reality a starfish is a neural network – basically a network of cells. Instead of having a head like a spider, the starfish functions as a decentralized network."[275]

– Ori Brafman and Rod A. Beckstrom

It's at this point, when you've already paid for your book, I should confess my poor history as a prognosticator. My specialty is being simultaneously correct and far off reality. The best example is on Election Day 2000, I said "we may wake up tomorrow and not know who the president is going to be." Correct, and far off reality.

In this vein, I wrote a 2003 piece talking about the success Howard Dean's presidential campaign had letting donors do much of their messaging for them to ask for donations and support.[276] I (correctly) posited this as a way of the future, but (far off reality) said campaigns may have to pull back the reins on this because of the dangers of loosely affiliated civilians doing messaging. My concern was of the microliterate, the profane, the misogynist, the racist, the other-ists, the ill-informed, and the indelicate making quasi-official campaign pronouncements.

So, yes, I accidentally invented Twitter. (rim shot)

Where I erred and erred significantly is to imagine that reins still would exist. Campaigns would still send approved messaging through approved channels and scripted surrogates. The conversation in the public, however, could not and would not be driven by the approved messaging. Like it or not, the relative power held by professionals waned as the power of unpaid advocates and detractors waxed.

Take the Sleeping Giants versus Breitbart effort discussed earlier. It wasn't a nonprofit organization that took on Breitbart's advertising revenues – it was two volunteers through a Twitter account.

A nonprofit example is the Ice Bucket Challenge. If you're like me, you had board members and leaders asking you why you didn't do something like that when it came out.

The origin is muddled, with some crediting friends Pete Frates, Pat Quinn, and Corey Griffin with creating the challenge. Others point to Jessica Lagle challenging friends to support an evangelical mission in Africa before completing the "24-hour cold water challenge" in March 2014.[277] Variants were used to raise much for cancer research, a specific cancer case in Indiana, firefighters, and various pet causes of golfers.

Later, the Golf Channel showed what was a small social media effort on their Morning Drive program and performed the challenge live. A little over two weeks later Matt Lauer did the Ice Bucket Challenge on *The Today Show* at the challenge of Greg Norman.

That same day, golfer Chris Kennedy did the challenge, then challenged his cousin whose husband had ALS. **This was the first time the challenge was associated with ALS in a mass setting**. Before that, people donated to a charity of their choice.

That's right – while the Ice Bucket Challenge raised both money and awareness for the ALS Association in the United States and the Motor Neurone Disease Association in the UK, it was created by neither. It wasn't even associated with ALS until *after* it had been shown on *The Today Show*.

Like political professionals, what we can control is an ever-decreasing portion of the communications about us. And, as we try to control what we can't control, we only prevent ourselves from being talked about, a greater sin.

In *The Starfish and the Spider*, Ori Brafman and Rod Beckstrom talk about the decentralized starfish – cut off a leg and it grows back. Looking at organizations as diverse as the Apache, the women's rights movement, abolitionists, GE, and Al-Qaeda, they find decentralized organizations are antifragile, gaining from being attacked and mutating to fit the terrain.

Hierarchical spider systems in the nonprofit world can't adapt this way. You can imagine the chaos if the leadership at a large charity were attacked. In fact, you need not imagine it. When Wounded Warrior Project had news organizations exaggerating and fabricating charges against it[*], the board purged much of the executive team. Program expenses[†] went from $262 million in FY15 to $166 million in FY17, meaning these news reports and the resulting chaos cost almost $100 million in funding for veterans' services per year. The organization is still trying to find its new normal as it works to help veterans do the same.[‡]

Now, imagine a leadership crisis at Black Lives Matter, the Tea Party, or Alcoholics Anonymous. The first question would be "what leadership?". In a network, there are nodes that are more important to some than to others. The loss of these nodes, however, leads to a replacement or a rewiring around that missing node. Every person in the network is valuable; no one is invaluable.[§] In fact, the cofounders of Black Lives Matter eschew the idea of a leaderless organization; they instead talk about being leader-full organizations that survive leadership transitions.[278][279]

The growth potential is also near limitless, especially when compared with a model of getting work only or mostly from those paid

---

[*] I recommend Doug White's report at http://www.thenonprofittimes.com/wp-content/uploads/2016/09/WWP-Report-by-Doug-White.pdf for an account of this. Suffice it to say, if the term "fake news" had been en vogue at the time, this would have been it, with several statements fabricated and others misleading. Add in a splash of overhead-based bashing from Charity Navigator, and you have a hit job on Wounded Warrior Project.

[†] See, I'm doing it too – using program expenses as a proxy for impact! Shame on me.

[‡] And doing a good job on a worthy mission from most accounts.

[§] While not a positive example, think of the number of times the number two or three person in Al Qaeda was caught or killed in the decade after 9/11. Defense against the Dark Arts professors and Spinal Tap drummers had greater longevity and job security. And yet the organization (unfortunately) continued on.

for their time. Consider the battle between one of the largest corporations on earth paying experts spending whatever it took to capture all human knowledge versus a network of volunteers giving their time to accomplish the same task. Or, in other words, Microsoft Encarta versus Wikipedia.

For those who don't remember Microsoft Encarta, that's the point. It was "a digital multimedia encyclopedia published by Microsoft Corporation from 1993 to 2009. Originally sold on CD-ROM or DVD, it was also later available on the World Wide Web via an annual subscription." And, yes, I got that description from Wikipedia, along with a description of a reason for Encarta's demise: "By the time of the announcement of its closure in April 2009, Encarta had about 62,000 articles, most behind a paywall, while the English Wikipedia had over 2.8 million articles in open access."[280] In a twist that should (but won't) have economics professors frantically rewriting their $130 intro textbooks, monetary incentives as a tool got their keisters handed to them by non-tangible incentives.

What if we took off all controls, starting the purging fire with our 298-page brand standards guide? Probably not as much bad as we'd think. That said, it's super scary. As you've probably found in your life, all other people are flawed. People who are not you can say things that are wrong, against your policies, or illegal; I once saw a field employee do all three in one tweet, a 140-character record that stood until June 16, 2015.

Quality is also an issue on two extremes. On one, you can have representatives who seem borderline illiterate. On the other, you can have experts who are challenged to communicate with the general public. (I just waded through an article tweeted out by a nonprofit called "Using an epigenetic mechanism, romidepsin restored gene expression and alleviated social deficits in animal models of autism." If this is the article it intended to go to a lay audience, I would love to see the one it decided was too technical.)

Even if these downsides make us shy from a total bonfire of our brand books and approval processes, what happens if we push the balance to the volunteer? Brafman and Beckstrom talk about this with the concept of a hybrid organization – a centralized organization that has elements of decentralization, allowing stakeholders to have a role. Amazon rates no products.* Wikipedia writes no articles. Kiva creates no stories and has no programs in the classical sense. Rather, all these and more are created by allowing those in their network to create.

We can get value if we empower volunteers with the tools to report, fundraise, advocate, and provide programs. It may be that the nonprofit of the future looks less like a hierarchy than a loosely affiliated network or, at least, incorporates more of this network into their hierarchy.

Supporters as reporters and fundraisers

In 2004, there was still some debate about whether online donations were ever going to be a significant part of nonprofit revenues. That same year, a knitting blogger who goes by the name Yarn Harlot† created a fundraising campaign for Médecins Sans Frontières (Doctors Without Borders) called Tricoteuses sans Frontières (Knitters Without Borders). She put up a page on her blog talking about the important work that MSF does and urged her followers to join Knitters Without Borders in support.

Guess how much she raised.

Wrong. Too low.

By the sixth anniversary of the campaign, Knitters Without Borders had raised over a million dollars to support MSF. That's when the earthquake hit Haiti in 2010. It destroyed the hospital in which MSF was working.

---

* Amazon Choice looks like a rating system, but from the limited amount that Amazon has disclosed about this seal of approval, it appears that it is based on metrics that come from user reviews, low return rates, common purchasing patterns and other technical criteria (e.g., orderable from Amazon's Echo) rather than any subjective judgment on the part of Amazon or its employees.

† Stephanie Pearl-McPhee.

That's when the Yarn Harlot put up the Knit Signal. Picture a gif of Batman's Bat Signal, but a ball of yarn with two needles in it where the bat would be. This stimulated another round of funding for the organization and specifically for Haitian relief.

This story has a few remarkable aspects. First, knitters are more common and more organized than you literally knew. I married a knitter, so I kinda knew, but even I was surprised.

Second, the Knitters Without Borders logo, such as it is, is a parody of the MSF logo. Think for a moment about whether your communications or legal team would allow a knitting blog to parody your logo. I'm thinking it's actually more likely that on page 637 of your brand standards guide it specifically says "this logo may not be parodied on knitting blogs."

Third, here's part of Yarn Harlot's update on the Haitian earthquake:

> "I spoke briefly on the phone this morning with the MSF office here in Toronto, and they confirmed several things.
>
> Things are bad.
>
> The MSF Hospital has sustained damage that means it isn't functioning as a hospital right now. Staff have moved to the courtyard and set up tents and what materials they could retrieve from the building and are doing their best to help people as they can. Doctors who were providing maternity care are now running a trauma centre.
>
> They, and their sister offices in other countries spent all night figuring out who could go and how to get them there, and staff is packing as we read this to get there as fast as they can. They'll be taking inflatable surgery suites with them so they can use that instead of their damaged buildings.

> They believe that some of their staff are among the casualties.
>
> They recognize the power of Knitters Without Borders and the force that we can marshal in a pinch, and they are grateful that you've been able to help them in the past, and they would very much like your help now, and right away."[281]

Your strongest advocates can do some of your fundraising and audience-building for you if you'll let them. But it means losing control. You need to:

- Give them tools and permission. Consider the logo for Knitters Without Borders; what would your brand police do if someone ripped off and modified your logo? Yet allowing the crowd to mash up your tools has power. #GivingTuesday would not have spread as far if it were exclusive to its creators at the 92nd Street Y. Instead, different organizations can do different permutations on the logo (including one testicular cancer charity who turned the heart in the logo upside down), allowing it to spread.
- Keep them in the loop. "I spoke briefly on the phone this morning with the MSF office here in Toronto." She got the details in this post from MSF headquarters. While they were in the middle of dealing with an earthquake. You've likely been in those all-hands-on-deck moments at your organization. You plan. You huddle up. You execute. And you shrink from the rest of the world as if you were a frightened turtle, forsaking food, sleep, outside calls, and some hygiene. Not MSF. They talked to a key influencer of a committed, if seemingly odd*, community. Not later that week when things died down. Not

* Odd for a nonprofit, that is. Being part of a knitting community is not odd at all.

when they got to it after finding out what staff members they lost. That day.

- Recognize their power and appreciate them. "They recognize the power of Knitters Without Borders and the force that we can marshal in a pinch" and "they are grateful that you've been able to help them in the past, and they would very much like your help now, and right away." Flattery will get you everywhere.

In return for loosening its grip, MSF reached people where their tribe lived speaking to a truly unique donor identity. No amount of money could have created that exposure to that audience that way. (They would clearly have more work to do after this acquisition to get those who came for the knitting to stay for the borderless doctors; this can be filed under "good problem to have.")

Your most committed supporters will do this type of reporting. The ACLU has created a digital organizing infrastructure that allows volunteers to create their own organizing events. They can also highlight issues they feel worthy of praise or scorn that filter up to the national level. The national level then works to support and recruit additional resources for these local campaigns. All while reporting on these efforts to supporters eager to hear how goes the fight.[282]

Perhaps in the last section when you were reading about localization, you wondered how you could create a great localized experience. After all, putting [City Name] localizers in your direct mail copy is a technique without a lot of substance. Often, the story isn't from there, the money isn't going there, and the reporting back on what-your-gift-did won't mention it. Moreover, you simply don't have the resources to research and put out thousands of stories for each town and hamlet you serve.

Your supporters can. Whether it is to a geographically localized community, a hobby-based identity like knitters, or simply high-engagement volunteers telling their own stories, individuals within those community are better at the stories that will engage their supporters than you. In peer-to-peer fundraising, signs the fundraiser is committed to your organization are 28 times more powerful than signs your organization is effective.[283] This isn't your failing. It's simply because your supporters are closer to their networks than you. They are willing to put that closeness to work for you. It's time to let them.

A decentralized organization means empowering everyone who has the stories with the tools to tell them. Whether it's through access to your blogging platform and social media, this involves training your supporters – paid and unpaid – how to put their own stories into the world. This can be unpolished; unpolished also can mean genuine.

We've opened the door to this somewhat with peer-to-peer fundraising, largely around events. For some reason, for constituents to tell our story, they must travel at least 3.1 miles or dress in fancy clothes. But this artifice is falling away. In the UK, participation event revenue is declining[284], with even the largest stalwart events decreasing.[285] Similarly, in North America, participation rates dropped 5% to 11%[286] in 2016 from 2015, which was down from previous years.[287] Across Europe and the United States, half marathons participation declined by a quarter and 5Ks by 13% since 2016.[288] This decrease happened while engagement increased in other peer-to-peer fundraising platforms. Thus, friends asking friends still works; you just have a diminished need to wear running shoes or high heels to do so.*

What if your constituents could use your system to send fundraising letters to their friends? They have the stories, the address, and the signature line; you have access to bulk postage and laser versioning. After all, you likely are spending on algorithms that tell you this person is like this other person, whether lookalike audiences online or modeled cooperative lists offline. This is the human-powered equivalent. The bonus is the letter comes from someone who speaks their language, knows their concerns, and has social capital with them. More simply, remember the 50% gain you could get from localizing your story in the last section? This could be created by volunteers rather than by staff.

---

* Running shoes = 5Ks. High heels = galas. You could do them in reverse; I don't recommend it.

The power of crowdsourcing isn't just useful in fundraising; it has also proven itself in mission areas, as we'll see next.

Supporters as eyes and ears

Let's say you wanted to study how bird migratory patterns are changing as a result of human-made climate change.[289] How would you get your data?

You could put bands on the birds to learn whether (and when and where) you see the same bird again. Lightweight geolocators can be attached to birds. That, however, is limited by the number of birds you can catch. You could use satellite data to track them; that is limited by the resolution of satellites. In short, finding, identifying, and counting birds is a human-run enterprise.[290]

Humans are already doing this work individually. More than 45 million Americans watch birds, 86% at their homes and 36% taking trips to observe birds in the wild.[291] What if you could get their data and aggregate it for scientists?

That's what the Cornell Lab of Ornithology does with its eBird program. Started in 2002, this system allows birders to enter their pictures and observations of birds around the world (the platform is available in 27 languages as of this writing). In the average month, 7.5 million bird observations are reported into eBird. These data are available free of charge to scientists and back to the birders who supply the data, allowing them to learn what birds have been reported around them and around the world.

As with Wikipedia, volunteers have quality control issues with volunteers; also as with Wikipedia, volunteers are both issue and answer. Hundreds of volunteer experts comb through the submissions for accuracy with rare bird finds getting special scrutiny. About two percent of submissions are rejected.[292] Algorithms can also ferret out human errors by controlling for the expertise of the observer.[293]

Since Cornell Lab started using citizen scientists, as it calls these volunteer data-gatherers, more than 150 peer-reviewed scientific papers have used their data to expand our understanding of the avian world.[294] Moreover, these endeavors spread a love of science and nature to those without letters after their name, allowing citizen scientists to be part of something bigger.

While Cornell Lab may be the vanguard, it is not alone in harnessing citizen scientists to improve our understanding of the world. Volunteers have mapped mammals along the Appalachian Trail, listened for calling frogs, tracked bee populations, monitored monarch butterflies, and helped scientists map illnesses in bird populations for the first time.[295] Citizen astronomers from Zooniverse's Exoplanet Explorers team discovered a planet missed by NASA's algorithms.[296]

This eyes and ears approach is not limited to scientists. The Southern Poverty Law Center encourages its supporters to #ReportHate, letting them know about bias incidents (after notifying law enforcement, of course). In the month following the 2016 U.S. presidential election, volunteers tracked over a thousand incidents of bias-related harassment, intimidation, and assault[297], the highest for November since data collection began in 1992. Lest you think this is false alerts or people more likely to report violence rather than an actual uptick, it also correlates to hate crime data from police.[298] Eyes-and-ears volunteers are accurate collectors of data for hate as well as birds.

You may remember a couple of chapters ago when we talked about a content-driven media-organization approach to bringing new constituents, then new donors, into an organization. One of the central challenges of such a strategy is grist for the mill – how do you continually create content of interest to your constituents? Herein, we have at least part of an answer: you let them create it. Even if your eyes-and-ears approach starts as a glorified crowdsourced clipping service on issues of importance, that still gives you the news and updates necessary to test issues and stories on social networks (especially on Twitter, where logorrhea can be a strategic advantage) to see which take off. You even start with an advantage – you know the story was of interest to at least one of your supporters.

Supporters need not act only as a human-powered Google News Alert. From your constituent submissions, you can act as the aggregator and create white papers, reports, and other newsworthy content (whether you are looking to engage traditional news sources or feed your own media organization). Donors to the Southern Poverty Law Center get several reports throughout the year about the rise or fall of hate groups, some powered by #ReportHate reports. And birders using eBird and its resulting apps can have their birdwatching experience enriched by the data collected by like-minded birders.

This creates a virtual circle of constituents providing information, having that information enhanced, and getting that data back in forms that validates volunteers' effort in collecting it and providing new insights for them. All this deepens their experience with, and attachment to, the nonprofit. And that's just the side benefit – the information also establishes the nonprofit as a trusted expert, allows them to specify and localize their pitch, and gives them an opportunity to attract new constituents.

Supporters as staff proxies

> *"Designing merchandise, setting up our website and crowdfunding, and managing production were my favorite parts of organizing the march because I was able to use my professional skills for such an important cause. For anyone coming in to grassroots organizing work for the first time, I would highly recommend thinking about what your skills are already and how you can volunteer to help instead of thinking you need to learn new skills or feeling like you don't have anything to offer."*[299]
>
> – Bob Bland, one of many organizers of the Women's March

One of the secrets of the 27,000 pieces of feedback I discussed earlier is that not all feedback is created equal. Amidst the fog of "Keep up the good work!" and "Please send me less mail" comments – valuable to be sure, but limited in scope – are comments like these:

> "I would love to find a way to volunteer with your organization that uses my work skills – marketing/ communication/writing/editing – please let me know if you have any needs."
>
> "I wish my culinary skills were able to be put to use for this organization."
>
> "I would like to get more involved in any events happening in Colorado. I am not a good salesperson but I can talk on the phone for hours, I can walk, I can help out at events."

The person on the other side of the keyboard is someone who wants to help. Moreover, they want to help in a specific way, using their skill set to greatest advantage.

Most nonprofits are not set up for this. We have a more industrial mindset. We want a specific outcome and know where volunteers fit into the widget-making process, where their cog fits in our machine. It does not matter whether you are a lawyer, a communications professional, a programmer, or a baker: you will be asked to make cupcakes for the bake sale. This is a good use of time and energy for only one of these volunteers. The organization pays for lawyers, communications professionals, and programmers internally or externally; they don't want volunteers, what with their unreasonable demands for no money.

The excuse most often used – that volunteers are not qualified to do the work – does not hold water. One organization estimated that for a national conference of about 500 people, they spent $500,000 and over a year of planning. That figure is about half staff time and half hard costs. This section's header quote about enjoying being called upon to use your skills comes from Bob Bland. She and countless others organized the 2017 Women's March with 750,000 people, plus or minus a quarter million, in Washington, DC, and over 1% of the total US population across the country.[300] They did it in about 11 weeks. They did it for free.

Our default, however, is still to pay people to do the work. Much of this is because it is how it has always been done. If you are working to register voters, for example, you hire someone to stand at a densely populated location or knock on every door in a neighborhood. This can be hundreds of dollars per person registered to vote.

Jeremy Smith, a former Army combat engineer in Afghanistan, and Madeline Eden, CTO at a blockchain company, imagined an easier way. They created Register2Vote, a site that allowed Texans to fill out registration forms online. Users still had to mail in a form (Texas makes it very hard to register to vote and to register others to vote*), but one step easier is still easier. With some advertising, they were able to register people for $2 to $3 per registration.[301]

Getting people to find the site and register got a passive stream of registrants. What about active outreach? Smith and Eden reached out to Tech for Campaigns, a group of tech-savvy volunteers, to see if anyone could help them create a system that mapped unregistered households.

Enter Erez Cohen, formerly of Mapsense and Apple Maps, now a volunteer at Tech for Campaigns. He served as the team lead for a group of volunteers who created a tool called Map the Vote. The team created a clever solution to finding unregistered households:

- Take a dataset of all addresses.
- Subtract the addresses that have registered voters at them.
- Take the resulting dataset of addresses without registered voters and display them 20 at a time to volunteers, with the ability to record results in the app, getting the necessary materials to those interested to register.[302]

---

* For Texas, difficulty in registering to vote is a feature, not a bug.

Cohen reports that more people elected to register and not once had they engaged in a face-to-face conversation. It beats the heck out of malls, concerts, and unfocused door knocking.

They wanted to do a mapping project, so they recruited a product lead on Apple Maps who wanted to make a difference. You can too. On your file are advertisers, copywriters, marketers, tech wizards, designers, etc., etc. Even if you think your constituent base is uniquely bereft of talent, corporations' social responsibility programs often allow employees to volunteer with nonprofits to use their unique skills. If you have no corporate partners, people in between jobs looking to hone their skills and resumes are likely volunteers. Sites like VolunteerMatch can also help you recruit those who wish to use their talents for good.

Your files, your corporate partners, your local community: they've been giving money because that's what you've been asking for. What if you asked for volunteers like Erez who can give you something unique? And what if you listened when people told you what they want to do?

Daniel Pink writes about three keys in his excellent *Drive: The Surprising Truth about What Motivates Us*[303*]:

- Autonomy: the desire to direct our own lives.
- Mastery: the desire to improve at something that matters.
- Purpose: the desire to serve something larger than ourselves.

We nonprofits have purpose coming out the ying-yang. As such, we have a leg up on many day jobs. Purpose is why the plastic surgeon whose day job is tummy, chins, and implants might want to help fix burns and cleft palates in their off-hours. What we often lack are the other legs of the motivation stool: the opportunities for volunteer to use the skills they like using (autonomy) and want to improve (mastery).

I'm a Tech for Campaigns volunteer. I've been a campaign volunteer (and staff) on and off for over two decades. I'm an introvert, so cold calling and door knocking were necessary evils. I felt no

[*] I will not be insulted if you put this book down right now to pick his up; it's worth it.

autonomy in having to do them and had no desire to master them. Not surprisingly, I put more time and effort into my campaigns working with Tech for Campaigns than any others.* I chose the work I did (autonomy), chose the candidates for whom I worked (purpose), and worked with talented professionals from whom I learned (mastery).

People work better when their skills are used. People work harder, longer, and more often when they enjoy the work. These should not be controversial statements; you've seen them in your own life. Yet we want volunteers to make widgets instead of letting a million flowers bloom.

Why staff?

The Women's March story shows the promise of a volunteer-led model. It also shows the challenges of that same model. The third Women's March in 2019 faced controversy over some of the co-organizers' ties to and failures to denounce Louis Farrakhan and his alleged† anti-Semitic, homophobic, and transphobic comments.[304] Speakers and activists who spoke at previous conferences withdrew[305] and the march denounced anti-Semitism while defending the organizers.[306] Some local marches were cancelled[307] and others broke off from the national march.[308] This isn't the first such potential schism: the original name for the march was the Million Women March, something the (largely white women) original organizers did not know had already been done by (largely African-American women) activists in Philadelphia in 1997.

Would this all be fixed with staff? No. One doesn't get millions organizing around an intersectionalist‡ message without some

* Other than when campaigns were my full-time job.

† I encourage you to read the comments themselves and make the determination as to how much the word alleged here is being used for legal reasons only.

‡ If you are not familiar with intersectionality, I'm almost certainly the wrong person to talk about it; Kimberlé Crenshaw is the right person. But to drastically oversimplify,

intersecting. The women's rights movement split in 1869 over whether black men should get the right to vote. Change is messy. Many things that turn out to be inclusive were once exclusive.[309]

That said, staff-free or staff-limited movements have this messiness built into their DNA. Wikipedia, as an example, catalogues its own controversies on the "List of Wikipedia controversies"[310] page and has a list of topics that are constantly being circularly edited.[311] Lest you think these are all serious policy disagreements, their "Lamest edit wars" page[312] discusses biting controversies like whether the "outta" in Weird Al's "Straight O/outta Compton" should be capitalized*, how tall Andre the Giant was†, and whether the octothorpe (#) in the programming language C# is a number sign or the musical sharp symbol.

Trivial though these may be, they illustrate the challenges to a largely volunteer-based model. Control and getting to a shared vision are hard even when you have a paycheck as leverage. There also isn't always a match. It may be difficult to fathom how someone's welding skills are going to help with the fight against feline diabetes. But you can still ask. People are generally happy to tell you what they would like to do. My wants and desires? Are you kidding? I'm my own favorite topic!

---

intersectionality talks about how we exist at the intersections of categories like sex, gender, sexual preference, race, ethnicity, etc. Furthermore, when we experience oppression or bias, it is not along the lines of just one of these categories: the experience of an African-American homosexual woman isn't the experience of a white straight women + white homosexual man + black straight man; further, viewing it this way would test to normalize classifications like white, male, and straight, treating any other classification as "other." Solutions thus also differ across intersections. A traditional political organizing strategy for the category of "African-Americans" would be to organize at churches; an African-American homosexual woman may be alienated from church. Thus, when I speak of messiness, it isn't so much that the movement is messy; it's that we humans are – gloriously, wonderfully messy.

* Hence the O/outta formulation here – you think I want to subject myself to those zealots on the side you disagree with? Clearly, I'm with whatever you believe.

† Tall. Hence the name.

Also, expertise, central purpose, tool creation for volunteers, and minor trivia like making sure everything is done legally all have their value. So you may not want to go full starfish.

You may, however, find value in changing your default. Instead of needing a reason to use volunteers, what happens if you need a reason not to use volunteers? This simple shift in mindset could help open your organization's eyes to the rich tapestry of skills your supporters bring to the table and the types of things you can accomplish together.

The conglomerate nonprofit: Structuring for the storm

"When bad men combine, the good must associate; else they will fall one by one, an unpitied sacrifice in a contemptible struggle."[313]

– Edmund Burke

In their classic *The Why Axis*, Uri Gneezy and John List talk about Brian Mullaney, founder of WonderWork. In it, they discuss his goal of creating "a General Motors of Compassion with different charity brands that tackle single causes... Just like GM has Chevrolet and Cadillac, we will have a blindness brand, a club foot brand, a burns brand, a hydrocephalic brand, and a hole-in-the-heart brand." This innovative structure allowed him, he said, to share administrative costs across multiple organizations. Additionally, it would be able to cross-sell donors with different offers without the list costs that would normally plague new donor acquisition. In theory, a donor could be a donor to all five WonderWork brands or as many as fit with their identity.

Unfortunately, *The Why Axis* chose a poor example for its points. WonderWork declared bankruptcy six years after its founding after legal judgments against it. Mullaney resigned from the organization amid "allegations of fraud and misdeeds." The bankruptcy court found the charity used false and misleading statements, lacked appropriate Board oversight, and failed a litany of tasks, including reporting obligations, restricting assets properly, matching donations, and basic accounting. It also concluded that "from its inception, [it] has been a fundraising vehicle in search of a mission."[314]

Perhaps it is because of what happened to WonderWork that nonprofits don't engage in this type of diversification. However, the existence of a Ponzi or Madoff doesn't invalidate the need to save money; likewise, the existence of a WonderWork shouldn't invalidate the model. The fundamental idea behind multiple brands is a sound one.

With winter at our heels, it's time to look at new structures and alliances. Breaking down barriers allows us to huddle together for warmth.

After all, as of this writing, one nonprofit represents every 220 American or 330 UK citizens (approximately). Overlap and inefficiencies abound, as do possibilities for creating wholes greater than their parts.

Some of this is in cost saving. Double-entry accounting doesn't have an environmentalist way to do it; few animal rights issues need to be negotiated into a lease; no special anti-cancer provisions are needed in a retirement plan. Staff for these positions could be held in common. Common purchasing also yields negotiating leverage for everything from health plans to databases to #10 envelopes.

While a mundane advantage, these costs can often prove fatal to the new nonprofit. As states invent new nonprofit filing requirements, for example, a cause looking for a national footprint must navigate these waters lest it be dashed upon the rocks. It is valuable, then, to have a legal guide who knows the rapids.

A conglomerate organization can also make life easier for its donors. The original WonderWork promise was an internal-focused one – if we have associated brands, we can get more from donors. Let's flip that on its head, focusing it on donors – if we have associated brands, donors can support organizations that know more about them and can cater to their needs.

Starting with an example from the for-profit world, how many times in your life will you be asked if you want your receipt? We each have our preferences for this. Perhaps your preferences are no receipts unless you are traveling, in which case you would prefer email receipts to paper receipts if possible. Or no receipts for purchases under $100.[315] It seems this should be something programmed into your credit/debit card, allowing the cashier to honor your preferences and save a bit of work.

Now, think about your preferences as a donor.[*] You only want to make monthly donations unless there's a disaster… or you never want to make a monthly donation. You don't like mail requests after a nasty third grade paper cut… or the latest X organization[†] hack makes you glad you never put your credit card online. You hate the premiums nonprofits send… or you are re-wallpapering a room and are only 17 mail pieces short of the address labels you need to finish the job. You like reading each mail piece even if you don't give to them… or only give after your tax refund and at the end of the year; any other asks are worthless to you and the organization.

If you donate to ten organizations, you must train all ten organizations on these things, or you must grin and bear it when they mess them up. We nonprofits are the "do you want a receipt?" cashier; we ask when it would be better to know.

These are the picayune examples. More important are the identities discussed earlier. In the current world, when you give to the hospital that saved your life when you were vacationing in Blefuscu, other organizations don't know why you made that gift. (Often, the Blefuscudian hospital also doesn't know why you made that gift.) As a result, you get solicited by other hospitals, as if you gave willy-nilly to hospitals, and by other Blefuscudian institutions, as if you were a local looking to support local organizations. They don't know why, so they assume, making the proverbial ass out of u and me.[‡] It is like Amazon who, after you looked at a bed one time, turned your web browsing into bedsbedsbedspillowsbedsbedsbedsbedsblanketsbedsbedsbeds for the next month.[§]

A coordinated, cooperative, or conglomerated organization can know. Moreover, it can know identity across missions. Tell them once

---

[*] If you are a nonprofit professional but not a donor, reconsider either one of those two things.

[†] Probably Target.

[‡] Yes, this isn't technically a proverb. But it probably will be in a couple hundred years. I'm ahead of the curve.

[§] And Amazon is actually good at this!

that you give because you are a parent and your asks across organizations will focus on this parent identity. If you are a religious person, your appeals from even secular organizations will talk about the religious reasons to give. Shared first-party data has the win-win of getting you appeals that appeal to you more, with the result of you giving more and feeling better doing it.

How do we get to this brave new world? Structures and techniques abound from loose alliances to mergers to incubating your own ideas. The central message is that no one solution will work for all, but one or more of them may work for you.

The incubator

The founder story is a well-worn path. A young man has an idea in his dorm/garage.* Through hard work, Sorkinesque dialogue, and a bit of the con man's arts, he works to bring this idea to fruition. He does this first with, then against, the friends whose friendship he will eventually sacrifice to his ambition. Eventually, he will rule all he surveys in his computer/social network/gambling/criminal empire, but at what cost? It's a familiar narrative.

Back in the real world, founding needs friends. What do Tesla Motors, YouTube, LinkedIn, Yelp, Reddit, and Kiva.org have in common? All were founded, co-founded, or led by former PayPal staff who left after eBay acquired the company. They stayed in touch. They worked for and with each other at future companies. They invested in each other's companies. They formed a network and an informal incubator of ideas.

Sometimes this incubation is formal. Y Combinator selects companies for investment where they give seed capital and get seven percent equity. They mentor, train, provide shared services, and

* In fairness, it's only *usually* young (Breaking Bad and The Founder are counter examples) and *usually* men (Molly's Game is a counter example), but the exceptions show the frequency of the rule in most constructed narratives.

generally steward these companies into larger enterprises. You've likely heard of some of their successes – Dropbox, Airbnb, Reddit, Twitch, Instacart – and likely not of others, but the total valuation of these companies is now over $100 billion. They are one of many in the for-profit world.

Nonprofit incubators are fewer and farther between, usually local in nature and focus. The challenge is that we do not have $100 billion as the pot of gold at the end of the rainbow. While saving 100,000 lives may have a greater impact than $100 billion, we don't think that way around investment outcomes. Nor do we think of nurturing new nonprofits, or focuses, within our own organizations. This is a pity, as one of the four predictors of whether an innovative philanthropy endeavor will survive is whether its leaders have the time to try, fail, and adjust.[316]

When for-profits think this way, and nonprofits do not, the relationship and power dynamic between the two changes.

Take the example of distracted driving. When cell phone usage became more ubiquitous, so too did distracted driving crashes. In fact, many Americans believe that cell phone road deaths are equal to or more than drunk driving deaths.

(Side note: this is not the case. In the last years for which we have data, 10,874 Americans died in drunk driving crashes.[317] Fewer than 500 fatal crashes involved cell phone use as a distraction.[318] This is the availability heuristic at work: you can look at the car next to you at a stoplight and see the driver is texting. It is far more difficult for you to look at the car next to you and see that the driver is drunk. We can more easily recall cell phone use and driving, so that gets moved up in our mental queue. Incidentally, both are dangerous. Most of the reason that cell phone crashes don't cause more fatalities is they tend to happen at lower speeds, more often damaging vehicles and lives without causing fatalities. If you are reading this on your phone while driving, please stop either reading or driving.)

Anyway, in 2010, Google searches for "texting and driving" surpassed "drinking and driving." They haven't looked back. It's a clear issue of public concern. Why, then, was there no MADD-like nonprofit to serve this need? In fact, a few smaller and more disparate nonprofits did crop up.

At the time, MADD looked at taking distracted driving into their mission. One side said that the victims and survivors of drunk driving crashes expected the organization to focus on them and their core issue. The other argued that distracted driving and drunk driving share legislation, strategies for helping victims and survivors, and natural allies. Either decision could be justified. In the end, MADD decided not to add this to their mission. This likely made sense from a programmatic sense. Researchers who have studied diversification in program activities found they "experience some initial positive efficiencies and very low levels but then very quickly become more inefficient at increasingly unrelated levels."[319] In other words, focus is important for efficiency.

Into the void stepped AT&T. In 2010, it created their It Can Wait anti-distracted driving campaign. Since 2010, it has been the largest U.S. effort to prevent texting and driving. The campaign is doing many things a nonprofit would normally do – collecting petition signatures and pledges, distributing awareness materials, advocating for stronger laws, putting out advertising and providing programmatic tool-kits – without the nonprofit arm.

The campaign made sense for several business reasons. At the fore is an excellent opportunity for positive branding. Normally, a company would partner with a nonprofit for this positive branding, but when you do it yourself, you get to put your logo on it. Consider the 2010-2013 results for the It Can Wait campaign:

- 4 million pledges
- 5 million page views
- 3.5 million ItCanWait.com visits
- 4 billion media impressions
- Social media reach to 310 million unique user accounts

Among other successes.[320] AT&T reports an 11 to 29 percent increase in net promoter score among those who have seen It Can Wait ads. The campaign has significant reach and impact. These would not be possible through the auspices of a separate nonprofit organization – AT&T's logo would be second, if at all, in branding efforts.

This would seem to be a win-win: the large pocketed telecom providing advocacy and effort so a nonprofit doesn't have to. But that advocacy will never focus on the role of that telecom. Over MADD's almost 40-year history, it has run the gamut of relationships with the alcohol industry from alliance to open warfare. It Can Wait will not and cannot run afoul of the telecom industry because it is that industry.* This means the focus of these campaigns is on how the technology is used, rather than on the technology itself. As Ian Crouch put it in the New Yorker:

> "Many of us believe the responsibility lies with those using their phones at the wheel and no one else. Lawsuits by accident victims or their families against mobile carriers or device makers have gained little traction in the judicial system, which may reflect a wider cultural sentiment: few of us would be inclined to blame these accidents on Apple or Samsung or Verizon or A.T.& T. the way we draw connections between, for instance, cigarette producers and victims of lung cancer or kids with asthma. That's because, unlike cigarettes, there is a safe way to use cell phones and mobile networks.
>
> And yet, rather than distancing themselves from the dangers of distracted driving, or waiting for pressure to mount from outsiders, the major national carriers, led by A.T.& T., have become the loudest and most coherent

* I'm not arguing an equivalency between the two industries here, just a similarity in situation.

> voices on the issue. And so, when we think about texting and driving, we think of them."[321]

By controlling the organization, AT&T influences the narrative of how these crashes come about. This may be benign in this case. But think of your own organization: is there an area into which you have debated expanding your mission? What would happen if another organization moved into that void?

With an incubator model, MADD would not have faced the yes/no binary as to whether to take on distracted driving. Rather, it could have allowed a new organization to use shared resources (and be compensated for same.) The expertise MADD has in traffic safety and victim services, the relationships, a sympathetic donor file, and the signaling of a strong United States brand name: all these would have conferred significant advantage on a fledgling organization, allowing them to centralize disparate advocacy groups. This is important for a new nonprofit: if you think it is hard to acquire donors for an established organization and brand name, try acquiring them without.

Such incubation need not be limited to mission extensions; you could also expand based on donor identity. For example, many secular organizations and missions have a devoted following from those who give for religious reasons. Let's take an animal welfare organization. A donor may be giving because they believe in Proverbs 12:10 ("The righteous care for the needs of their animals"[*]).[†] You will likely get more from that donor, and giving them more satisfaction in their giving, if you can tie their gift to the reason they are making it: to help all of God's creatures.

If this were the mass market message, however, it would turn off those whose reason for giving is secular. Earlier, we discussed different messages for each of these groups. This could be made even more

---

[*] Exact wording depending on version.

[†] There is an animal rescue organization called Proverbs 12:10 Animal Rescue in Nashville, in fact.

compelling with a different brand, and brand offer, to these donors. That's just for one donor identity.

When the new organization matures, it could remain one organization with multiple brands (or sub-brands) or split into separate organizations with strong kinship and shared innovation. The latter is likely better because of the value of focus. But either beat the alternatives: a space that will be filled by a future competitor, a for-profit, or no one at all.

Mergers and acquisitions

Incubation is the alpha, where for-profits have a structure and we do not. Now let's talk about the omega. Nonprofits are not immune from the market. Some nonprofits are better and some worse. Some organizations are worth more than their balance sheet, some less. And some nonprofits will live; some will die.[*]

We are like the for-profit sector in this way, except no nonprofit in my memory has been bailed out as too big to fail. In March 2015, the Federation Employment and Guidance Service announced it was closing. This $250 million nonprofit had 120,000 people reliant on it for employment, housing, health care, and other human services in New York. City and state agencies that used FEGS were left scrambling to find replacement providers.

Both systemic and idiosyncratic factors contributed to FEGS's fall, ably summarized in the Human Services Council report on the closing.[322] Government reimbursement rates are insufficient to cover indirect costs and were often late, forcing human services organizations to take usurious gap loans.[†] Salaries were so low that employees were themselves getting social safety net services. Partners were left unaware

---

[*] There is plenty of room for debate on how much the live/die dichotomy is correlated with the better/worse dichotomy.

[†] I'm writing this section during a government shutdown; history is likely to repeat itself with nonprofits that are providing federal government services currently.

of the fiscal challenges. Risk management strategies were inadequate or non-existent. Perhaps you recognize these issues from a nonprofit near you. They look remarkably like sector-wide issues covered in Gregory and Howard's *The Nonprofit Starvation Cycle*[323] stemming from an excessive focus against overhead costs.

One factor goes unmentioned in the report, however. When a for-profit company flounders, it can turn to mergers and acquisitions to save employees and the company functions. It can also engage in M&A from a position of strength; sometimes it is involved involuntarily. These deals can be for all or part of a company. Bankers stand at the ready to assist. As with incubators, nonprofits largely lack the infrastructure, and the vocabulary for mergers and acquisitions.

I once had the honor of serving on the board of a local early childhood developmental education organization. A similar organization that served two nearby communities (with state contracts to provide services) had to shut down. The board and organizational leadership at our nonprofit weighed if we would expand to none, one, or both communities. In the end, we decided to take on one community; another organization would take on the other.

The trick? We could not take on any of the infrastructure of the closing organization. We had to find new facilities, hire new staff, and re-recruit those to whom we wanted to provide services. Since the state contract was also not transferrable, we had to fund the new venture from our existing reserves with the hope of being able to reclaim revenues retroactively. Donor lists were lost, so people who wanted to help developmental challenged kids in their own community did not know how to, losing those dollars for this specific charity and possibly the charity sector overall.

Thankfully, we had a talented and dedicated staff who I swear had a pact to only sleep after the expansion was running smoothly. However, with a functional nonprofit mergers and acquisition sector, this could have been an orderly dividing of assets rather than one of the more organized, efficient scrambles I've seen. Lost in this description of it is the parents who were told that the agency providing their child's special education care was shuttering and not knowing what would happen. We did our best to make that interval as short and painless as possible, but those kids still had pain, uncertainty, and lost time.

Like the for-profit sector, we should be able to merge for competitive advantage as well. Sometimes, we find groups that formed around identity that have such similar goals; it benefits them to address them together. So it was with the merger of Mayors Against Illegal Guns and Moms Demand Action – two very different supporter identities – to address gun violence under the banner of Everytown for Gun Safety. It is likely appropriate that this merger came under Mike Bloomberg, no stranger to M&A activity in the for-profit sector. It was buoyed by his policy acumen and personal net worth in support. It's also instructive that Everytown for Gun Safety kept the Moms Demand Action brand name, as the name alone drips with the identity of its desired supporters. The organization has also created Students Demand Action to focus on another identity of supporters (and, sadly, to serve those often impacted by gun violence). One is reminded of political campaigns' smart use of identity group + "for" + name of candidate, as in Firefighters for Kang/Kodos 2020.

Everytown's incubator + merger + identity-focus strategy is notable as an exception in the nonprofit sector. The more common example is Students Against Destructive Decisions and Mothers Against Drunk Driving. The two work on similar issues. MADD's supporter list has former SADD students in spades. And yet no common organization or formal alliance exists, to the point that, when MADD launched its high school program Power of You(th) in 2012, it could not use the SADD infrastructure to get it into high schools. With both duplication of effort and the loss of prospective supporters, this is an example of where one plus one could equal three but instead yields 1.5.

This is by no means a unique example. Let's say you are a strong environmentalist and you care about the future of the Chesapeake Bay in Maryland specifically. This type of place-based identity is fairly common; a lot of support of environmental groups can be explained by a person's attachment to a place or type of place (e.g., forest, mountains, water).[324] If you want to act on this identity, you could support the efforts of American Forests, American Hiking Society, Audubon

Society, Clean Water Action, Conservation Fund, Conservation International, Ducks Unlimited, Earthjustice, Environmental Defense Fund, Friends of the Earth, Food and Water Watch, Green Day, Green Faith, Greenpeace, League of Conservation Voters, National Fish and Wildlife Foundation, Waterkeeper Alliance, National Geographic Society, National Wildlife Federation, Nature Conservancy, Roots, Sierra Club, Union of Concerned Scientists, Wildlife Habitat Council, or World Wildlife Fund – all of who are national or international and whose work touches the Chesapeake.

Or you could engage in something statewide like Environment Maryland, Maryland Association for Environmental and Outdoor Education, Maryland Beatles, Maryland Conservation Council, Maryland Environmental Health Network, Maryland Environmental Services, Maryland Environmental Trust, Maryland League of Conservation Voters, or Maryland Ornithological Society.

Or if you wanted to get more local still you could support Alliance for the Chesapeake Bay, Anacostia Unplugged, Anacostia Watershed Society, Anne Arundel County Watershed Stewards Academy, Battle Creek Nature Education Society, Blue Water Baltimore, Chesapeake Bay Foundation, Chesapeake Bay Program, Chesapeake Bay Trust, Chesapeake Climate Action Network, Chesapeake Conservancy, Chesapeake Legal Alliance, Chesapeake Research Consortium, Chesapeake Rolling Stones, Choose Clean Water Coalition, Eastern Shore Land Conservancy, Elizabeth River Project, Finger Lakes Land Trust, Meadowview Biological Research Station, Oyster Recovery Partnership, Patuxent Tidewater Land Trust, Phish, Potomac Appalachian Trail Club, Potomac Conservancy, Smithsonian Environmental Research Center, or Southern Maryland Resource Conservation and Development.*

---

* Some of these names take "the" or "The" in front of them; some do not. I hope your reading experience was not diminished by my lack of desire to seek out 42 sets of brand standards.

A single donor identity could contribute to a lot of only semi-distinguishable organizations. To reinforce this, I added five band names to the list*; kudos to you if you spotted them. This is not to pick on environmental groups generally or the Chesapeake in particular; throw a dart at a sector and location and you will find a similar rich, messy tapestry.

Donor identities clearly intersect here, with some organizations appealing to users of the land like hunters, hikers, and boaters, others appealing to animal and wildlife advocates, and others to researchers. And you have folks who are focused on land versus water versus air versus climate. That said, the chances are very good effort overlaps between at least two of these organizations. Mergers and acquisitions would not go amiss in this crowded space, with the donor identities customized by you, a clever marketer.

Ideally, these mergers would happen before the doors are in danger of closing. If it is only the prospect of hanging in a fortnight that concentrates the mind, however, then better late than never. In 2017, the Canadian Cancer Society and the Canadian Breast Cancer Foundation merged after revenue declines of 16% and 33%, respectively.[325] In one year, the CCS went from nearly a $25 million shortfall to nearly an $8 million surplus. Both organizations wanted to maintain a presence throughout Canada, but found efficiencies in centralized and shared HR, IT, communications, and marketing staff.[326]

One wonders if giants like Junior Diabetes Research Foundation and the American Diabetes Association or the American Cancer Society and Susan G. Komen will find it similarly in their interests to join forces. They don't currently; nonprofits of more than $50 million in revenue currently engage in M&A at one-tenth the rate of our for-profit brethren.[327] This is a pity, as a study of Chicago nonprofit mergers and acquisitions found that both acquiring and acquired nonprofits felt they'd improved their impact 88% of the time.[328]

---

* Green Day, the Roots, the (Maryland) Beatles, the (Chesapeake) Rolling Stones, and Phish.

It is time to give our organizations permission to explore mergers, acquisitions, and alliances. If you waited too long to incubate an idea and a competitor emerged, you may be able to join forces profitably. If a nonprofit with whom we make common cause is in danger of default and you feel like you can make more out of their donor base than it can, begin the due diligence process. Sometimes, M&A can solidify strategic advantage or guarantee survival in the for-profit world. So too can it be with us.

Co-ops and exchanges

I know. You can't believe I'm recommending list cooperatives given what I said about them earlier. Note that I didn't argue that they weren't the most effective means of cold list acquisition* – they usually are.

The challenges with list cooperatives are:

- Cost – you pay more for a modeled list.
- Loss of control of your list – if a name on your list is designated as a good name, it could be rented out scores of time, giving other nonprofits the opportunity to become the preferred nonprofit for your best donors.
- Using only transactional data – the co-op knows the amount, frequency, and timing of interactions. It does not, however, know donor identities that would cause someone to become attached to one organization or another. As discussed earlier, you could have two people who look alike in every other way, but whose spouses passed away from different diseases and thus support entirely different charities.
- Lack of insight into the post-acquisition relationship. Let's say you are a donor who writes checks to ten different organizations

* This may be damning with faint praise, however.

every December. You only want one mailing per year from that organization (plus an acknowledgment letter to make sure they got your gift). You will have to tell each organization this is your wish individually. Additionally, if you are giving to ten organizations per year, you will likely be rented to scores more – you will also have to educate these upstarts about your giving pattern.

You may have a fellow traveler non-profit to your organization, similar in brand, identity, organizational, or lifecycle. For whatever reason, you don't want to start M&A proceedings, but a tighter association could benefit you both. You could set up your own list exchange with this organization or your own co-operative among several organizations. Further, these relationships could be set up with rules that eliminate the four drawbacks above, with shared first-party data (including preferences) and rules governing access timing and quantity.

This structure could be used among affiliated organizations. For example, the U.S. Olympic and Paralympic Committee has national governing bodies for each of the sports in the Olympic Games, each their own separate organization. Each maintains its own database and marketing program. But a donor to or member of USA Field Hockey is more likely to also be a Team USA donor than a random person off the street. That person is more likely to donate if Team USA can talk to them more about field hockey than sports in which they have little to no interest. Conversely, a Team USA donor, asked about their favorite sport, is a likely candidate for being a part of the national governing body of that sport as well. It benefits both to share information and names.

Similarly, this model works for the knotty, fraught relationships between international, national, regional, state, and/or local offices. Internecine battles over "my donors" versus "your donors" could be replaced by donations going to the programs and locations the donor desires. If a donor says they want their donations to benefit nationally, great; if they want it to go locally, also great. This strategy helps you fulfill on the donor-directed enterprise of a couple sections ago by not only getting the donor's preference but reflecting it back by soliciting the donor from the correct entity or entities.

This sharing need not apply only to formally affiliated organizations. In October 2017, the Boy Scouts of America announced it would start accepting girls into their programming; in May 2018, it announced it would drop "Boy" from the name of their flagship program. And in November 2018, the Girl Scouts sued Boy Scouts for trademark infringement and unfair competition.

Setting aside debates over the merits of the lawsuit, of single-sex versus co-educational programs, of sex/gender binaries, and probably a bunch of other things, what if these two organizations worked together to recruit support and membership? After all, it is a safe wager that if an older sibling is a scout, a younger sibling is more likely to be a scout regardless of the sex/gender of the siblings.

An agreement could be built around intake and survey forms where both Boy Scouts and Girl Scouts ask about family make-up and ages. If the Boy Scouts discovered that their new Cub Scout had a baby brother, that's great marketing information for them. But if it found out about a baby sister, this lead would go into the cooperative database for the Girl Scouts marketing when the timing was right (and vice versa). And, to encourage both organizations to be diligent about collecting this information, a traditional payment structure for leads could be set up to benefit the organization that did more giving than taking.*

These shared systems also would focus on how donors are communicated with outside of a one-organization, or one-department, bubble. Take the example of an organization† our family has given to through both national fundraising and local events. When we moved more than three years ago, the organization's direct marketing

---

* You could also have a shared database for those in the neighborhood who are a soft touch for buying cookies or cookie dough or the like to support local kids, but please don't: I'm trying to lose a few pounds.

† This organization will remain nameless because 1) it is a good organization we still support and 2) we've had this problem with multiple organizations; singling out one would do no good.

immediately switched to our new address. However, we are still being solicited by the 5K event in our old location by email as if we had never left (and we've received no asks from our new location's 5K).

Everyone in this scenario is doing the right thing to reach their own limited goals. The local office is working doggedly toward their goal to increase walkers and walker retention. Trying to reactivate lapsed walkers makes sense, if you don't have the critical piece of information that we now live 600+ miles away.* The direct marketer is running frequent change-of-address checks on their file – bully for them. Over in another silo the online walk system is working to maximize shareholder/owner value, so it hasn't fixed a default unsubscribe page that only allows you to opt out of all communications or all walk communications, with no ability to change an address or walk of choice.

The problem isn't with the actions; it's with the goals. Systems must be in place where the old walk can give a name to the new walk, or the national direct marketer can switch a person's walk locality. Further, incentives must exist to do so. If systems and incentives work and donors can move successfully, the national organization, both local organizations, and the donor all win: a rare win-win-win-win scenario.

This is a structure where the clear benefits for the organizations (less expensive names, controls over donor solicitation, and shared learnings) are also benefits for donors (communications from only organizations that fit my interests and respect my preferences).

Some may argue for donor privacy. I would submit is it already non-existent when we rent, exchange, and co-op our names already. The least we can do is to work for that experience to be a more positive one for the donor, helping control the amount of mail they get and make it relevant to their lives.†

---

* That said, one would think part of this journey would be to figure out if we enjoyed the walk experience. One would be wrong.

† And also giving the donor easy control over their communication. Yes, all these points work best together.

Advocacy extension

In the United States, the 501(c) section for exempt organizations, along with limitations on lobbying, was codified in the Revenue Act of 1954. So, remember when Marty McFly travels back in time to when a shop owner said "A colored mayor. That'll be the day!"?* One year before that. That's when our nonprofit structures were created in the United States. It may be time for a change. And with winter on our heels, it may be time to entertain those possibilities.

The 2017 tax law change may have unintentionally opened the door for this type of change. The new tax law increases the amount you can take as a standard deduction on your taxes. Normally you would prepare your taxes both ways and see whether itemized deductions or standard deductions would have you pay less in taxes.† If the standard deduction is bigger than itemized deductions, fewer people will itemize. This means fewer people will get any tax benefit from donating to charities. Specifically, the Joint Committee on Taxation and the American Enterprise Institute separately estimate that 27-28 million fewer people will take a charitable deduction, falling from about 30% of taxpayers to about 5% of taxpayers.[329] These are the same five percent of donors who are seeing their giving increase post the tax law change while the other 95% are seeing their giving fall.

The bargain that nonprofits struck for tax deductibility under the 501(c)3 structure is that we will not be political organizations. We won't electioneer. We won't donate to political candidates. We won't endorse candidates. We will have only a skeleton force of paid lobbyists.

If tax deductibility no longer matters and the deal is off on one side, it's off on both sides: we need not fight political fights with both hands

---

* Don't remember Marty McFly doing this? This supports the point – he traveled back in time 30 years in the movie *Back to the Future*; now that movie is over 30 years old.

† Or have a computer do it.

tied behind our backs. That is, we can shift from (c)3 organizations to (c)4s and mix it up.

There's no better time to engage in politics. As a sector, we have an obligation to advocate for ourselves. After all, if you aren't at the table, you are on the menu. The last Congress were 101 educators, 28 doctors (plus two nurses and a pharmacist), 26 farmers/ranchers, 21 communications professionals, 21 insurance agents/execs, 18 management consultants, 18 bankers, 16 military reserves or National Guardspeople, 11 accountants, 10 law enforcement officers, 8 ministers, 8 engineers, and on and on.[330]

But no nonprofit executives.

This isn't to say our leaders are ignorant of nonprofits. In the United States, from Trump's America First Policies to Bernie Sanders' Our Revolution, they are experienced with setting up (c)4 organizations to funnel money for their own political ends.

The type of on-the-ground work that charities do, however, is generally foreign to most politicians. So, when ignorance abounds, the best we can hope for is benign neglect. The worst are efforts to repeal laws like the Johnson Amendment (prohibiting churches from becoming political soapboxes), postal "reforms" over the cost of mailing that would hit us hard, and tax bills that affect giving.

This paltry understanding of Nonprofit World's operations occurs despite the size and importance of Nonprofitland. If the global nonprofit sector were a country, we'd be the 16th largest economy in the world, ahead of powerhouses like Saudi Arabia.* We must be able to stand up for ourselves at full voice.

Beyond our sector concerns, government action, or inaction, can be a significant headwind or tailwind to our missions. And if what we've traded the volume of our voice for is no longer valuable, we can take back that trade. Sticking to the (c)3 rules could be more hindrance than help; we may have nothing to lose but our chains.

---

* And yet, imagine the uproar if one of our executives had a journalist disassembled with a bone saw.

This is almost certainly too extreme – it is unlikely that we will see St. Jude or United Way running partisan get-out-the-vote efforts any day soon. That said, even if it doesn't change our organization's decision calculus, it may change our donors' decisions. Some donors likely have not given to (c)4 advocacy organizations because of the lack of tax deductibility. If tax deductibility no longer matters, these donors will rationally make the shift to where their giving can have a greater impact.[*]

The world, or at least many perceptions of the world, is politicized. Razor purchases became polarized when one company said people should act better toward each other. A popular sport became polarized when some players kneeled to protest and an apparel company became polarized when one of the faces of that protest was one of the company's endorsement faces. A carbonated sugar water company became polarized when it implied their product, when combined with a celebrity, could cure social division. People think differently of you from a distance if you wear a certain color hat. The markers of identity and tribe are manifold and manifest. It's difficult to say nonprofits can or will be immune from the pull of ideologic left and right, when those poles are where energy and dollars are flowing.

Take the rational reasons, add in ideological pulls, season to taste, and multiply over the full donor base: you have a likely shift of funds from semi-political (c)3s to fully political (c)4s in the United States. After all, while donors to nonprofits have decreased, donors to political campaigns have increased. In the 2018 election cycle, .47% of Americans gave $200 or more[331] to a political campaign.[332] That doesn't sound like a lot, except that it's more than double the proportion of people who gave (.23%) during the previous mid-term cycle.[333]

---

[*] This is not an insult to (c)3 organizations' effectiveness. Rather, it's an assumption that each organization will rationally allocate resources to the most effective efforts. If you are rationally allocating resources, it is better to have all the options another organization has, plus some. As this is where (c)4s stand in relation to (c)3s, they can be more efficient.

What is an organization to do? If you have political inclinations that can't be fully served in a (c)3 structure, now is the time to embark on your (c)4 and perhaps your political action committee ambitions if you don't have them. If you do, it's time to double down.

We previously discussed the NRA's formation of identity – advocacy can be a great way to form this identity. Consider what one prominent nonprofit leader said about the NRA model:

> "I think that is what the NRA has done well ... building an affinity with its brand, their own members ... they have built the idea of the 'NRA voter.' … I think the NRA has been very successful as a single-issue advocacy organization for many years and making their members feel affiliation with the brand and making members want to show up with each other in support of the causes that national [organization] suggests to them."[334]

Who was this NRA ally from the far right of the political spectrum? ACLU national director Faiz Shakir. Not surprisingly, as ACLU's membership swells in reaction to current politics, they are looking to emulate some of the NRA's identity-bolstering tactics like voter registration, get-out-the-vote efforts, and grading politicians' votes (you can read more about this in an aptly titled piece "The ACLU Wants to Be the NRA, Without All the Guns"[335]). This type of identity formation may not be limited to the ACLUs, NRAs, Planned Parenthoods, and Sierra Clubs of the world. One could even see a world where nonpartisan nonprofits split into liberal, conservative, and neutral versions of themselves to avail themselves of both solutions across the ideological spectrum and the identity-forming potential of ideology. For those who are involved in politics, in for a penny, in for a pound.

At the very least, we should be able to stand up for ourselves and our missions. It is allowable for 501(c)3s to run get-out-the-vote and voter registration efforts if they are nonpartisan. This is another way to increase your political heft without going full (c)4 – if your membership all votes, and politicians know your membership all votes, they can weigh that in their decision-making. Consider this statement from Billy Shore, founder of Share our Strength:

> "We intend to reach out to donors, volunteers, and grantees to make sure they know that the efforts we've worked on so hard for so long – from protecting the vital nutritional assistance provided by the Supplemental Nutrition Assistance Program to increasing participation in school breakfast and summer meals – could succeed or fail based on the composition of the next Congress.
>
> We won't urge them to vote for specific candidates, but we will urge them to vote … There is nothing more nonpartisan, patriotic, or American than encouraging people to vote. Every nonprofit and civic organization should assume some responsibility for at least communicating with its donors, volunteers, and others who have a stake in their causes. The reach and influence nonprofits have are valuable assets. Not to deploy them on behalf of a stronger civic society is not only counterproductive but also civically and morally irresponsible."[336]

Note the difference between "political" and "partisan" in this case. Share our Strength works with executives and legislatures of all parties, as its mission to end childhood hunger in the United States is, or should be, non-partisan. That doesn't make it apolitical – the stakes are high for them on what political decisions are reached. So too for all our missions.

In short, politics should not be verboten. Some organizations will likely benefit from zagging as others zigging, avowing and remaining studiously nonpartisan and perhaps even apolitical. But if someone votes because you encouraged them on an issue you share as your common mission, you've built a stronger bond built between you and that supporter.

Non-profits selling goods

Fully hybrid organizations start by integrating a for-profit model for revenue generation model with non-profit mission that can receive donations. This is an interesting structure, but not the point of this section. If you are considering creating an organization like this, I recommend *In Search of the Hybrid Ideal*[337] and *Effective Social Enterprise – A Menu of Legal Structures*.[338]

What I'm talking about here is traditional nonprofits selling things. To do this, I must first talk about unrelated business income tax (UBIT) and tax code changes. I apologize for this; I promise I'll also talk about British monsters, ocean conservancy, and mindfulness.

If you are a nonprofit and you sell a good or service, you pay taxes on the income unless the sale is related to your mission. To drastically oversimplify, the museum gift shop doesn't pay taxes; the museum restaurant does. To un-oversimplify, some gift shop items will require taxation – things that are ornamental, useful, or a souvenir unrelated to the museum; some will not – those that are related to the organization and the mission.[339]

So, using the Art Institute of Chicago as an example, a postcard of American Gothic would not incur tax. A postcard with Wrigley Field and "Wish You Were Here" would incur tax. A postcard of American Gothic and "Wish You Were Here" lives in the grey area that keeps attorneys employed.

A point on unrelated business income tax: it is a tax; it is not a contract with Satan. Believe it or not, this is a necessary clarification. Many nonprofits avoid selling goods altogether and those that do aim to minimize it. In that, we could be missing another revenue stream, which harms our viability.

This is especially true given additional changes to the tax code. Before 2017, UBIT was a graduated scale with brackets from 15% for under $50,000 up to 35% for $10 million-plus. With the tax bill, UBIT is now paid at a 21% flat tax rate.

A brief aside: this change appears stupid. The goal of UBIT is to discourage nonprofits from shifting from their philanthropic purposes to selling stuff. Thus, it makes sense to have a gradual disincentive for more sales; this does the opposite. Additionally, it's harder to go from $0 to $1 than from $10,000,000 to $10,000,001 – presumably you would want the latter dollar to be taxed more because it's easier to get. So I'm not advocating for this change.

I am, however, advocating you take advantage of this change: lemons to lemonade and all that. Selling goods has fixed costs that don't change no matter how much you sell. As you sell more, these costs become amortized over more revenues, so your margins go up. With no tax disincentive, a higher margin business has no penalties.

This is not to say your staff should stop fundraising and start stamping out widgets. There may, however, be products that fit with your mission close enough to avoid UBIT or, at least, to have synergy with your brand and with your donor's identities.

Take the example of Scope, a UK nonprofit helping those facing disabilities achieve equality. I mention their mission because, even in the UK, while 70% had heard of the organization, only 10% knew what it did.[340] One of their key donor identities was mothers sympathetic to the cause, saying things like "I thought parenting was tough, but it must be ten times harder with a disabled child."[341] The key, then, was to bolster their maternal identity, allowing them to model positive helping behavior for their kids and giving them the tools to feel like a better mother.

Enter Mindful Monsters, a card and activity set rolled out monthly that helps parents instill mindfulness in their kids. With your 7.50-pound monthly or 75-pound annual gift, you get a starter pack with seven activity cards, a parent's guide, and monster stickers, with more activity cards each month. The monsters focus on four themes of mindfulness: concentration, positivity, relaxation, and creativity.[342] Educational experts crafted the package so it would be effective for kids and a positive experience for parents.

Notice disability equality doesn't come up in this description. Rather, Scope saw the needs of their target audience. Instead of a glossy brochure, set of address labels, or full-color calendar, they created a premium that appealed to those needs. As a result, Scope reports it was able to lower monthly donor acquisition costs by 75%, cut time to break even in half, and retain these donors far better than average.[343] The retention did not happen by happenstance – it used the first year of Mindful Monster time to engage donors about Scope and what their donation was doing, in the hopes of converting them to longer-time purely philanthropic donors.

You may recognize this strategy from the international relief organization that benefited from educating its low commitment, and only low commitment, donors. You also may recognize this as a media organization strategy from earlier in this book except, instead of using content to acquire a constituent, they were able to use it to acquire and retain monthly donors. Nice work if you can get it.*

In the United States, would you have to pay tax on the sale of these cards? This goes into the grey area I spoke about earlier. You could argue that helping mothers is part of your mission, but that's a bit thin. Or you could argue that it's a premium like many other organizations give out and a minimal part of the donation you are getting in return. How successful that would be depends on the cost of the programs and the quality of your aforementioned attorneys.

My guess is you would have to pay the tax. Let us say that the costs for the program are a full quarter of the donation amount and judged to be unrelated to your mission. You would pay a tax of 21% on that 25%, or 5.25%. Raise your hand if you would be willing to make "only" 94.75% of a monthly donation if you could reduce your other acquisition costs by 75% for donors that retain better. Of course, your mileage may vary, but a focus on creating content or goods that your donor identities want to consume is an effective way to bring those donor identities to you.

---

* And you can get it if you try.

Some will complain this is us competing with for-profits. Yes. It is. But they started it. If we are not careful, they will finish it.

Take the example of 4Ocean. Technically speaking, this is a company that sells bracelets, one for $20, with a different design every month and the opportunity to get a monthly subscription.

You would be excused if you thought 4Ocean was a nonprofit. Their proposition is that for every bracelet sold, it will remove a pound of plastic from the ocean, which is recycled to make the bracelets. In fact, that's what it leads with, asking you to help end the ocean plastic crisis together with a live tracker of how many pounds of trash it has removed. All this is pitched before you ever find out your part in the process is to buy a bracelet. Their TV advertising reads like a nonprofit script, other than "give" and "donate" are replaced by "buy." This is the same model discussed above for Mindful Monsters except a for-profit is running the whole thing.

On the one hand, good for them. Milton Friedman may or may not have been correct when he said the one and only social responsibility of business is to increase its profits[344], but even under that model, kudos to the company that can maximize its profits by doing some measure of social good. A 4Ocean model for business leads to better oceans than a traditional business model. Andrew Cooper, 4Ocean's co-founder, makes this explicit as part of their goal:

> "We live in a world of consumerism and every purchase we make is a vote and it's the big brands that are counting the ballots. If we can teach people to use their dollar to vote for a company that's doing good they will listen and these big brands will start using ocean plastic in their products. … The reason why these big companies aren't doing things like this is because there's not enough attention on it right now. But if we can raise enough awareness, they'll start doing it."[345]

At the same time, consider what is lost by this not being done by a nonprofit (wherein the $20 would be a donation and the bracelet a premium given to donors). If a nonprofit finds a way to turn the $20 into more than a pound of plastic removed, they have an obligation to increase the plastic removed. If 4Ocean finds a way to turn the $20 into more than a pound of plastic removed, they have an obligation to increase their profits.

When asked why they didn't structure as a nonprofit, Alex Schulze, the other co-founder, said:

> "A non-profit is typically reliant on grants and other funding that you have to get that can be pulled away at any time. By creating a demand for this plastic in the ocean, it doesn't matter what happens. It's not like we're just trying to do this locally, we're trying to start a global movement that can truly change things. I think that with a business, Andrew and I have had the opportunity to scale quickly. We've gone from just the two of us cleaning to around 200 people. I think that that type of growth would not have been possible if we were a non-profit."[346]

I'm rooting for them and business models like them. It's important to know, however, that purposed-driven businesses don't just compete against non-purposed-driven businesses; they compete against nonprofits. And if we do remain reliant on grants and other funding that can be pulled away at any time (or concerned about how low can we go on our overhead percentage), we won't be able to compete.

Previous analyses of nonprofits have pointed the need to adhere to a vision first as a weakness. Goals like paying a living wage, lower priced products for lower-income people, or healthier products, they say, get in the way of competing in the marketplace. [347]

Call me crazy, but to the extent that marketplaces and ethics conflict, this seems like more of a problem with the marketplace, not the ethics. That said, we need not be consigned to the competitive basement. If, like Scope and Mindful Monsters, we can bring in product purchasers as donor or potential donors, we have an additional revenue stream that for-profits will not. As such, we may be able to overcome market-based barriers like having ethics.

The battle has begun as to where the money from product sales should go; will we take the field or surrender?

The direct donation hybrid organization

While we are talking about adding different models to our organizations, how about an if-you-can't-beat-them-join-them approach to crowdfunding and direct donation sites? As we discussed in the donor-directed enterprise section, some like their gift to go to a very specific person, place, or issue. We can profit by accommodating this, even if these decisions are colored by color and don't address systemic, underlying issues. By hybridizing, we can compensate for these deficits with our under-restricted funds.

These direct donations don't just have the advantage of localization and individualization; they also have a goal-focused advantage. People love to complete a goal. Kiva has found that when an individual fundraising goal was 0-33% complete, the average hourly progress toward goal was 6.7%. When it was 33-66% complete, progress was 10.8% per hour; for the final third, it was 12.8% per hour.[348] In other words, proximity to your goal creates an energy and momentum that makes accomplishment of that goal more likely.

Let's combine the advantage of a discrete, smaller goal with the our underlying-issue-addressing-juggernaut organization. Take a disease charity for polythelia sufferers. The organization works diligently toward a cure and assisting with research efforts. It also provides awareness activities and helps those diagnosed with the malady understand and live with their disease. While this is plenty of mission for any one organization, it will field questions consistently as to whether it helps sufferers financially. This is an issue faced by many organizations, regardless of whether they indirectly help disease sufferers or crime victims or elite athletes or children's education: they will always get questions as to whether they can help in a specific case.

Our hypothetical polythelia organization could add a crowdfunding operation to its main site or outsource it to a third-party. In either case, it would likely lose a few direct gifts from those who felt the best way to honor their friend with the disease was to donate to the general cause. However, it gains the name and data of someone who cares about a person with the disease (and, potentially, the requirement to serve someone who receives direct assistance, saving on costs). This data, plus the positive brand associations from being the one-stop polythelia shop, would be missed if that sufferer had to run a campaign on an unrelated third-party site. If someone is going to compete with you, it might as well be you, using the funds to offset where you would normally put general mission funding.

Let's also think bigger. What if we could take that energy and focus it on a systemic goal rather than fixing one situation?

Such is the idea of social finance's pay-for-success projects. These projects take government's social goals, accomplish them through nonprofit service providers, and fund them with private investments. The government then reimburses the investors based on the level of service accomplished – if goals are achieved, investors get their principle back plus interest. The idea is a win-win-win-win: people in need get services; nonprofits get upfront funding; governments only pay for results; and philanthropists/impact investors put their capital to work to maximize their results.[349] This also gets additional skin in the game: for example, if you have a social impact bond with an organization, you are also more likely to help them revamp their IT infrastructure or purchase a table at their gala.

That idea is spreading: from their 2010 creation, social impact bonds have proliferated to 108 projects in 24 countries.[350] These are not without growing pains. If a significant goal is maximizing your outcome* metric[351], you would likely turn away the hardest cases. For

---

* Some terminology here:

- Inputs: what resources do we have to get our job done? The biggest of these, of course, are time and money, but people and expertise also fall into this

example, if your goal was to decrease recidivism, you would logically reject those most likely to recommit a crime from even entering your program lest they ruin your stats.

Also, rather than funding innovation, these bonds have instead funded programs based on well-established models.[352] This is what you'd want if you were an investor looking to get return on investment, but not so much if your goal is significant leaps in effectiveness. Nonprofits report additional hurdles and onerous oversight pressures from investors.[353] They've also tended to shift, rather than increase, resources.[354] And, of course, organizations with less quantifiable outcomes like arts and advocacy organizations find this quantification nearly impossible. Imagine trying to implement a bond focused on getting seven percent more art appreciation out of the populace.

These are not reasons to reject the funding mechanism. Instead, they are cautions against silver-bullet thinking.

What if we could democratize the funding stream and shift it from impact investing to philanthropy? That is, using Kiva/microfinance as a

---

category. Picture the Apollo 13 scene where they must turn this filter into this CO2 scrubbing filter with this box of stuff. Inputs are the box of stuff.

- Activities: what do you do with your resources? We love to talk about these. We give our programs fancy trademarked names and want our donors to care about these.
- Outputs: what do you get by using your resources? A training program creates people who are trained. A research effort creates a white paper and a study. Everyone loves to talk about outputs because there is a number: we filled X beds, we had a Y% graduate rate, we served Z meals.
- Outcomes/impacts: what is the effect of your outputs? A humanitarian delivery of food doesn't end when the food reaches the dock — the output is reduced hunger among this target population. Some people look at outcomes and impacts as separate things, with outcomes being a short-term implication and impacts being the long-term impact. For me, there's short-term, medium-term, and long-term impacts of the action.

The further downstream you can look at this, the better. Too often, we get stuck talking about how great our program is (activities) and the number of peoples served as if they were widgets (outputs), when we should focus on impacts – the dent we are making in the world.

model, we could change the front end of this system to be financed by supporter loans (with no interest and some risk of loss). Governments still repay if agreed-upon criteria are met. This has the potential to take our win-win-win-win and make it even better:

- Donors get a warm glow of helping instead of seven percent interest. Lest you think people won't do this, remember people are giving right now with a zero percent chance of financial repayment.
- More people in need get services. Opening this to the public increases available funding. Perhaps with a loan structure, a $20 donor can now justify a $50 loan with a 90% chance of repayment. They can also make that $50 loan multiple times assuming repayment. This gets additional money in the sector and additional skin in the game.
- Nonprofits get upfront funding, plus a built-in set of supporters for sustaining the program once the seed funding is no longer in place. Plus, they are not limited by existing models; they can innovate and/or focus on more at-risk populations with the only limitation the support of their donors/loaners.
- Governments only pay for results and aren't on the hook for interest.

Oculus's VR headsets, the Tile locator app, the Veronica Mars movie, the Pebble smartwatch – all these crowdfunded efforts exist because democratized funding met idea, fell deeply in love, and started having entrepreneurial kids. It's time for us to put a nonprofit spin on these and do what we do best – have a great impact and spread joy.

Some combination thereof

This list is neither exhaustive nor exclusive. We could see a wonderfully messy goulash of models with organizations:

- Outsourcing the sale of goods in their name, taking licensing revenue **and potential donor names** instead (essentially cause-related marketing, but instigated by the nonprofit with a sharing of the most important asset of the customer file).
- Similarly outsourcing their direct donation efforts to existing direct donation sites, turning these companies into vendors instead of competitors.
- Using democratized pay-for-success fundraising to fund their internal incubation of new ideas and missions.
- Using list exchanges as a way of building common ties toward mergers.
- Creating cooperatives of ideas instead of (or in addition to) lists. I've helped organize a discussion of test results among disparate nonprofits for years, in which organizations agree to share their own interesting results to learn others' results. We can learn much from each other with intellectual cooperation.
- Creating cooperatives for shared gift processing. In politics, ActBlue provides online fundraising and organizing tools to Democratic campaigns and progressive causes; Patriot Pass has been announced as the Republican answer.[355] These shared platforms allow donors who have shared information and usability across campaigns; campaign staff and volunteers get access to this cross-campaign data, giving them a better understanding of donors' issues and desires. Nonprofits could benefit from doing likewise to understand their donors. Shared platforms among nonprofits could also ban pernicious practices like hostage taking of recurring donors should someone ever wish to switch.
- Creating shared services. Some tasks in the nonprofit world are required but create no advantage: state fundraising registrations, real estate management, joint cost allocation coding, etc. Instead of each organization having 10% of a person dedicated to each, why not have a shared organization where one person handles each of these for ten organizations?

And more. In short, our organization boundaries are and should be fluid. We can raise more and do more if we remember:

- We are stronger when we work together.
- We can organize around the supporter, not the mission or organization.
- We can have a spectrum of relationships between fully separate and fully combined.
- We can raise funds beyond donations.

Conclusion

> *"In many ways, the work of a critic is easy. We risk very little, yet enjoy a position over those who offer up their work and their selves to our judgment. We thrive on negative criticism, which is fun to write and to read. But the bitter truth we critics must face is that in the grand scheme of things, the average piece of junk is probably more meaningful than our criticism designating it so. But there are times when a critic truly risks something, and that is in the discovery and defense of the new. The world is often unkind to new talent, new creations. The new needs friends."*[356]
>
> – Peter O'Toole as Anton Ego

Here, in order, are the top 10 grossing movies of 2018 in the United States:

1. Extension of a movie universe
2. Sequel in an extended movie universe
3. Sequel
4. Sequel
5. Sequel
6. Remake
7. Extension of a movie universe
8. Sequel
9. Sequel in an extended movie universe
10. Prequel[*]

---

[*] Black Panther, Avengers: Infinity War, Incredibles 2, Jurassic Park: Fallen Kingdom, Deadpool 2, The Grinch, Aquaman, Mission: Impossible – Fallout, Ant-Man and the Wasp, Solo: A Star Wars Story.

You must get to numbers 13, 14, and 16 to find movies not based on another movie.*

Why, you may ask, am I bringing this up in a book about nonprofits? It's because of the eternal struggle of explore or exploit. We've faced it since our ancestors debated whether to stay at this hunting spot or move on to the next in hopes of greater game or fears of overhunting.

We face it in marketing. Is this control package or "best practice" so good that we should exploit it for another year? Or should we risk a test and, if so, how much?

Think of this like a pharmaceutical or consumer goods company. What percentage of your budget are you going to set aside for your R&D budget? Some organizations have set up a pilot program to test radical change with a small portion of their file, so most of their effort can be focused on exploiting what they have while a skunk works aims to overthrow the control.

The answer to the explore versus exploit spectrum is: it depends. And it depends on where you are in the lifecycle of your nonprofit.

If you are looking to create an enterprise that will stand for a thousand more years, you should bias toward exploring and experimentation. After all, the faster you can get to the best strategies, the more of your thousand years you will have to exploit them. On the flip side, if you are looking to finish your endeavor soon, it makes no sense to test significantly but rather to exploit everything you've already learned.

So the answer to why Hollywood is rife with recapitulation is that it is in exploit mode. It knows what works. And it knows they don't have long left in the current model. Between CGI actors, AI editors, theater attendance at a two-decade low, inefficiencies in labor contracts, threats from streaming services, piracy, a new generation of non-moviegoers, and competition from international culture makers, Hollywood is being disrupted. It knows it. Hence, today we drink, for tomorrow we die. Why risk John Carter when you can make Bond 25, Bourne 6, Harry

* Bohemian Rhapsody, A Quiet Place, and Crazy Rich Asians.

Potter 11, Star Wars 12, Furious 10, or Marvel whatever-number-we're-on[*]?

This is a path available to us should we wish it. We can do what we've always done. We can nibble around the edges, focusing on our subject line test, optimizing our envelope teaser, and driving out costs. This is efficiency. It's not a bad thing. It's learning to run faster as the treadmill increases its speed. If we can do it well enough, maybe we can make it to retirement having made some gains in funding our missions.

If that is your goal, hopefully you found some tips here worth using: a dab of donor preferences here, an identity statement there, and you have a path to some incremental results, all without changing too much.

But I'm hoping that dipping your toe into the water is the prelude to something bigger. We too are being disrupted. This isn't something we can incrementally solve. Nor can we can solve it by finding another channel. It will help for a time, but the Law of Shitty Clickthroughs means that's a temporary salve.

If you are exploiting while others are exploring, those explorers will win in the long run.

It's instructive to look at those who have not made this leap. For example, I can date myself well by saying I've been alive for the creation, rise, and largely fall of large chain bookstores.

When I was born, you got a book at an independent bookstore or at a mall bookstore. Then came Barnes and Noble and Borders, which featured cheaper prices, greater selection, and less direct customer service.

The first to die was the mall bookstore: B. Dalton, Waldenbooks, Crown Books, etc. They were unable to compete on price, selection, or customer service. (Now the mall itself is contracting.) Independent bookstores were hurt, especially those competing on cost. A select few

---

[*] It depends on whether you count one or both Hulk movies, the Deadpool movies, licensed IP movies like X-Men and the first five Spider-Men, and bad movies like the three Fantastics Four. Also, it is likely that all these numbers will be out of date when you read this anyway.

made it through by focusing on customer service and personality, building relationships with their patrons that a website can't replicate.

The long-term problem with the chain bookstore focusing on price and selection is if you can't offer the lowest and the largest. Amazon hit the big box bookstores hard. Customers who'd flocked to Messrs. Noble and Barnes for lower costs and greater selection saw lowest cost and greatest selection elsewhere and left. Borders closed completely by the end of 2010; Barnes and Noble has contracted to survive including firing all full-time employees in early 2018.[357]

On the other hand, independent bookstores are having a renaissance for those who want to touch, smell, and talk about books, especially for niche book types. It turns out that book people want book experiences more than they wanted coffee experiences. They've grown by 31% since 2009[358], spurred by the availability of books from wholesalers within hours to facilitate local events.[359]

It's to the point where the most dated period piece from Tom Hanks's movies from the 1990s isn't the one where he faced discrimination for his sexual orientation, supported women trying to make it in a men's world, was a Wall Street asshole, or fought Nazis. These still seem strangely and sadly relevant.

It's *You've Got Mail* – the one where the heartless big box bookstore owner put the independent bookstore out of business while winning her heart with online chatting that used full words, capitalization, and punctuation – that doesn't fit. Just the sound of a modem coming online (is it R2D2 being tortured? a feral vacuum cleaner? what happens when you spill grape juice in a synthesizer?) makes this a museum piece. Tom Hanks' character who seeks out chain bookstore expansion likely would not have stayed employed through 2010.

Why this trip down book-acquisition memory lane? Because nonprofits are being disrupted in the same ways.

Instead of a wide selection of books, we have a wide selection of nonprofits. We compete with the traditional organizations and, if our business is giving a hit of dopamine for doing good, we face ever more competition. Get the brand that is donating a part of their profits to charity. Use the "donate a dollar" at check out. Buy something from the neighborhood kid selling something for some club. Knock doors for or donate to a favorite political candidate.

If we are selling the same thing as everyone else, we will see low retention rates, dropping donor rolls, and difficulty in acquisition. In short, we will see what we are seeing. But forever.

We also have a wider selection in how a donation can be used. It is better to give without restrictions. We want unrestricted giving. We should get unrestricted giving. But none of these are guarantees that we will get unrestricted giving. People like to know their specific impact. Sites like Kiva, DonorsChoose, GoFundMe, and a myriad of sites of others allow you to give directly to the specific person or people or cause you want. Sure, they won't solve systemic issues and will (unintentionally, to be sure) reinforce existing biases, but the pitch seduces. If they are not yet competing with you for directed donations, know that the emphasis is on the "yet."

Instead of the low costs of books, donors are looking for low overhead. These sites have it. Some nonprofits have been competing on costs with matches and multipliers and 90%+ to missions and Charity Navigator seals. But like the Borders and B&Ns of years past, those organizations will be left behind in this arms race by direct giving organizations or organizations that set their organizational structure up to deliver 100% to the mission. Those who have competed on cost become McDonalds if someone were to deliver a ten-cent hamburger. Those nonprofits competing on cost also won't be able to compete with organizations that have invested in deepening their relationship with donors. Your overhead rate may be lower, but that doesn't matter if donors looooooooove your competition.

Instead of the customer service gap between big bookstores and independents on customer service, we nonprofits have disruptors working to own the donor relationship. Facebook, Google, and other for-profits are offering us nearly limitless scope, but at the price of being our gatekeepers. It is but a short step to them being our wardens. It benefits these intermediaries for us to be interchangeable widgets they can play off against each other, all while gathering the data on why and how people give. Once there, it can be used to sell to our competitors or, worse, become our competitors.

Like our big bookstores before, we are trying to sail between the Scylla of the small, nimble, focused, and donor-directed organizations and Charybdis of the massive, efficient, and crushing organizations.*

The answer is not to compete on that axis. The answer isn't wider; it's deeper – deeper in the relationships we build with donors and in the warm feelings we give them.

It means knowing them, showing them that you know them, and owning the donor relationship and data from stem to stern.

It means allowing them to drive with us: how they want to hear from us, how their support will be used, how they can make an impact with more than their money.

It means starting our relationships by giving, not asking. And not giving things: giving ideas, information, and salves that speak to who I am and the moment in which I find myself.

And it means questioning our dichotomies, our neat lines we've tried to draw between volunteer and staff and between this organization and another.

If a better model existed, it would be fine for us to be left in the evolutionary dust with others more adapted to the times. No such model exists.

Government can't do what we do. Samuel Broder, the former director of the National Cancer Institute once said that "If it was up to the NIH to cure polio through a centrally directed program… You'd have the best iron lung in the world but not a polio vaccine." Our messy spectrum of solutions is also beautiful and effective. We cannot, should not, count on government to solve our ills.

If it were up to private industry to take out social ills, we would have solutions for the ills most profitable to solve: many drugs[360], few

* Scylla and Charybdis are the sea monsters that Odysseus has to say between in the Odyssey. Scylla is a six-headed monster; Charybdis a whirlpool that threatens the ship.

mosquito nets.[361]. One can see the iron lung being more profitable and thus more worth the efforts of a for-profit over the non-recurring revenue of a vaccine. The incentives of the free market do not always line up with incentives for the greater good. It takes significant regulation and restructuring of incentives, for example, for a for-profit prison to want to decrease, instead of increase, recidivism.

If it were up to directed donation sites, we could get financing for individuals to receive iron lungs for those who couldn't afford them by running a GoFundMe or the like. This is better than those folks not getting iron lungs. Funding skews, however, to the telegenic and to those who look like the donor. It also avoids the hard questions of funding iniquities and better solutions.

It took Basil O'Connor and the March of Dimes to cure polio. Fundraising to treat *and* cure the disease, their efforts raised the equivalent of seven billion dimes (in 1930-1950s dollars) for the fight against polio.[362] March of Dimes funded Salk's research, Sabin's oral vaccine, and treatment for millions of polio patients. At its peak, polio paralyzed, then killed, a half a million people every year.[363] In 2018, 29 cases were reported worldwide.[364]

To be sure, it also took government and industry and direct support for patients. But it was the nonprofit, the cause, the mission in the center that focused our efforts to a truly philanthropic goal.

This model is not a relic of a bygone era. From 2000 to 2018, the Michael J. Fox Foundation received and spent $800 million (in 2000-2010s dollars) to understand and fight Parkinson's. They've turned Parkinson's research from a dead end to something scientists vie to work on. A 2011 seed grant has turned into Inbrija, which doesn't cure Parkinson's, but does provide a rescue inhaler like the ones vital for asthma sufferers.[365] It strives still for a cure, but in the process has made the lives of Parkinson's patients much better.

Ignorance, malfeasance, pestilence, and famine: these are the intractable foes we've chosen for ourselves. We choose to face down the most powerful. We choose to comfort the poor, one of whose most powerful advocates said we will always have the poor with us. We choose to stare Death itself in the face and try to make it blink first.

We didn't choose nonprofits because they are easy. We choose them because they work. If it were easy, someone would have made an app for it.

So why do we fight to sustain ourselves for this generation and the ones to come? Because we nonprofits are worth fighting for.

Acknowledgements

To my family, especially my wife Megan, my parents Royal and Bonny, and my kids, Sophie and Drew. They who tolerated me working on the book and talking about the book and thinking about the book and temporarily putting aside the things that are important in life to work on the book and generally wandering around life going "bookbookbookbookbookbook." They also proofread and hired an editor and designed the cover with me and workshopped jokes with me* and generally did everything short of deserving a co-author credit. Special thanks to Sophie, who woke me up before the dawn frequently enough to find time to work on it.

To those who brought me into this wonderful nonprofit world. It starts with Karen Sprattler and the Mothers Against Drunk Driving public policy team taking a chance on me to work on state legislation, then Chuck Hurley leaping into faith with my move over to fundraising. In addition to them, I had the privilege of working for and learning from folks like Debbie Weir, Vicki Knox, Guy Fischer, Cathey Wise and working with many other talents too numerous to name for fear of omission. Thank you also to the amazing volunteers and board members of MADD. I hope you see yourself in these pages, in the commitment that comes connection to a cause and in the power of volunteers to create change.

To those who taught me marketing, direct marketing, and fundraising. This starts with business school professors, where I must single out Dr. David Rados's nonprofit marketing class that I did not think I would need at the time. In early professional life, Steven Kappel at Fleetguard/Nelson and Casey Smith and Luther Cale at HealthStream were great teachers to me. Thank you also to Bobby Frist, who tolerated the many mistakes I made while learning and taught me about leadership. In the nonprofit world, Ray Grace and Geoff Peters taught

* Believe it or not, there were jokes that bad enough to be cut. Thank my family for this small blessing.

me how to run direct marketing fundraising when I didn't know how. Now, I have the pleasure of working with and writing with Roger Craver. I owe him much, from learning from him from afar when he was the titular Agitator to fulfilling a dream of writing for the same to teaching me on the job at DonorVoice to helping birth this book into the world.

To the DonorVoice team – Kevin, Josh, Julie, Kiki, Stephanie, Craig, Charlie, Ilja, and Andrew – who accepted me into their weird, brilliant, powerful family. I thought I knew what small-but-mighty was before you; I did not. So much of the work within this book is theirs/ours; I hope only to have done it some measure of justice.

To the researchers and nonprofit thinkers who populate the parts of the book the DonorVoice team did not. Newton said "If I have seen further it is by standing on the shoulders of Giants"; my view is likely still obstructed by these folks' heads – I have climbing left to do. Specifically, thank you to Shannon McCracken of the Nonprofit Alliance, who read and commented and caught errors I did not.

To the nonprofits. Not just for the case studies, although I am there also in debt. Not just for the camaraderie with nonprofit leaders, although I hope I sharpen their steel half as much as they do mine. But for choosing to be the fulcrum by which we move the world.

References

[1] Martin, G. R. R. (1996). *A Game of Thrones.* (New York, NY: Bantam Books).
[2] Blackbaud estimates that from 2015 to 2018, overall giving has increased nine percent in the United States. They also record from 2017 to 2018, it increased 1.9% for Canadian charities, increased 4% for Australian and New Zealand charities, and decreased 4.2% for UK charities. Blackbaud. 2018 Charitable Giving Report by Blackbaud. Retrieved June 5, 2019, from https://institute.blackbaud.com/asset/2018-charitable-giving-report. If this book is ever translated into other languages, I will work to look up trends in other countries but for right now I have trouble enough with my native tongue.
[3] Individual giving in the United States has been consistent at 2.1% for the past six years and around 2% since data are available. Giving USA. (n.d.). Giving USA 2018: The Annual Report on Philanthropy for the Year 2017. Retrieved June 5, 2019, from https://www.givinginstitute.org/page/GivingUSA.
[4] Blackbaud has a 1.5% increase in total giving from 2017 to 2018: Blackbaud. 2018 Charitable Giving Report by Blackbaud. Retrieved June 5, 2019, from https://institute.blackbaud.com/asset/2018-charitable-giving-report/.
[5] Epsilon. (2019). Not-for-profit giving trends 2018, from https://us.epsilon.com/resources/not-for-profit-sector-trends.
[6] Fundraising Effectiveness Project. (2019). 2018 Fundraising Effectiveness Survey Report, from http://afpfep.org/reports/.
[7] Indiana University Lilly Family School of Philanthropy. Generosity for Life data. Retrieved June 5, 2019, from http://generosityforlife.org/.
[8] Blackbaud. Vital Signs: Monitoring Giving Patterns in the Donor Marketplace. Retrieved June 5, 2019, from https://institute.blackbaud.com/asset/vital-signs-monitoring-giving-patterns-in-the-donor-marketplace/.
[9] Blackbaud. 2018 Charitable Giving Report by Blackbaud. Retrieved June 5, 2019, from https://institute.blackbaud.com/asset/2018-charitable-giving-report/.
[10] Lindsay, D. (2017, October 3). Fewer Americans Find Room in Their Budgets for Charity, Chronicle Data Shows. Chronicle of Philanthropy, from https://www.philanthropy.com/article/Share-of-Americans-Who-Give-to/241345/.
[11] Indiana University Lilly Family School of Philanthropy. Generosity for Life data. Retrieved June 5, 2019, from http://generosityforlife.org/generosity-data/data-tools/generosity-reports;
Lindsay, D. (2017, December 05). Donor States of America. Retrieved June 5, 2019, from https://www.philanthropy.com/article/Donor-States-of-America/241895?cid=cpfd_home.
[12] Lindsay, D. (2017, December 05). Donor States of America. Retrieved June 5, 2019, from https://www.philanthropy.com/article/Donor-States-of-America/241895?cid=cpfd_home.

---

[13] Blackbaud. (2016). DonorCentrics™ Index of Direct Marketing Fundraising 2015 Fourth Calendar Quarter Results. Retrieved June 5, 2019, from https://www.blackbaud.com/files/resources/target-index-results-summary-q4-2015.pdf.
[14] Fundraising Effectiveness Project. (2019). 2018 Fundraising Effectiveness Survey Report, from http://afpfep.org/reports/.
[15] Blackbaud. (n.d.). The Next Generation of American Giving. Retrieved June 5, 2019, from https://institute.blackbaud.com/asset/the-next-generation-of-american-giving-2018/.
[16] Indiana University Lilly Family School of Philanthropy. Generosity for Life data. Retrieved June 5, 2019, from http://generosityforlife.org/generosity-data/data-tools/generosity-reports;
Wallace, N and Myers, B. In Search of ... America's Missing Donors. *Chronicle of Philanthropy*. Retrieved June 5, 2019, from https://www.philanthropy.com/interactives/Disappearing;
Lindsay, D. (2017, December 05). Donor States of America. Retrieved June 5, 2019, from https://www.philanthropy.com/article/Donor-States-of-America/241895?cid=cpfd_home.
[17] Wallace, N and Myers, B. In Search of ... America's Missing Donors. *Chronicle of Philanthropy*. Retrieved June 5, 2019, fromhttps://www.philanthropy.com/interactives/Disappearing.
[18] Meer, J., Miller, D., & Wulfsberg, E. (2017). The Great Recession and Charitable Giving. Applied Economics Letters. doi:10.3386/w22902, from http://people.tamu.edu/~jmeer/MMW_Great_Recession_and_Giving.pdf.
[19] Malmendier, U., & Nagel, S. (2011). Depression Babies: Do Macroeconomic Experiences Affect Risk-Taking? The Quarterly Journal of Economics, 126(1). doi:10.3386/w14813, from https://academic.oup.com/qje/article-abstract/126/1/373/1901343.
[20] Meer, J. (2013). The Habit of Giving. Economic Inquiry, 51(4), 2002-2017. doi:10.1111/ecin.12010, from https://onlinelibrary.wiley.com/doi/pdf/10.1111/ecin.12010.
[21] Saez, E., & Zucman, G. (2014). Wealth Inequality in the United States since 1913: Evidence from Capitalized Income Tax Data. NBER WORKING PAPER SERIES. doi:10.3386/w20625, from http://www.nber.org/papers/w20625.pdf
[22] Collins, C., Flannery, H., & Hoxie, J. (2016). Gilded Giving: Top-Heavy Philanthropy in an Age of Extreme Inequality, from http://www.ips-dc.org/wp-content/uploads/2016/11/Gilded-Giving-Final-pdf.pdf.
[23] Blackbaud. (2016). DonorCentrics™ Index of Direct Marketing Fundraising 2015 Fourth Calendar Quarter Results, from https://www.blackbaud.com/files/resources/target-index-results-summary-q4-2015.pdf.
[24] Fundraising Effectiveness Project. (2019). 2018 Q4 Quarterly Fundraising Report, from https://afpglobal.org/sites/default/files/attachments/2019-02/FEP2018Q4Report.pdf.

---

[25] Larimer, S. (2015, July 1). Girl Scouts Choose Transgender Girls over $100,000 Donation. Washington Post. Retrieved June 6, 2019, from https://www.washingtonpost.com/news/morning-mix/wp/2015/06/30/girl-scouts-choose-transgender-girls-over-100000-donation/.
[26] Ellinger, N. (2019, March 17). Three Scenarios for the Future of Individual Giving. Retrieved June 6, 2019, from http://agitator.thedonorvoice.com/three-scenarios-for-the-future-of-individual-giving/.
[27] Fundraising Standards Board. (2016). *FRSB Investigation into Charity Fundraising Practices instigated by Mrs. Olive Cooke's Case* (Rep.). Retrieved June 6, 2019, from https://www.civilsociety.co.uk/uploads/assets/uploaded/9f5da72e-a00b-4d0a-83ec1a732f6d72ba.pdf.
[28] Sharman, A. (2015, May 19). Family of Olive Cooke say charities are not responsible for her death. Retrieved June 13, 2019, from https://www.civilsociety.co.uk/news/family-of-olive-cooke-say-charities-are-not-responsible-for-her-death.html.
[29] Barraza, J. A., & Zak, P. J. (2009). Empathy toward Strangers Triggers Oxytocin Release and Subsequent Generosity. *Annals of the New York Academy of Sciences, 1167*(1), 182-189. doi:10.1111/j.1749-6632.2009.04504.x, from http://www.nexthumanproject.com/references/Empathy_Towards_Strangers_Claremont.pdf.
[30] Lin, P., Grewal, N. S., Morin, C., Johnson, W. D., & Zak, P. J. (2013). Oxytocin Increases the Influence of Public Service Advertisements. *PLOS One, 8*(2). doi:10.1371/journal.pone.0056934, from http://www.ncbi.nlm.nih.gov/pmc/articles/PMC3584120/.
[31] Barraza, J. A., & Zak, P. J. (2009). Empathy toward Strangers Triggers Oxytocin Release and Subsequent Generosity. *Annals of the New York Academy of Sciences, 1167*(1), 182-189. doi:10.1111/j.1749-6632.2009.04504.x, from http://www.nexthumanproject.com/references/Empathy_Towards_Strangers_Claremont.pdf.
[32] Gęsiarz, F., & Crockett, M. J. (2015). Goal-directed, habitual and Pavlovian prosocial behavior. *Frontiers in behavioral neuroscience*, *9*, 135. Retrieved June 13, 2019, from http://www.ncbi.nlm.nih.gov/pmc/articles/PMC4444832/.
[33] McClure, S. M., Li, J., Tomlin, D., Cypert, K. S., Montague, L. M., & Montague, P. R. (2004). Neural correlates of behavioral preference for culturally familiar drinks. *Neuron*, *44*(2), 379-387. Retrieved June 13, 2019, from https://www.sciencedirect.com/science/article/pii/S0896627304006129.
[34] Harbaugh, W. T., Mayr, U., & Burghart, D. R. (2007). Neural responses to taxation and voluntary giving reveal motives for charitable donations. *Science*, *316*(5831), 1622-1625. Retrieved June 13, 2019, from https://www.ncbi.nlm.nih.gov/pubmed/17569866.
[35] Kean, S. (2015, May). The Man Who Couldn't Stop Giving. *The Atlantic*. Retrieved June 13, 2019, http://www.theatlantic.com/magazine/archive/2015/05/the-man-who-couldnt-stop-giving/389531/

---

36 M+R. (2019). *2019 Nonprofit Benchmarks*. Retrieved June 6, 2019, from https://mrbenchmarks.com/#!/fundraising-messages.

37 Jarcho, J. M., Berkman, E. T., & Lieberman, M. D. (2010). The Neural Basis of Rationalization: Cognitive Dissonance Reduction during Decision-Making. *Social Cognitive and Affective Neuroscience,6*(4), 460-467. doi:10.1093/scan/nsq054, from https://www.ncbi.nlm.nih.gov/pmc/articles/PMC3150852/.

38 Sargeant, A. (2001). Managing donor defection: Why should donors stop giving? New Directions for Philanthropic Fundraising, 2001(32), 59-74. doi:10.1002/pf.3204, from http://www.campbellrinker.com/Managing_donor_defection.pdf.

39 Francis, N., & Holland, N. (1999). The Diary of a Charity Donor: An Exploration of Research Information from the Royal Mail Consumer Panel and Mail Characteristics Survey. *International Journal of Nonprofit and Voluntary Sector Marketing*, 4(3), 217-223. doi:10.1002/nvsm.74.

40 Rothschild, M. L. (1979). Marketing Communications in Nonbusiness Situations or Why It's so Hard to Sell Brotherhood like Soap. *Journal of Marketing, 43*(2), 11-20. doi:10.1177/002224297904300202, from https://www.jstor.org/stable/1250737?seq=1#page_scan_tab_contents.

41 Epley, N. (2008). Solving the (Real) Other Minds Problem. *Social and Personality Psychology Compass, 2*(3), 1455-1474. doi:10.1111/j.1751-9004.2008.00115.x, from https://faculty.chicagobooth.edu/nicholas.epley/Epley2008OtherMinds.pdf.

42 EMarketer. (2015). *Programmatic Advertising 2015*(Rep.), from http://www.emarketer.com/public_media/docs/Programmatic_Advertising_2015-Executive_Summary-10082015.pdf.

43 Godin, S. (2017, February 19). The Opposite of "More." Retrieved June 6, 2019, from https://seths.blog/2017/02/the-opposite-of-more/.

44 Samek, A., & Longfield, C. (2019). Do Thank-You Calls Increase Charitable Giving? Expert Forecasts and Field Experimental Evidence. *SSRN Electronic Journal.* doi:10.2139/ssrn.3371327, from https://papers.ssrn.com/sol3/papers.cfm?abstract_id=3371327.

45 Donkers, B., Diepen, M. V., & Franses, P. H. (2017). Do charities get more when they ask more often? Evidence from a unique field experiment. *Journal of Behavioral and Experimental Economics, 66*, 58-65. doi:10.1016/j.socec.2016.05.006, from http://repub.eur.nl/pub/19423/ERS-2010-015-MKT.pdf.

46 Schulman, K. (2018, January 22). How Amnesty Increased First Year F2F Retention by 12 Points. Retrieved June 6, 2019, from https://www.institute-of-fundraising.org.uk/blog/how-amnesty-increased-first-year-f2f-retention-by-12-points/.

47 Marden, L. (2016, December 13). Retrieved June 06, 2019, from https://www.youtube.com/watch?v=26IWoeXL1nw.

48 DonorTrends. Mail Smarter. Retrieved June 06, 2019, from http://www.thedonorvoice.com/wp-content/uploads/2017/05/Mail-Smarter-DonorTrends-Case-Study.pdf.

49 Abila. (2015, April 15). *Abila Engagement Study Finds Disconnects between Nonprofit Practices and Donor Preferences*[Press release]. Retrieved June 6, 2019,

from https://www.abila.com/company/press-releases/abila-engagement-study-finds-disconnects-between-nonprofit-practices-donor-preferences/.
[50] Lyons, D. (2017). *Disrupted: My Misadventure in the Start-Up Bubble*. New York, NY: Hachette Books.
[51] EveryAction. (2019). *2018 Email Deliverability Study* (Rep.). Retrieved June 6, 2019, fromhttps://act.everyaction.com/email-deliverability-study-18.
[52] M+R. (2019). *2019 Nonprofit Benchmarks*. Retrieved June 6, 2019, from https://mrbenchmarks.com/. Also, previous year's versions, available at the same site.
[53] Damgaard, M. T., & Gravert, C. (2017). Now or never! The effect of deadlines on charitable giving: Evidence from two natural field experiments. *Journal of Behavioral and Experimental Economics, 66*, 78-87. doi:10.1016/j.socec.2016.04.013, from ftp://ftp.econ.au.dk/afn/wp/14/wp14_03.pdf.
[54] Damgaard, M. T., & Gravert, C. (2018). The hidden costs of nudging: Experimental evidence from reminders in fundraising. *Journal of Public Economics, 157*, 15-26. doi:10.1016/j.jpubeco.2017.11.005, from https://www.sciencedirect.com/science/article/pii/S0047272717301895.
[55] Damgaard, M. T., & Gravert, C. (2017). Now or never! The effect of deadlines on charitable giving: Evidence from two natural field experiments. *Journal of Behavioral and Experimental Economics, 66*, 78-87. doi:10.1016/j.socec.2016.04.013, from ftp://ftp.econ.au.dk/afn/wp/14/wp14_03.pdf.
[56] Damgaard, M. T., & Gravert, C. (2018). The hidden costs of nudging: Experimental evidence from reminders in fundraising. *Journal of Public Economics, 157*, 15-26. doi:10.1016/j.jpubeco.2017.11.005, from https://www.sciencedirect.com/science/article/pii/S0047272717301895.
[57] Damgaard, M. T., & Gravert, C. (2018). The hidden costs of nudging: Experimental evidence from reminders in fundraising. *Journal of Public Economics,157*, 15-26. doi:10.1016/j.jpubeco.2017.11.005, from https://www.sciencedirect.com/science/article/pii/S0047272717301895.
[58] Chen, A. (2014, July 18). The Law of Shitty Clickthroughs. Retrieved June 8, 2019, from https://andrewchen.co/the-law-of-shitty-clickthroughs/
[59] DaCosta, M. (Director). (1962). The Music Man. Retrieved June 8, 2019, from https://www.youtube.com/watch?v=g8LHlJSBkg0.
[60] Benway, J. P. (1998, October). Banner blindness: The irony of attention grabbing on the World Wide Web. In *Proceedings of the Human Factors and Ergonomics Society Annual Meeting* (Vol. 42, No. 5, pp. 463-467). Sage CA: Los Angeles, CA: SAGE Publications. Retrieved June 8, 2019, from http://www.ruf.rice.edu/~lane/papers/banner_blindness.pdf.
[61] Pernice, K. (2018, April 22). Banner Blindness Revisited: Users Dodge Ads on Mobile and Desktop. Retrieved June 8, 2019, from https://www.nngroup.com/articles/banner-blindness-old-and-new-findings/.
[62] Craver, R. (2015, April 17). Raise More, Ask Less - Part 4. Retrieved June 8, 2019, from http://agitator.thedonorvoice.com/raise-more-ask-less-part-4/.

---

[63] Lucker, J., Hogan, S. K., & Bischoff, T. (2017). Predictably inaccurate: The Prevalence and Perils of Bad Big Data. *Deloitte Review*. Retrieved June 8, 2019, from https://www2.deloitte.com/content/dam/insights/us/articles/3924_Predictably-inaccurate/DUP_Predictably-inaccurate-reprint.pdf.

[64] Livingston, G. (2015, May 07). Family Size Among Mothers. Retrieved June 8, 2019, from https://www.pewsocialtrends.org/2015/05/07/family-size-among-mothers/.

[65] Brockell, G. (2018, December 12). Dear Tech Companies, I Don't Want to See Pregnancy Ads after My Child was Stillborn. *Washington Post*. Retrieved June 8, 2019, from https://www.washingtonpost.com/lifestyle/2018/12/12/dear-tech-companies-i-dont-want-see-pregnancy-ads-after-my-child-was-stillborn/.

[66] Lucker, J., Hogan, S. K., & Bischoff, T. (2017). Predictably inaccurate: The Prevalence and Perils of Bad Big Data. *Deloitte Review*. Retrieved June 8, 2019, from https://www2.deloitte.com/content/dam/insights/us/articles/3924_Predictably-inaccurate/DUP_Predictably-inaccurate-reprint.pdf.

[67] Faulkner, K. (2016, December 6). Fines Handed to the RSPCA and British Heart Foundation for Snooping on Donors' Finances Could Have Been 10 Times Bigger. *Daily Mail*. Retrieved June 8, 2019, from https://www.dailymail.co.uk/news/article-4007640/Fines-handed-RSPCA-British-Heart-Foundation-snooping-donors-finances-10-times-bigger.html.

[68] Nonprofit Times. (2017, September 19). EU Clamping Down on Data Use for Marketing. *Nonprofit Times*. Retrieved June 8, 2019, from https://www.thenonprofittimes.com/npt_articles/eu-clamping-data-use-marketing/.

[69] Rosling, H., Rosling, O., & Rulund, A. R. (2018). *Factfulness: ten reasons we're wrong about the world - and why things are better than you think*. First edition. New York: Flatiron Books.

[70] Althoff, T., & Leskovec, J. (2015, May). Donor Retention in Online Crowdfunding Communities: A Case Study of Donorschoose. org. In *Proceedings of the 24th International Conference on World Wide Web* (pp. 34-44). International World Wide Web Conferences Steering Committee. Retrieved from https://www.ncbi.nlm.nih.gov/pmc/articles/PMC4827627/.

[71] Jobs, S. (2010, June 26). Retrieved June 13, 2019, from https://www.youtube.com/watch?time_continue=97&v=39iKLwlUqBo.

[72] Which was a good movie with a couple flaws certainly not in need of recutting by misogynists.

[73] Radojev, H. (2017, November 1). Cancer Research UK Opt-in Percentage for Telephone 'In Single Figures'. *Civil Society*. Retrieved June 8, 2019, from https://www.civilsociety.co.uk/news/cancer-research-uk-opt-in-rates-for-telephone-tracking-at-single-figures.html.

[74] Stewart, R. (2018, January 27). Cancer Research Hopes to Reap Rewards from Embracing GDPR Changes Early. The Drum. Retrieved June 8, 2019, from https://www.thedrum.com/news/2018/01/17/cancer-research-hopes-reap-rewards-embracing-gdpr-changes-early.

---

[75] Hardin, G. (1968). The Tragedy of the Commons. *Science, 162*(3859), 1243-1248.
[76] Naik, P., & Piersma, N. N. (2002). *Understanding the Role of Marketing Communications in Direct Marketing* (No. EI 2002-13).
[77] Diamond, W. D., & Noble, S. M. (2001). Defensive Responses to Charitable Direct Mail Solicitations. *Journal of Interactive Marketing, 15*(3), 2-12. Retrieved June 8, 2019, from https://www.researchgate.net/profile/Stephanie_Noble/publication/227945639_Defensive_responses_to_charitable_direct_mail_solicitations/links/57b5e18308ae19a365fc4d04.pdf.
[78] Breeze, B. (2010). How donors choose charities. *London: University of Kent.* Retrieved June 8, 2019, from http://www.cgap.org.uk/uploads/reports/HowDonorsChooseCharities.pdf.
[79] Donkers, B., van Diepen, M., & Franses, P. H. (2017). Do Charities Get More When They Ask More Often? Evidence from a Unique Field Experiment. *Journal of Behavioral and Experimental Economics, 66*, 58-65. Retrieved June 8, 2019, from http://repub.eur.nl/pub/19423/ERS-2010-015-MKT.pdf.
[80] Harbaugh, W. T., Mayr, U., & Burghart, D. R. (2007). Neural Responses to Taxation and Voluntary Giving Reveal Motives for Charitable Donations. *Science, 316*(5831), 1622-1625. Retrieved June 8, 2019, from http://science.sciencemag.org/content/316/5831/1622.
[81] Apogee. (2016). Your Donors Are Cheating On You! (Rep.). Retrieved June 8, 2019, from http://marketing.infogrouptargeting.com/acton/fs/blocks/showLandingPage/a/4454/p/p-00ed/t/page/fm/0.
[82] Sharp, B. (2016). How Brands Grow. Melbourne: Oxford University Press. doi:https://doi.org/10.1108/10610421211215715.
[83] Number one is pleading poverty, which is another way of saying you didn't make the case strong enough. Sargeant, A. (2001). Managing Donor Defection: Why Should Donors Stop Giving? New Directions for Philanthropic Fundraising, 2001(32), 59-74. doi:10.1002/pf.3204, from http://www.campbellrinker.com/Managing_donor_defection.pdf.
[84] Sargeant, A. (2001). Managing Donor Defection: Why Should Donors Stop Giving? New Directions for Philanthropic Fundraising, 2001(32), 59-74. doi:10.1002/pf.3204, from http://www.campbellrinker.com/Managing_donor_defection.pdf.
[85] Breeze, B. (2010). How Donors Choose Charities. *London: University of Kent.* Retrieved June 8, 2019, from http://www.cgap.org.uk/uploads/reports/HowDonorsChooseCharities.pdf.
[86] Breeze, B. (2010). How Donors Choose Charities. *London: University of Kent.* Retrieved June 8, 2019, from http://www.cgap.org.uk/uploads/reports/HowDonorsChooseCharities.pdf
[87] Breeze, B. (2010). How Donors Choose Charities. *London: University of Kent.* Retrieved June 8, 2019, from http://www.cgap.org.uk/uploads/reports/HowDonorsChooseCharities.pdf

---

[88] Small, D. (2018, June 1). Hearts, Minds and Money: Maximizing Charitable Giving. Retrieved June 8, 2019, from https://knowledge.wharton.upenn.edu/article/maximizing-charitable-giving/.
[89] Perry, S. (2013, June 17). The Stubborn 2% Giving Rate. *Chronicle of Philanthropy*. Retrieved June 8, 2019, from https://www.philanthropy.com/article/The-Stubborn-2-Giving-Rate/154691.
[90] LaBarge, M. C., & Stinson, J. L. (2014). The Role of Mental Budgeting in Philanthropic Decision-Making. *Nonprofit and Voluntary Sector Quarterly*, *43*(6), 993-1013. Retrieved June 8, 2019, from https://journals.sagepub.com/doi/abs/10.1177/0899764013489776.
[91]LaBarge, M. C., & Stinson, J. L. (2014). The Role of Mental Budgeting in Philanthropic Decision-Making. *Nonprofit and Voluntary Sector Quarterly*, *43*(6), 993-1013. Retrieved June 8, 2019, from https://journals.sagepub.com/doi/abs/10.1177/0899764013489776.
[92] Schwab, K. (2016). The Fourth Industrial Revolution. New York, NY: Crown Business.
[93] Kessler, J. B., & Milkman, K. L. (2016). Identity in Charitable Giving. *Management Science*, *64*(2), 845-859. Retrieved June 8, 2019, from https://site.stanford.edu/sites/default/files/kesslermilkman_identityincharitablegiving.pdf.
[94] Tybout, A. M., & Yalch, R. F. (1980). The Effect of Experience: A Matter of Salience?. *Journal of Consumer Research*, *6*(4), 406-413.
[95] Godin, S. (2013, July 26). "People Like Us Do Things like This." Retrieved June 13, 2019, from https://seths.blog/2013/07/people-like-us-do-stuff-like-this/.
[96] Barrett, B. (2016, March 27). Netflix's Grand, Daring, Maybe Crazy Plan to Conquer the World. *Wired*. Retrieved June 13, 2019, from https://www.wired.com/2016/03/netflixs-grand-maybe-crazy-plan-conquer-world/ .
[97] Ellinger, N. (2018, March 21). How Donors Choose Among Nonprofits: The Role of Identity. Retrieved June 15, 2019, from http://agitator.thedonorvoice.com/how-donors-choose-among-nonprofits-the-role-of-identity/.
[98] Drezner, N. D. (2018). Philanthropic mirroring: Exploring identity-based fundraising in higher education. *The Journal of Higher Education*, *89*(3), 261-293. Retrieved June 8, 2019, from https://www.tandfonline.com/doi/abs/10.1080/00221546.2017.1368818.
[99] Green, D. (2019, February 14). From Saturation to Success: Acquisition Breakthroughs! Lecture presented at 2019 ANA DC Nonprofit Conference, Washington DC. Retrieved June 8, 2019, from https://www.ana.net/miccontent/show/id/er-dmanp-feb19-saturation-to-success.
[100] Kahan, D. M. (2017). Misconceptions, Misinformation, and the Logic of Identity-Protective Cognition. *Yale Law & Economics Research Paper No. 587*. Retrieved June 8, 2019, from https://papers.ssrn.com/sol3/papers.cfm?abstract_id=3046603.
[101] Sweeny, K., Melnyk, D., Miller, W., & Shepperd, J. A. (2010). Information Avoidance: Who, What, When, and Why. *Review of General Psychology*, *14*(4), 340-353. Retrieved June 8, 2019, from

https://www.researchgate.net/publication/232602336_Information_Avoidance_Who_What_When_and_Why.
[102] Feinberg, M., & Willer, R. (2015). From Gulf to Bridge: When Do Moral Arguments Facilitate Political Influence?. *Personality and Social Psychology Bulletin, 41*(12), 1665-1681. Retrieved June 8, 2019, from http://journals.sagepub.com/doi/abs/10.1177/0146167215607842.
[103] Althoff, T., & Leskovec, J. (2015, May). Donor Retention in Online Crowdfunding Communities: A Case Study of Donorschoose.org. In *Proceedings of the 24th International Conference on World Wide Web* (pp. 34-44). International World Wide Web Conferences Steering Committee. Retrieved June 8, 2019, from https://www.ncbi.nlm.nih.gov/pmc/articles/PMC4827627/.
[104] Perkins, J. (2007, November 8). MySpace.com: A Place for Donors? Retrieved June 8, 2019, from http://www.care2services.com/care2blog/myspacecom-a-place-for-donors.
[105] Benton, J. (2016, March 17). NPR Decides It Won't Promote Its Podcasts or NPR One on Air. *Nieman Lab*. Retrieved June 8, 2019, from https://www.niemanlab.org/2016/03/npr-decides-it-wont-promote-its-podcasts-or-npr-one-on-air/.
[106] Levitt, T. (1960, July/August). Marketing Myopia. Harvard Business Review, 3-13.
[107] National Public Radio. (2018, March 28). *NPR Maintains Highest Ratings Ever* [Press release]. Retrieved June 15, 2019, from https://www.npr.org/about-npr/597590072/npr-maintains-highest-ratings-ever.
[108] Ellinger, N. (2017, April 20). Three off-ramps from the volume hamster wheel. Retrieved June 15, 2019, from http://agitator.thedonorvoice.com/three-off-ramps-from-the-volume-hamster-wheel/.
[109] Roman, E. (2017, January 24). Don't Take It Personally, But Innovators Are Done With Personas. *CMO*. Retrieved June 13, 2019, from https://www.cmo.com/features/articles/2017/1/16/why-personas-dont-work-and-what-innovators-are-doing-differently.html.
[110] Wachter-Boettcher, S. (2017). Technically Wrong: Sexist apps, biased algorithms, and other threats of toxic tech. New York: W.W. Norton & Company.
[111] Starbuck, W., & Farjoun, M. (Eds.). (2009). *Organization at the Limit: Lessons from the Columbia Disaster*. John Wiley & Sons.
[112] Schulman, K. (2014, November 06). How Nonprofits Can Stop Donor Churn before It Starts. Retrieved June 8, 2019, from https://www.slideshare.net/kschulman14/how-nonprofits-can-stop-donor-churn-before-it-starts.
[113] Ellenberg, J. (2015). *How Not to be Wrong: The Power of Mathematical Thinking.* NY, NY: Penguin Books.
[114] Wald, A. (1980). A Method of Estimating Plane Vulnerability based on Damage of Survivors, CRC 432, July 1980. *Center for Naval Analyses*.
[115] Rosenthal, H. (1986, July 16). Widow of Challenger Pilot Files First Damage Lawsuit In Shuttle Explosion. *Associated Press*. Retrieved June 8, 2019, from https://www.apnews.com/8db5a70bdf454ed28d24e3eeef177496.

[116] Petterson, E. (2017, October 24). Weinstein Co. Sued by Actress for Failing to Control Harvey. *Bloomberg News.* Retrieved June 8, 2019, from https://www.bloomberg.com/news/articles/2017-10-25/weinstein-co-sued-by-actress-for-failing-to-control-harvey.

[117] Duhigg, C. (2012). *The power of habit: Why we do what we do in life and business.* New York: Random House.

[118] Fried, J., & Hansson, D. H. (2010). *Rework.* New York, NY: Currency.

[119] Sargeant, A., & Jay, E. (2011). *Building Donor Loyalty: The Fundraisers Guide to Increasing Lifetime Value.* John Wiley & Sons.

[120] Slovic, P., Västfjäll, D., Erlandsson, A., & Gregory, R. (2017). Iconic Photographs and the Ebb and Flow of Empathic Response to Humanitarian Disasters. *Proceedings of the National Academy of Sciences*, *114*(4), 640-644. Retrieved June 9, 2019, from https://www.ncbi.nlm.nih.gov/pmc/articles/PMC5278443/.

[121] Eisensee, T., & Strömberg, D. (2007). News Droughts, News Floods, and US Disaster Relief. *The Quarterly Journal of Economics*, *122*(2), 693-728. Retrieved June 9, 2019, from https://econpapers.repec.org/article/oupqjecon/v_3a122_3ay_3a2007_3ai_3a2_3ap_3a693-728..htm

[122] Ingraham, C. (2015, October 15). Most Gun Owners Don't Belong to the NRA — and They Don't Agree With It Either. *Washington Post.* Retrieved June 9, 2019, from https://www.washingtonpost.com/news/wonk/wp/2015/10/15/most-gun-owners-dont-belong-to-the-nra-and-they-dont-agree-with-it-either/.

[123] Pew Research Center. (2018, September 18). Section 2: Opinions of Gun Owners, Non-Gun Owners. Retrieved June 9, 2019, from http://www.people-press.org/2013/03/12/section-2-opinions-of-gun-owners-non-gun-owners/.

[124] Parker, K., Horowitz, J. M., Igielnik, R., Oliphant, J. B., & Brown, A. (2017, July 10). America's Complex Relationship with Guns: Views on Gun Policy in the U.S. Retrieved June 9, 2019, from https://www.pewsocialtrends.org/2017/06/22/views-on-gun-policy/.

[125] Lacombe, M. (2018, February 23). This is How the NRA 'Politically Weaponized' Its Membership. *Washington Post.* Retrieved June 9, 2019, from https://www.washingtonpost.com/news/monkey-cage/wp/2017/10/11/this-is-how-the-nra-politically-weaponized-its-membership/.

[126] Paynter, B. (2018, November 28). Facebook Gave away $7 Million in Seconds on Giving Tuesday. *Fast Company.* Retrieved June 9, 2019, from https://www.fastcompany.com/90273801/facebook-gave-away-7-million-in-seconds-on-giving-tuesday.

[127] Facebook. (n.d.). Fundraising and Donations on Facebook. Retrieved June 9, 2019, from https://www.facebook.com/help/1640008462980459.

[128] Google. (n.d.). FAQs - Donations Help. Retrieved June 9, 2019, from https://support.google.com/donations/answer/7567250?hl=en.

---

[129] Haynes, E. (2019, February 7). Facebook Plans New Instagram Fundraising Tool. *Chronicle of Philanthropy*. Retrieved June 9, 2019, from https://www.philanthropy.com/article/Facebook-Plans-New-Instagram/245635.
[130] Angwin, J., Varner, M., & Tobin, A. (2019, March 09). Facebook Enabled Advertisers to Reach 'Jew Haters'. Retrieved June 9, 2019, from https://www.propublica.org/article/facebook-enabled-advertisers-to-reach-jew-haters.
[131] Limp, D. (2016, August 24). Introducing the Kindle Reading Fund. Retrieved June 9, 2019, from https://blog.aboutamazon.com/community/introducing-the-kindle-reading-fund.
[132] Gershgorn, D. (2016, August 23). The Unbreakable Genius of Mark Zuckerberg. *Popular Science*. Retrieved June 9, 2019, from https://www.popsci.com/mark-zuckerberg.
[133] Elgan, M. (2016, February 15). The Surprising Truth about Facebook's Internet.org. *Computer World*. Retrieved June 9, 2019, from https://www.computerworld.com/article/3032646/internet/the-surprising-truth-about-facebooks-internetorg.html
[134] Williams, M. (2015, November 24). Google's Loon Balloons Now Fly for Three Months. *Computer World*. Retrieved June 9, 2019, from https://www.computerworld.com/article/3008459/internet/googles-loon-balloons-now-fly-for-three-months.html.
[135] Strom, S., & Helft, M. (2011, January 30). Google Finds It Hard to Reinvent Philanthropy. New York Times. Retrieved June 10, 2019, from https://www.nytimes.com/2011/01/30/business/30charity.html.
[136] Eliot, T.S. *The Love Song of J. Alfred Prufrock*, 1915.
[137] Gevelber, L. (2015, December). Why Consumer Intent Is More Powerful Than Demographics. Retrieved June 10, 2019, from https://www.thinkwithgoogle.com/marketing-resources/micro-moments/why-consumer-intent-more-powerful-than-demographics/.
[138] McCullough, D. G. (2017). *The Johnstown Flood*. New York, NY: Simon & Schuster Paperbacks.
[139] World Digital Library. (n.d.). Johnstown, Pennsylvania, 1904. Retrieved June 10, 2019, from https://www.wdl.org/en/item/9571/.
[140] MacLaughlin, S. (2017, September 19). Giving When Disaster Strikes. *Huffington Post*. Retrieved June 10, 2019, from https://www.huffpost.com/entry/giving-when-disaster-strikes_b_59c0e106e4b0c3e70e742793.
[141] Sullivan, P. (2016, April 26). Notre-Dame Donation Backlash Raises Debate: What's Worthy of Philanthropy? *New York Times*. Retrieved June 10, 2019, from https://www.nytimes.com/2019/04/26/your-money/notre-dame-donation-backlash-philanthropy.html.
[142] Edge Research. (2018). *Reactive Giving Understanding the Surge in Cause-Related Giving* (Rep.). Retrieved June 10, 2019, from http://www.edgeresearch.com/reactive-giving/.

---

[143] Edge Research. (2018). *Reactive Giving Understanding the Surge in Cause-Related Giving* (Rep.). Retrieved June 10, 2019, from http://www.edgeresearch.com/reactive-giving/.
[144] Albrecht, L. (2018, January 10). Shark Charities Flooded with Donations after Trump Says He Hopes Sharks Die. *MarketWatch*. Retrieved June 10, 2019, from https://www.marketwatch.com/story/shark-charities-flooded-with-donations-after-trump-says-he-hopes-sharks-die-2018-01-23.
[145] Guynn, J. (2018, June 18). Facebook Fundraiser to Help Immigrant Children Tops $20 Million with Global Donations. *USA Today*. Retrieved June 10, 2019, from https://www.usatoday.com/story/tech/2018/06/18/facebook-campaign-raising-millions-reunite-immigrants-children/712502002/.
[146] Tversky, A., & Kahneman, D. (1973). Availability: A Heuristic for Judging Frequency and Probability. *Cognitive Psychology*, *5*(2), 207-232.
[147] Frechete, M. (2016, December 28). The Availability Heuristic and Marketing. Retrieved June 10, 2019, from http://www.digitalmktggeek.com/the-availability-heuristic-bias/.
[148] Read, J. D. (1995). The Availability Heuristic in Person Identification: The Sometimes Misleading Consequences of Enhanced Contextual Information. *Applied Cognitive Psychology*, 9(2), 91-121. . doi:10.1002/acp.2350090202.
[149] Edge Research. (2018). *Reactive Giving Understanding the Surge in Cause-Related Giving* (Rep.). Retrieved June 10, 2019, from http://www.edgeresearch.com/reactive-giving/.
[150] Tang, J., Zhang, Y., Sun, J., Rao, J., Yu, W., Chen, Y., & Fong, A. C. M. (2011). Quantitative study of individual emotional states in social networks. *IEEE Transactions on Affective Computing*, *3*(2), 132-144. .). Retrieved June 10, 2019, from http://keg.cs.tsinghua.edu.cn/jietang/publications/TAC11-Tang-et-al-social-emotion-analysis.pdf
[151] Dooley, R. (2017, July 18). Sex, Lies, and Our Secret Motivators. Retrieved June 10, 2019, from https://www.neurosciencemarketing.com/blog/articles/sex-lies.htm.
[152] Manucia, G. K., Baumann, D. J., & Cialdini, R. B. (1984). Mood influences on helping: Direct effects or side effects?. *Journal of personality and social psychology*, *46*(2), 357. Retrieved June 10, 2019, from http://psycnet.apa.org/doi/10.1037/0022-3514.46.2.357,
[153] Merrill, L., & Koutmeridou, K. (2018, August). *Applying Behavioral Science to Fundraising*. Live performance in Bridge Conference, Washington, DC. Retrieved June 10, 2019, from https://imgsvr.eventrebels.com/ERImg/02/30/25/4185501/133957-3-45701.pdf.
[154] Schneider, C. R., Zaval, L., Weber, E. U., & Markowitz, E. M. (2017). The Influence of Anticipated Pride and Guilt on Pro-Environmental Decision Making. *PLOS One*, *12*(11), e0188781. Retrieved June 10, 2019, from https://journals.plos.org/plosone/article?id=10.1371/journal.pone.0188781.

---

[155] Loeb, P. as quoted in Craver, R. (2018, September 06). Raging All The Way To The Bank. Retrieved June 13, 2019, from https://agitator.thedonorvoice.com/raging-all-the-way-to-the-bank/.
[156] McCord, J., Puzzo, J., & Copley, C. (Writers). (2018, February). *Unexpected Disruptions: When Disaster Strikes*. Live performance in DMANF 2018 Nonprofit Conference, Washington, DC. Retrieved June 10, 2019, from http://dmafiles.org/wp-content/uploads/2018/02/Unexpected-Disruptions-From-Disasters.pdf.
[157] Okada, A., Ishida, Y., & Yamauchi, N. (2018). In Prosperity Prepare for Adversity: Use of Social Media for Nonprofit Fundraising in Times of Disaster. In *Innovative Perspectives on Public Administration in the Digital Age* (pp. 42-64). IGI Global.
[158] Uehlein, M. (2016, February 22). How the Human Rights Campaign Made History at the Supreme Court - A Multichannel Case Study. Retrieved June 10, 2019, from https://medium.com/@mikeuehlein/how-the-human-rights-campaign-made-history-at-the-supreme-court-a-multichannel-case-study-12e91908d92d.
[159] Internal Revenue Service. (2018, December 12). Lobbying. Retrieved June 10, 2019, from https://www.irs.gov/Charities-&-Non-Profits/Lobbying.
[160] Internal Revenue Service. (2019, February 25). Measuring Lobbying Activity: Expenditure Test. Retrieved June 10, 2019, from https://www.irs.gov/charities-non-profits/measuring-lobbying-activity-expenditure-test.
[161] Lee, Y. H., & Hsieh, G. (2013, April). Does Slacktivism Hurt Activism?: The Effects of Moral Balancing and Consistency in Online Activism. In *Proceedings of the SIGCHI Conference on Human Factors in Computing Systems* (pp. 811-820). ACM. Retrieved June 10, 2019, from http://faculty.washington.edu/garyhs/docs/lee-chi2013-slacktivism.pdf.
[162] Daigneault, S., Davis, M., & Sybrant, M. (2011). *Connecting Online Advocacy and Fundraising* (Rep.). Retrieved June 10, 2019, from https://www.blackbaud.com/files/resources/downloads/WhitePaper_ConnectingOnlineAdvocacyAndFundraising.pdf.
[163] Kristofferson, K., White, K., & Peloza, J. (2013). The Nature of Slacktivism: How the Social Observability of an Initial Act of Token Support Affects Subsequent Prosocial Action. *Journal of Consumer Research*, *40*(6), 1149-1166. Retrieved June 10, 2019, from http://jcr.oxfordjournals.org/content/40/6/1149.
[164] Lacetera, N., Macis, M., & Mele, A. (2016). Viral Altruism? Charitable Giving and Social Contagion in Online Networks. *Sociological Science*, *3*. Retrieved June 10, 2019, from https://www.sociologicalscience.com/download/vol-3/march/SocSci_v3_202to238.pdf.
[165] Hutchinson, A. (2015, October 25). How Salad Can Make Us Fat. *New York Times*. Retrieved June 10, 2019, from https://www.nytimes.com/2015/10/25/opinion/sunday/how-salad-can-make-us-fat.html.
[166] Young, L., Chakroff, A., & Tom, J. (2012). Doing Good Leads to More Good: The Reinforcing Power of a Moral Self-concept. *Review of Philosophy and Psychology*,

3(3), 325-334. Retrieved June 10, 2019, from http://moralitylab.bc.edu/wp-content/uploads/2011/10/YoungChakroffTom.pdf.

[167] Council for Aid to Education. (2018, February 6). *Colleges and Universities Raised $43.60 Billion in 2017* [Press release]. Retrieved June 10, 2019, from https://cae.org/images/uploads/pdf/VSE-2017-Press-Release.pdf.

[168] Elliott, M. (2017, November 17). The 15 Biggest College Alumni Networks in the U.S. Retrieved June 10, 2019, from https://www.cheatsheet.com/money-career/biggest-college-alumni-networks-in-us.html/.

[169] National Highway Traffic Safety Administration. (2018). 2017 Data: Alcohol-Impaired Driving (Rep.). Washington, DC: NHTSA. DOT HS 812 630. Retrieved June 10, 2019, from https://crashstats.nhtsa.dot.gov/Api/Public/ViewPublication/812630.

[170] Winfrey, O. (Writer). (2008). *Oprah Winfrey's Speech at Stanford's Commencement*. Live performance in Stanford, CA.

[171] Shotton, R. (2018). *The Choice Factory: 25 Behavioural Biases That Influence What We Buy*. Petersfield, Hampshire: Harriman House.

[172] Howell, J. L., & Shepperd, J. A. (2012). Behavioral Obligation and Information Avoidance. *Annals of Behavioral Medicine*, *45*(2), 258-263. Retrieved June 10, 2019, from https://www.researchgate.net/publication/233887883_Behavioral_Obligation_and_Information_Avoidance.

[173] Sorkin, A. (Writer). (2001, November 7). War Crimes [Television series episode]. *The West Wing*. New York, NY: NBC.

[174] Sørum, B. (2014, July 09). Slides and Resources from IoF National Convention: "From Good Intentions to More Web Donations." Retrieved June 10, 2019, from https://beateinenglish.wordpress.com/2014/06/18/slides-and-resources-from-iof-national-convention-from-good-intentions-to-more-web-donations/,

[175] Except that it was in Norwegian, which I don't speak. Thanks Sørum, B. (2014, July 09). Slides and Resources from IoF National Convention: "From Good Intentions to More Web Donations." Retrieved June 10, 2019, from https://beateinenglish.wordpress.com/2014/06/18/slides-and-resources-from-iof-national-convention-from-good-intentions-to-more-web-donations/ (and Google Translate!).

[176] Giddens, J. (2018, May 11). How an End-of-Article Call-to-Action Affects Donor Conversion Rate. Experiment ID: #8983. Retrieved June 10, 2019, from https://www.nextafter.com/research/2018/05/how-an-end-of-article-call-to-action-affects-donor-conversion-rate/.

[177] Gaines, C. (2018, May 17). How Cutting through the Clutter with a Content Offer Can Impact Name Conversion. Experiment ID: #9027. Retrieved June 10, 2019, from https://www.nextafter.com/research/2018/05/how-cutting-through-the-clutter-with-a-content-offer-can-impact-name-conversion/.

[178] Gaines, C. (2018, May 12). How Using an Inline Form for a Particular Kind of Offer on the Homepage Impacts Name Conversion. Experiment ID: #8978. Retrieved

June 10, 2019, from https://www.nextafter.com/research/2018/05/how-using-an-inline-form-for-a-particular-kind-of-offer-on-the-homepage-impacts-name-conversion/.
[179] Content Marketing Institute. (n.d.). What is Content Marketing? Retrieved June 10, 2019, from https://contentmarketinginstitute.com/what-is-content-marketing/.
[180] Guéguen, N., & Jacob, C. (2001). Fund-raising on the Web: The Effect of an Electronic Foot-in-the-Door on Donation. *CyberPsychology & Behavior*, *4*(6), 705-709. Retrieved June 10, 2019, https://pdfs.semanticscholar.org/3b33/3339ff15d901ad27a453b10bbe35b5996e00.pdf.
[181] M+R. (2019). *2019 Nonprofit Benchmarks*. Retrieved June 6, 2019, from https://mrbenchmarks.com/.
[182] Delany, C. (2018, December 14). This Election Cycle, The DCCC Showed Why We Pay to Build Email Lists. Retrieved June 10, 2019, from http://www.epolitics.com/2018/12/14/this-election-cycle-the-dccc-showed-why-we-pay-to-build-email-lists/.
[183] Wallace, N (@nicoleCOP). (2018, April 12). Digital-ad campaigns don't have to be expensive. Kennedy Center tested the waters, spending $1,979 on ads that brought in 757 email addresses. During 35 Days of Giving campaign, people on that list gave $6,105. #18NTC [Tweet]. https://twitter.com/nicolecop/status/984524529065218051.
[184] Miller, K. L. (2013). *Content Marketing for Nonprofits: A Communications Map for Engaging Your Community, Becoming a Favorite Cause, and Raising More Money*. San Francisco, CA: Jossey-Bass. pg. 105.
[185] Thompson, D. (2017). *Hit Makers: The Science of Popularity in an Age of Distraction*. New York, NY: Penguin Press.
[186] Barsch, J. D., & Isaacs, S. L. (2017). *The Google Ad Grants Playbook: The Definitive Guide to Breakthrough Nonprofit Growth ... on Googles Dime*. Rapid City, SD: Josh Barsch/Steve L. Isaacs.
[187] Sloane, G. (2017, July 11). Facebook Unleashes Ads on Messenger as Main App Starts Running out of Space. *Ad Age*. Retrieved June 10, 2019, from https://adage.com/article/digital/facebook-messenger-start-showing-ads-u-s-homescreens/309710/.
[188] Rodriguez, J. (2018, May 24). Facebook Ads CPM, CPC, & CTR Benchmarks for Q1 2018. Retrieved June 11, 2019, from https://blog.adstage.io/2018/05/24/facebook-ads-q1-2018.
[189] Price, R. (2018, July 25). Facebook's User Growth has Stalled, or Gone in Reverse, in Its Most Profitable Markets. Retrieved June 11, 2019, from https://www.businessinsider.com/facebook-maus-daus-stalled-us-shrinking-europe-2018-7.
[190] Hopper, K. (2019, January 31). 2018 EOY Fundraising: The Good, the Bad, and the Meh. Retrieved June 11, 2019, from https://www.mrss.com/lab/2018-eoy-fundraising-the-good-the-bad-and-the-meh/.
[191] Nielsen. (2018). *The Nielsen Total Audience Report Q1 2018*(Rep.). Retrieved June 11, 2019, from http://www.nielsen.com/content/dam/corporate/us/en/reports-downloads/2018-reports/q1-2018-total-audience-report.pdf.

---

[192] Sluis, S. (2018, May 10). Digital Ad Market Soars To $88 Billion, Facebook And Google Contribute 90% Of Growth. Retrieved June 11, 2019, from https://adexchanger.com/online-advertising/digital-ad-market-soars-to-88-billion-facebook-and-google-contribute-90-of-growth/.

[193] NextAfter. (2018, August 29). *Cracking the Code of Facebook Fundraising.* Webinar. Retrieved June 11, 2019, from https://www.nextafter.com/events/cracking-the-code-of-facebook-fundraising/.

[194] Dastin, J. (2018, October 9). Amazon Scraps Secret AI Recruiting Tool that Showed Bias against Women. *Reuters*. Retrieved June 11, 2019, from https://www.reuters.com/article/us-amazon-com-jobs-automation-insight/amazon-scraps-secret-ai-recruiting-tool-that-showed-bias-against-women-idUSKCN1MK08G .

[195] Care2. (2017). *How World Animal Protection Reached Highly Engaged Donors Who Continue to Give* (Rep.). Retrieved June 11, 2019, from http://www.care2services.com/wap-care2-case-study.

[196] Cialdini, R. B. (1993). *Influence: The Psychology of Persuasion*. New York: Quill.

[197] Ariely, D., & Loewenstein, G. (2006). The Heat of the Moment: The Effect of Sexual Arousal on Sexual Decision Making. *Journal of Behavioral Decision Making, 19*(2), 87-98. Retrieved June 11, 2019, from http://people.duke.edu/~dandan/webfiles/PapersPI/Sexual%20Arousal%20and%20Decision%20making.pdf. And yes, they describe the procedure for arousal for those curious about such things.

[198] De Pelsmacker, P., Geuens, M., & Anckaert, P. (2002). Media Context and Advertising Effectiveness: The Role of Context Appreciation and Context/Ad Similarity. *Journal of Advertising*, *31*(2), 49-61. Retrieved June 11, 2019, from https://www.tandfonline.com/doi/abs/10.1080/00913367.2002.10673666.

[199] Yi, Y. (1990). Cognitive and Affective Priming Effects of the Context for Print Advertisements. *Journal of Advertising*, *19*(2), 40-48. Retrieved June 11, 2019, from https://www.tandfonline.com/doi/abs/10.1080/00913367.1990.10673186.

[200] Moorman, M., Neijens, P. C., & Smit, E. G. (2002). The Effects of Magazine-Induced Psychological Responses and Thematic Congruence on Memory and Attitude toward the Ad in a Real-Life Setting. *Journal of Advertising*, *31*(4), 27-40. Retrieved June 11, 2019, from https://www.tandfonline.com/doi/abs/10.1080/00913367.2002.10673683.

[201] Lord, K. R., Burnkrant, R. E., & Unnava, H. R. (2001). The Effects of Program-Induced Mood States on Memory for Commercial Information. *Journal of Current Issues & Research in Advertising*, *23*(1), 1-15. Retrieved June 11, 2019, from https://www.tandfonline.com/doi/abs/10.1080/10641734.2001.10505110,

[202] Deppe, M., Schwindt, W., Kraemer, J., Kugel, H., Plassmann, H., Kenning, P., & Ringelstein, E. B. (2005). Evidence for a Neural Correlate of a Framing Effect: Bias-Specific Activity in The Ventromedial Prefrontal Cortex during Credibility Judgments. *Brain Research Bulletin*, *67*(5), 413-421. Retrieved June 11, 2019, from https://www.ncbi.nlm.nih.gov/pubmed/16216688.

---

[203] Weingarten, G. (2007, April 8). Pearls Before Breakfast: Can One of the Nation's Great Musicians Cut through the Fog of a D.C. Rush Hour? Let's Find out. *Washington Post*. Retrieved June 12, 2019, from http://www.washingtonpost.com/wp-dyn/content/article/2007/04/04/AR2007040401721_pf.html.
[204] Maheshwari, S. (2018, July 20). Revealed: The People Behind an Anti-Breitbart Twitter Account. *New York Times*. Retrieved June 12, 2019, from https://www.nytimes.com/2018/07/20/business/media/sleeping-giants-breitbart-twitter.html,
[205] Maheshwari, S. (2017, March 26). Brands Try to Blacklist Breitbart, but Ads Slip Through Anyway. *New York Times*. Retrieved June 12, 2019, from https://www.nytimes.com/2017/03/26/business/media/breitbart-advertising-blacklist.html.
[206] Maheshwari, S., & Wakabayashi, D. (2017, March 22). AT&T and Johnson & Johnson Pull Ads From YouTube. *New York Times*. Retrieved June 12, 2019, from https://www.nytimes.com/2017/03/22/business/atampt-and-johnson-amp-johnson-pull-ads-from-youtube-amid-hate-speech-concerns.html.
[207] Nicas, J. (2017, March 24). Google's YouTube Has Continued Showing Brands' Ads With Racist and Other Objectionable Videos. *Wall Street Journal*. Retrieved June 12, 2019, from https://www.wsj.com/articles/googles-youtube-has-continued-showing-brands-ads-with-racist-and-other-objectionable-videos-1490380551.
[208] Genuardi, P. (2019, June 12). Re: Random Question [Letter to N. Ellinger].
[209] Genuardi, P. (2019, June 12). Re: Random Question [Letter to N. Ellinger].
[210] This is because of a heady mix of social pressure, laws, genetic selection for those who care for their children, and sleeplessness-induced Stockholm syndrome. A not-insubstantial part of this book was written between when my daughter got up and when my daughter should get up. I'm editing this footnote at 3:52 A.M.
[211] Ipcar, M. (2014, August 20). Publishers: 'Look beyond native advertising to native advocacy'. *Digiday*. Retrieved June 12, 2019, from https://digiday.com/media/publishers-look-beyond-native-advertising-native-advocacy/.
[212] Alliance for Audited Media. (2018, December 31). Total Circ for Consumer Magazines. Retrieved June 12, 2019, from http://abcas3.auditedmedia.com/ecirc/magtitlesearch.asp.
[213] Foley, J. (Director). (1992). *Glengarry Glen Ross* [Motion picture]. United States: New Line Cinema.
[214] Alter, A. L., & Oppenheimer, D. M. (2009). Uniting the Tribes of Fluency to Form a Metacognitive Nation. *Personality and Social Psychology Review, 13*(3), 219-235. doi:10.1177/1088868309341564. Retrieved June 12, 2019, from http://pages.stern.nyu.edu/~aalter/tribes.pdf.
[215] Reber, R., Winkielman, P., & Schwarz, N. (1998). Effects of Perceptual Fluency on Affective Judgments. *Psychological Science*, *9*(1), 45-48.Retrieved June 12, 2019, from http://psy2.ucsd.edu/~pwinkiel/reber-winkielman-schwarz-Fluency-PS-1998.pdf.

---

[216] Jacoby, L. L., & Brooks, L. R. (1984). Nonanalytic Cognition: Memory, Perception, and Concept Learning. In *Psychology of Learning and Motivation* (Vol. 18, pp. 1-47). Academic Press. Retrieved June 12, 2019, from http://www.sciencedirect.com/science/article/pii/S0079742108603588.
[217] Alter, A. L., & Oppenheimer, D. M. (2006). Predicting Short-Term Stock Fluctuations by Using Processing Fluency. *Proceedings of the National Academy of Sciences, 103*(24), 9369-9372. Retrieved June 12, 2019, from http://pages.stern.nyu.edu/~aalter/PNAS.pdf.
[218] Laham, S. M., Koval, P., & Alter, A. L. (2012). The Name-Pronunciation Effect: Why People like Mr. Smith more than Mr. Colquhoun. *Journal of Experimental Social Psychology, 48*(3), 752-756. Retrieved June 12, 2019, from https://ppw.kuleuven.be/okp/_pdf/Laham2012TNPEW.pdf.
[219] New York Times. (2014, January 17). The New York Times's Most Visited Content of 2013. Retrieved June 12, 2019, from https://www.nytco.com/press/the-new-york-timess-most-visited-content-of-2013/.
[220] Rudd, M., Aaker, J., & Norton, M. I. (2014). Getting the Most out of Giving: Concretely Framing a Prosocial Goal Maximizes Happiness. *Journal of Experimental Social Psychology, 54*, 11-24. doi:10.1016/j.jesp.2014.04.002. Retrieved June 12, 2019, from https://dash.harvard.edu/bitstream/handle/1/12534961/rudd,aaker,norton_getting-the-most-out-of-giving.pdf?sequence=3.
[221] Loftus, E. F., & Palmer, J. C. (1974). Reconstruction of Automobile Destruction: An Example of the Interaction between Language and Memory. *Journal of Verbal Learning and Verbal Behavior, 13*(5), 585-589. Retrieved June 12, 2019, from https://webfiles.uci.edu/eloftus/LoftusPalmer74.pdf.
[222] Heath, C., & Heath, D. (2007). *Made to Stick: Why Some Ideas Survive and Others Die*. New York, NY: Random House.
[223] Regan, D. T. (1971). Effects of a Favor and Liking on Compliance. *Journal of Experimental Social Psychology*, 7(6), 627-639.
[224] As quoted in Wallis, D. (2012, November 8). Getting into a Benefactor's Head. *New York Times*. Retrieved June 12, 2019 from https://www.nytimes.com/2012/11/09/giving/understanding-donor-behavior-to-increase-contributions.html.
[225] Flynn, F. J. (2003). What Have You Done for Me Lately? Temporal Adjustments to Favor Evaluations. *Organizational Behavior and Human Decision Processes, 91*(1), 38-50.
[226] Chuan, A., Kessler, J. B., & Milkman, K. L. (2018). Field Study of Charitable Giving Reveals that Reciprocity Decays over Time. *Proceedings of the National Academy of Sciences, 115*(8), 1766-1771. Retrieved June 12, 2019 from http://www.pnas.org/content/early/2018/02/06/1708293115.
[227] Burk, P. (2003). *Donor-Centered Fundraising: How to Hold on to Your Donors and Raise Much More Money*. Burk and Associates.

---

[228] Grow, P. (2011, August 31). Could You Borrow the Smartest Thing I Ever Did? Retrieved June 13, 2019, from https://www.pamelagrow.com/1682/could-you-borrow-the-smartest-thing-i-ever-did/
[229] Burnett, K., & Fowler, J. (2016). The Donor's Choice: An Early Fundraising Preference Service That's Worked Brilliantly since 1986. Retrieved June 12, 2019, from http://www.kenburnett.com/Blog64thedonorschoice.html.
[230] Craver, R. M. (2014). *Retention Fundraising: The New Art and Science of Keeping Your Donors for Life*. Medfield, MA: Emerson & Church.
[231] Howard, J. (1998, October 12). 27 Nashville Predators. *Sports Illustrated*. Retrieved June 12, 2019, from http://www.si.com/vault/1998/10/12/250208/27-nashville-predators .
[232] Shpigel, B. (2017, May 22). From Hockey 101 to a Ph.D in Nashville. *New York Times*. Retrieved June 12, 2019, from https://www.nytimes.com/2017/05/22/sports/hockey/from-hockey-101-in-nashville-to-a-phd-with-predators.html.
[233] Leipold, C. (2008). *Hockey Tonk: The Amazing Story of the Nashville Predators*. Nashville, TN: Thomas Nelson.
[234] Smith, R. W., & Schwarz, N. (2012). When Promoting a Charity Can Hurt Charitable Giving: A Metacognitive Analysis. *Journal of Consumer Psychology*, *22*(4), 558-564. Retrieved June 12, 2019, from https://dornsife.usc.edu/assets/sites/780/docs/12_jcp_smith__schwarz_charity.pdf.
[235] Hudson, D. (2014, July 10). What's a Welcome Series email worth? Retrieved June 13, 2019, from http://powerthruconsulting.com/case-studies/whats-email-welcome-series-worth/.
[236] Althoff, T., & Leskovec, J. (2015, May). Donor Retention in Online Crowdfunding Communities: A Case Study of Donorschoose.org. In *Proceedings of the 24th International Conference on World Wide Web* (pp. 34-44). International World Wide Web Conferences Steering Committee. Retrieved June 13, 2019, from https://www.ncbi.nlm.nih.gov/pmc/articles/PMC4827627/.
[237] WETA. (2019, January 14). What's a Donor Worth? WETA Utilizes Lifetime Value Analysis to Understand Passport Impact. Retrieved June 13, 2019, from http://www.pbs.org/development/2019/01/14/whats-a-donor-worth-weta-utilizes-lifetime-value-analysis-to-understand-passport-impact/.
[238] Jewison, N. (Director). (1991). *Other People's Money* [Motion picture]. United States: Warner Bros.
[239] Kiva. (2012). Kiva 2011 Annual Report (Rep.). Retrieved June 13, 2019, from https://www.kiva.org/cms/kiva-annual-report-2011.pdf.
[240] Kiva. (2019). Kiva 2018 Annual Report (Rep.). Retrieved June 13, 2019, from https://assets.brandfolder.com/pniefv-3n0hzc-29nvzj/original/Kiva%20AR2018%20v4-2%20highres.pdf.
[241] DonorsChoose.org. (2016). School Year in Review: 2015-2016. Retrieved June 13, 2019, from https://secure.donorschoose.org/about/year-in-review-2016.html.

---

[242] McLennan, K. (2018, August 09). Highlights from our 2017–2018 School Year in Review. Retrieved June 13, 2019, from https://www.donorschoose.org/blog/highlights-from-our-2017-2018-school-year-in-review/.
[243] Fundraising Effectiveness Project. (2019). 2018 Fundraising Effectiveness Survey Report. http://afpfep.org/reports/.
[244] American Red Cross. (2017, December 13). Red Cross Issues Hurricane Harvey Progress Report. Retrieved from https://www.redcross.org/about-us/news-and-events/news/Red-Cross-Issues-Hurricane-Harvey-Progress-Report.html.
[245] GoFundMe. (n.d.). About GoFundMe. Retrieved June 13, 2019, from https://www.gofundme.com/about-us.
[246] Jenq, C., Pan, J., & Theseira, W. (2015). Beauty, Weight, and Skin Color in Charitable Giving. *Journal of Economic Behavior & Organization*, *119*, 234-253. Retrieved June 13, 2019, from http://www.sciencedirect.com/science/article/pii/S0167268115001675.
[247] Edelman, B., Luca, M., & Svirsky, D. (2017). Racial Discrimination in the Sharing Economy: Evidence from a Field Experiment. *American Economic Journal: Applied Economics*, *9*(2), 1-22. Retrieved June 13, 2019, from https://www.aeaweb.org/articles?id=10.1257/app.20160213.
[248] Moleskis, M., Alegre, I., & Canela, M. A. (2018). Crowdfunding Entrepreneurial or Humanitarian Needs? The Influence of Signals and Biases on Decisions. *Nonprofit and Voluntary Sector Quarterly*, 0899764018802367. Retrieved June 13, 2019, from https://journals.sagepub.com/doi/abs/10.1177/0899764018802367
[249] Karlan, D., & Wood, D. H. (2017). The Effect of Effectiveness: Donor Response to Aid Effectiveness in a Direct Mail Fundraising Experiment. *Journal of Behavioral and Experimental Economics*, *66*, 1-8. Retrieved June 13, 2019, from http://papers.ssrn.com/sol3/papers.cfm?abstract_id=2421943.
[250] Palotta, D. (Writer). (2013, May 17). Giving It Away, Part 3: Do We Have the Wrong Idea About Charity? [Radio series episode]. In *TED Radio Hour*. NPR. Retrieved June 13, 2019, from https://www.npr.org/2013/07/05/181693499/do-we-have-the-wrong-idea-about-charity.
[251] Gneezy, U., Keenan, E. A., & Gneezy, A. (2014). Avoiding Overhead Aversion in Charity. *Science*, *346*(6209), 632-635. Retrieved June 13, 2019, from http://rady.ucsd.edu/docs/Science-2014-Gneezy-632-5.pdf.
[252] Gregory, A. G., & Howard, D. (2009, Fall). The Nonprofit Starvation Cycle. *Stanford Social Innovation Review*. Retrieved June 13, 2019, from https://ssir.org/articles/entry/the_nonprofit_starvation_cycle.
[253] Caviola, L., Faulmüller, N., Everett, J. A., Savulescu, J., & Kahane, G. (2014). The Evaluability Bias in Charitable Giving: Saving Administration Costs or Saving Lives?. *Judgment and Decision Making*, *9*(4), 303. Retrieved June 13, 2019, from http://journal.sjdm.org/14/14402a/jdm14402a.pdf.
[254] The Charity Commission for England and Wales. (2018). *Trust in Charities, 2018: How the Public Views Charities, What This Means for the Sector, and How Trust can be Increased* (Rep.). Retrieved June 13, 2019, from

https://assets.publishing.service.gov.uk/government/uploads/system/uploads/attachment_data/file/723566/Charity_Commission_-_Trust_in_Charities_2018_-_Report.pdf.

[255] Yörük, B. K. (2016). Charity Ratings. *Journal of Economics & Management Strategy*, *25*(1), 195-219. Retrieved June 13, 2019, from https://pdfs.semanticscholar.org/87a3/2bd98bb5f31a1325336da8e25437082493f6.pdf.

[256] Kiva. (2018). *2017 Form 990*(Rep.). Retrieved June 13, 2019, from https://www.kiva.org/cms/kiva_microfunds_2017_tax_return-_public_disclosure_copy.pdf.

[257] Kiva. (2018). Kiva 2017 Annual Report (Rep.). Retrieved June 13, 2019, from https://assets.brandfolder.com/pd9l7g-arj040-fwfyop/original/Kiva%202017%20Annual%20Report%20-%20Large_Updated.pdf.

[258] Gneezy, U., Keenan, E. A., & Gneezy, A. (2014). Avoiding Overhead Aversion in Charity. *Science*, *346*(6209), 632-635. Retrieved June 13, 2019, from http://rady.ucsd.edu/docs/Science-2014-Gneezy-632-5.pdf.

[259] Charity: water. (n.d.). The 100% Model. Retrieved June 13, 2019, from https://www.charitywater.org/our-approach/100-percent-model/.

[260] Charity: water. (2008). *Annual Report 2007*(Rep.). Retrieved June 13, 2019, from https://assets.ctfassets.net/2w85ks0ylymt/60E5Lyn1UQE8KMiYcsukCQ/59cfd42b3b9e70960b73ae147ce6ba6b/cw_07_annual_report.pdf.

[261] Charity: water. (2013). *Annual Report 2012*(Rep.). Retrieved June 13, 2019, from https://archive.charitywater.org/annual-report/12/.

[262] Charity: water. (2018). *Annual Report 2017*(Rep.). Retrieved June 13, 2019, from https://assets.ctfassets.net/2w85ks0ylymt/7eQgn7fKrSoKm4SQGSQoAk/3c5bea8efa6fea96a8ccdd85a19325c4/Annual_report_2017.pdf.

[263] Collins, J. C. (2005). *Good to great and the social sectors: why business thinking is not the answer*. New York, NY: HarperCollins.

[264] Eckel, C. C., Herberich, D. H., & Meer, J. (2017). A Field Experiment on Directed Giving at a Public University. *Journal of Behavioral and Experimental Economics*, *66*, 66-71.

[265] Helms, S., Scott, B., & Thornton, J. (2013). New Experimental Evidence on Charitable Gift Restrictions and Donor Behaviour. *Applied Economics Letters*, *20*(17), 1521-1526. Retrieved June 13, 2019, from https://ssrn.com/abstract=2093479 and http://dx.doi.org/10.2139/ssrn.2093479.

[266] Aknin, L. B., Dunn, E. W., Whillans, A. V., Grant, A. M., & Norton, M. I. (2013). Making a difference matters: Impact unlocks the emotional benefits of prosocial spending. *Journal of Economic Behavior & Organization*, *88*, 90-95. Retrieved June 13, 2019, from https://www.hbs.edu/faculty/Publication%20Files/aknin%20dunn%20whillans%20grant%20norton_e35af370-c8a9-42d0-ac4c-c5cd991161ef.pdf.

[267] Rote, C. (Writer). (2018, August). *Beyond A/B: Testing Thousands Of Communications At Once*. Live performance in Bridge Conference, Washington, DC. Retrieved June 13, 2019, from https://imgsvr.eventrebels.com/ERImg/02/30/25/4186072/133982-3-45701.pdf .

---

[268] Peters, K. (2015, September). How Soliciting the Donor's Opinion Affects the Gifts Acquired: Experiment ID: #2079. Retrieved June 13, 2019, from https://www.nextafter.com/research/2015/09/how-soliciting-the-donors-opinion-affects-conversion/.
[269] Peters, K. (2018, June). How Soliciting Donor Opinion during the Donation Process Impact Conversion: Experiment ID: #9091. Retrieved June 13, 2019, from https://www.nextafter.com/research/2018/06/how-soliciting-donor-opinion-during-the-donation-process-impact-conversion/.
[270] Moleskis, M., Alegre, I., & Canela, M. A. (2018). Crowdfunding Entrepreneurial or Humanitarian Needs? The Influence of Signals and Biases on Decisions. *Nonprofit and Voluntary Sector Quarterly*, 0899764018802367. Retrieved June 13, 2019, from https://journals.sagepub.com/doi/abs/10.1177/0899764018802367.
[271] Althoff, T., & Leskovec, J. (2015, May). Donor Retention in Online Crowdfunding Communities: A Case Study of donorschoose.org. In *Proceedings of the 24th international conference on world wide web* (pp. 34-44). International World Wide Web Conferences Steering Committee. Retrieved June 13, 2019, from https://www.ncbi.nlm.nih.gov/pmc/articles/PMC4827627/.
[272] Kessler, J. B., & Milkman, K. L. (2016). Identity in charitable giving. *Management Science*, *64*(2), 845-859. Retrieved June 8, 2019, from https://site.stanford.edu/sites/default/files/kesslermilkman_identityincharitablegiving.pdf.
[273] Shang, J., & Croson, R. (2006). The Impact of Social Comparisons on Nonprofit Fund Raising. In *Experiments Investigating Fundraising and Charitable Contributors* (pp. 143-156). Emerald Group Publishing Limited.
[274] Le, V. (2018, April 06). The Ethical Argument for General Operating Funds. Retrieved June 13, 2019, from http://nonprofitaf.com/2018/03/the-ethical-argument-for-general-operating-funds/.
[275] Brafman, O., & Beckstrom, R. A. (2008). *The Starfish and the Spider: The Unstoppable Power of Leaderless Organizations*. New York, NY: Penguin Books USA.
[276] Ellinger, N. (2003). Learning from Howard Dean. *Political Marketing Group Newsletter, 3*, 11-13.
[277] Heimans, J., & Timms, H. (2018). *New Power: How Anyone Can Persuade, Mobilize, and Succeed in our Chaotic, Connected Age*. New York, NY: Doubleday, 34.
[278] Johnson, K. (2018, February 12). Co-Founder of Black Lives Matter Talks Misconceptions and Plans for 2018. *Black Enterprise*. Retrieved June 13, 2019, from https://www.blackenterprise.com/co-founder-black-lives-matter-talks-blm-misconceptions-plans-2018/.
[279] Marguerite Casey Foundation. (2015, October 23). Alicia Garza: Black Lives Matter Proves that 'New Leaders Are Possible'. Retrieved June 13, 2019, from https://caseygrants.org/who-we-are/inside-mcf/alicia-garza-black-lives-matter-proves-that-new-leaders-are-possible/.

---

[280] Wikipedia. (2019, May 15). Encarta. Retrieved June 13, 2019, from https://en.wikipedia.org/wiki/Encarta.
[281] Pearl-McPhee, S. (2010, January 13). The Knit-Signal. Retrieved June 13, 2019, from https://www.yarnharlot.ca/2010/01/the_knitsignal/.
[282] Martinez, P. (2018, May 3). ACLU National Director calls NRA Tactics "Model Worthy of Emulation." *CBS News*. Retrieved June 13, 2019, from https://www.cbsnews.com/news/aclu-faiz-shakir-national-rifle-association-worthy-of-emulation-cbsn-interview-today-2018-05-03/.
[283] Chapman, C. M., Masser, B. M., & Louis, W. R. (2019). The Champion Effect in Peer-to-Peer Giving: Successful Campaigns Highlight Fundraisers More Than Causes. *Nonprofit and Voluntary Sector Quarterly*, *48*(3), 572-592. Retrieved June 13, 2019, from https://journals.sagepub.com/doi/abs/10.1177/0899764018805196 .
[284] May, M. (2018, August 15). Top 25 Fundraising Events Saw Overall Income Drop in 2017, Figures Show. Retrieved June 13, 2019, from https://fundraising.co.uk/2018/08/17/top-25-uk-fundraising-events-saw-overall-income-drop-2017-figures-show.
[285] Turner, R. (2019, February 06). Mass Participation. What Went Wrong? Retrieved June 13, 2019, from https://fundraising.co.uk/2019/02/06/mass-participation-went-wrong/amp/.
[286] Blackbaud. (2017). 2016 Blackbaud Peer-to-Peer Fundraising Study. Retrieved June 13, 2019, from https://hi.blackbaud.com/p2p/2016-Peer-to-Peer-Report-pub2017.pdf.
[287] Masterson, S. (2017, February 28). Can Nonprofits Really Raise Money With 5Ks? Retrieved June 13, 2019, from https://npengage.com/nonprofit-fundraising/can-nonprofits-really-raise-money-with-5ks/.
[288] McGuire, J. (2019, June 7). Running Event Participation is in Decline for the First Time in Years. *Runner's World*. Retrieved June 13, 2019, from https://www.runnersworld.com/uk/news/a27810909/running-event-participation-in-decline/.
[289] Yes, how. Not if. Consider (just to grab a few):
Walther, G. R., Post, E., Convey, P., Menzel, A., Parmesan, C., Beebee, T. J., ... & Bairlein, F. (2002). Ecological responses to recent climate change. *Nature*, *416*(6879), 389. Retrieved June 13, 2019, from https://www.nature.com/articles/416389a;
Inouye, D. W., Barr, B., Armitage, K. B., & Inouye, B. D. (2000). Climate change is affecting altitudinal migrants and hibernating species. *Proceedings of the National Academy of Sciences*, *97*(4), 1630-1633. Retrieved June 13, 2019, from https://www.pnas.org/content/97/4/1630.short;
McCarty, J. P. (2001). Ecological Consequences of Recent Climate Change. *Conservation biology*, *15*(2), 320-331. Retrieved June 13, 2019, from https://onlinelibrary.wiley.com/doi/abs/10.1046/j.1523-1739.2001.015002320.x;
Visser, M. E., Perdeck, A. C., van Balen, J. H., & Both, C. (2009). Climate Change Leads to Decreasing Bird Migration Distances. *Global Change Biology*, *15*(8), 1859-1865. Retrieved June 13, 2019, from https://onlinelibrary.wiley.com/doi/abs/10.1111/j.1365-2486.2009.01865.x;

Crick, H. Q. (2004). The Impact of Climate Change on Birds. *Ibis*, *146*, 48-56. Retrieved June 13, 2019, from https://onlinelibrary.wiley.com/doi/full/10.1111/j.1474-919X.2004.00327.x;
Miller-Rushing, A. J., Lloyd-Evans, T. L., Primack, R. B., & Satzinger, P. (2008). Bird Migration Times, Climate Change, and Changing Population Sizes. *Global Change Biology*, *14*(9), 1959-1972. Retrieved June 13, 2019, from https://onlinelibrary.wiley.com/doi/abs/10.1111/j.1365-2486.2008.01619.x; to grab just a few.

[290] Robbins, J. (2013, August 19). Crowdsourcing, for the Birds. New York Times. Retrieved June 13, 2019, from https://www.nytimes.com/2013/08/20/science/earth/crowdsourcing-for-the-birds.html.

[291] U.S. Department of the Interior, U.S. Fish and Wildlife Service, and U.S. Department of Commerce, U.S. Census Bureau. (2018). *2016 National Survey of Fishing, Hunting, and Wildlife-Associated Recreation* (Rep.). Washington, DC. Retrieved June 13, 2019, from https://wsfrprograms.fws.gov/Subpages/NationalSurvey/nat_survey2016.pdf.

[292] Robbins, J. (2013, August 19). Crowdsourcing, for the Birds. New York Times. Retrieved June 13, 2019, from https://www.nytimes.com/2013/08/20/science/earth/crowdsourcing-for-the-birds.html.

[293] Johnston, A., Fink, D., Hochachka, W. M., & Kelling, S. (2018). Estimates of Observer Expertise Improve Species Distributions from Citizen Science Data. Methods in Ecology and Evolution, 9(1), 88-97. Retrieved June 13, 2019, from https://besjournals.onlinelibrary.wiley.com/doi/full/10.1111/2041-210X.12838.

[294] Cornell Lab of Ornithology. (n.d.). Mission: Citizen Science. Retrieved June 13, 2019, from https://web.archive.org/web/20190204073247/http://www.birds.cornell.edu/page.aspx?pid=1664.

[295] Cohn, J. P. (2008). Citizen Science: Can Volunteers Do Real Research?. *BioScience*, *58*(3), 192-197. Retrieved June 13, 2019, from https://academic.oup.com/bioscience/article/58/3/192/230689.

[296] England, R. (2019, January 09). Citizen Astronomers Discover New Planet that NASA Algorithms Missed. Retrieved June 13, 2019, from https://www.engadget.com/2019/01/09/citizens-discover-new-planet-nasa-algorithms-missed/.

[297] SPLC HateWatch Staff. (2016, December 16). Update: 1,094 Bias-Related Incidents in the Month Following the Election. Retrieved June 13, 2019, from https://www.splcenter.org/hatewatch/2016/12/16/update-1094-bias-related-incidents-month-following-election.

[298] Janik, R. (2018, July 5). Hate Crimes are up in Major U.S. Cities for the Fourth Year in a Row, Study Says. Retrieved June 13, 2019, from https://www.splcenter.org/hatewatch/2018/07/05/hate-crimes-are-major-us-cities-fourth-year-row-study-says.

---

[299] The Women's March Organizers & Condé Nast. (2018). *Together We Rise: Behind the Scenes at the Protest Heard around the World.* New York, NY: Dey Street Books.
[300] Chenoweth, E., & Pressman, J. (2017, February 7). This is What We Learned by Counting the Women's Marches. *Washington Post.* Retrieved June 13, 2019, from https://www.washingtonpost.com/news/monkey-cage/wp/2017/02/07/this-is-what-we-learned-by-counting-the-womens-marches/.
[301] Martinez, A. G. (2018, October 23). In Texas, Techies Are Trying to Turn the Red State Blue. *Wired.* Retrieved June 13, 2019, from https://www.wired.com/story/flipping-texas-elections-voter-registration-tech/.
[302] Cohen, E. (2018, September 20). How I Used My Startup Knowledge to Remap Texas Politics. Retrieved June 13, 2019, from https://medium.com/@erex78/how-i-used-my-startup-knowledge-to-remap-texas-politics-80ea3c9e5f5f.
[303] Pink, D. H. (2011). *Drive: The Surprising Truth about What Motivates Us*. New York, NY: Riverhead Books.
[304] For example, Lang, M. J. (2018, November 21). Anger over Farrakhan ties prompts calls for Women's March leaders to resign. *Washington Post.* Retrieved June 13, 2019, from https://www.washingtonpost.com/local/anger-over-farrakhan-ties-prompts-calls-for-womens-march-leaders-to-resign/2018/11/21/6d925942-edb4-11e8-8679-934a2b33be52_story.html.
[305] For example, Sobel, A. (2018, October 30). Why #Metoo Activist Alyssa Milano Will Not Speak at Next Women's March. *Advocate.* Retrieved June 13, 2019, from https://www.advocate.com/women/2018/10/30/metoo-activist-alyssa-milano-wont-be-stopped.
[306] North, A. (2018, December 21). The Women's March changed the American left. Now anti-Semitism allegations threaten the group's future. Retrieved June 13, 2019, from https://www.vox.com/identities/2018/12/21/18145176/feminism-womens-march-2018-2019-farrakhan-intersectionality.
[307] Thomas, R. (2019, January 03). Women's March in New Orleans cancelled. Retrieved June 13, 2019, from http://www.wafb.com/2019/01/03/womens-march-new-orleans-cancelled/.
[308] Orso, A. (2019, January 16). Saturday's Women's March on Philadelphia: Dueling protests and uncertain weather. *Philadelphia Inquirer.* Retrieved June 13, 2019, from https://www.inquirer.com/news/womens-march-philadelphia-philly-women-rally-protest-weather-20190116.html.
[309] And, sadly, vice versa.
[310] Wikipedia. (2019, June 12). List of Wikipedia controversies. Retrieved June 13, 2019, from https://en.wikipedia.org/wiki/List_of_Wikipedia_controversies.
[311]Wikipedia. (2019, June 12). List of controversial issues. Retrieved June 13, 2019, from https://en.wikipedia.org/wiki/Wikipedia:List_of_controversial_issues.
[312] Wikipedia. (2019, June 12). Lamest edit wars. Retrieved June 13, 2019, from https://en.wikipedia.org/wiki/Wikipedia:Lamest_edit_wars.
[313] Burke, E. (1770). *Thoughts on the Cause of the Present Discontents.*

---

[314] Lillien, J. (2017). *United States Bankruptcy Court Southern District Of New York In Re Wonderwork, Inc., Debtor: Final Report Of Jason R. Lilien, Examiner* (Rep.). Retrieved June 13, 2019, from http://online.wsj.com/public/resources/documents/examinerreport.pdf.
[315] Comedian Mitch Hedberg: "I'll just give you the money, and you give me the doughnut. End of transaction. We don't need to bring ink and paper into this. I just can't imagine a scenario where I would have to prove that I bought a doughnut." From Steele, T. (2016, February 24). 'I can't imagine having to prove I bought a donut'. Retrieved June 13, 2019, from https://www.koin.com/entertainment/i-cant-imagine-having-to-prove-i-bought-a-donut/960296304.
[316] Simon, L., & Silard, T. (2018). Funding Innovations That Break the Mold. *Stanford Social Innovation Review*. Retrieved June 13, 2019, from https://ssir.org/articles/entry/funding_innovations_that_break_the_mold.
[317] National Highway Traffic Safety Administration. (2018). 2017 Data: Alcohol-Impaired Driving (Rep.). Washington, DC: NHTSA. DOT HS 812 630. Retrieved June 10, 2019, from https://crashstats.nhtsa.dot.gov/Api/Public/ViewPublication/812630.
[318] National Highway Traffic Safety Administration. (2017). Distracted Driving 2015 (Rep.). Washington, DC: NHTSA. DOT HS 812 381. Retrieved June 13, 2019, from https://www.nhtsa.gov/sites/nhtsa.dot.gov/files/documents/812_381_distracteddriving2015.pdf.
[319] Kistruck, G. M., Qureshi, I., & Beamish, P. W. (2013). Geographic and Product Diversification in Charitable Organizations. *Journal of Management*, *39*(2), 496-530.Retrieved June 13, 2019, from https://journals.sagepub.com/doi/abs/10.1177/0149206311398135?journalCode=joma.
[320] McDermott, J. (2014, August 16). AT&T's Anti-Texting Campaign: Lots of Impressions, Zero Success. Retrieved June 13, 2019, from https://digiday.com/media/att-asks-twitter-whether-anti-texting-driving-campaign-working/.
[321] Crouch, I. (2013, October 21). Why A.T. & T. is Talking About Texting and Driving. *The New Yorker*. Retrieved June 13, 2019, from https://www.newyorker.com/business/currency/why-a-t-t-is-talking-about-texting-and-driving
[322] Human Services Council. (n.d.). *New York Nonprofits in the Aftermath of FEGS: A Call to Action* (Rep.). Retrieved June 13, 2019, from https://humanservicescouncil.org/wp-content/uploads/Initiatives/HSCCommission/HSCCommissionReport.pdf.
[323] Gregory, A. G., & Howard, D. (2009, Fall). The Nonprofit Starvation Cycle. *Stanford Social Innovation Review*. Retrieved June 13, 2019, from https://ssir.org/articles/entry/the_nonprofit_starvation_cycle.
[324] Scannell, L., & Gifford, R. (2010). Defining place attachment: A tripartite organizing framework. *Journal of environmental psychology*, *30*(1), 1-10. Retrieved June 13, 2019, from https://www.sciencedirect.com/science/article/abs/pii/S0272494409000620

---

[325] Reguly, E. (2017, February 1). Donation Drop Forces Merger of Canada's Largest Cancer Charities. *The Globe and Mail.* Retrieved June 13, 2019, from https://www.theglobeandmail.com/news/national/rapid-donation-drop-forces-merger-of-canadian-cancer-society-breast-cancer-foundation/article33864407/,

[326] Ubelacker, S. (4, July 2018). Canadian Cancer Society turns around finances after cutting excess fat post-merger. *The Star*. Retrieved June 13, 2019, from https://www.thestar.com/news/gta/2018/07/04/canadian-cancer-society-turns-around-finances-after-cutting-excess-fat-post-merger.html.

[327] Foster, W., Cortez, A., & Milway, K. S. (2009, February 25). Nonprofit Mergers and Acquisitions: More Than a Tool for Tough Times. Retrieved June 14, 2019, from https://www.bridgespan.org/insights/library/mergers-and-collaborations/nonprofit-mergers-and-acquisitions-more-than-a-too.

[328] Haider, D., Cooper, K., & Maktoufi, R. (2016). *Mergers as a Strategy for Success 2016 Report from the Metropolitan Chicago Nonprofit Merger Research Project*(Rep.). Retrieved June 14, 2019, from Mission Strategy Consulting website: http://chicagonpmergerstudy.org/sites/default/files/pdfs/2016_Metro_Chicago_NPMerger_Research_Project_Report.pdf.

[329] NPQ Editors. (2018, September 27). Our Burning Platform for a Universal Charitable Deduction. *Nonprofit Quarterly*. Retrieved June 14, 2019, from https://nonprofitquarterly.org/our-burning-platform-for-a-universal-charitable-deduction/.

[330] Congressional Research Service. (2018). *Membership of the 115th Congress: A Profile* (United States, Congressional Research Service). Washington, DC. Retrieved June 14, 2019, from https://fas.org/sgp/crs/misc/R44762.pdf.

[331] Why use this as a benchmark? Because that's when reporting is required.

[332] OpenSecrets.org. (2019). Donor Demographics. Retrieved June 14, 2019, from https://www.opensecrets.org/overview/donordemographics.php?cycle=2018&filter=A.

[333] OpenSecrets.org. (2015). Donor Demographics. Retrieved June 14, 2019, from https://www.opensecrets.org/overview/donordemographics.php?cycle=2014&filter=A.

[334] Martinez, P. (2018, May 3). ACLU national director calls NRA tactics "model worthy of emulation." *CBS News*. Retrieved June 13, 2019, from https://www.cbsnews.com/news/aclu-faiz-shakir-national-rifle-association-worthy-of-emulation-cbsn-interview-today-2018-05-03/.

[335] Brustein, J. (2017, November 8). The ACLU Wants to Be the NRA, Without All the Guns. Retrieved June 14, 2019, from https://www.bloomberg.com/news/features/2017-11-08/the-aclu-wants-to-be-the-nra-without-all-the-guns.

[336] Shore, B. (2018, September 12). Stop Sitting on the Sidelines, Nonprofits, and Get Out the Vote. *Chronicle of Philanthropy*. Retrieved June 13, 2019, from https://www.philanthropy.com/article/Opinion-Getting-Out-the-Vote/244487.

[337] Battilana, J., Lee, M., Walker, J., & Dorsey, C. (2012). In Search of the Hybrid Ideal. *Stanford Social Innovation Review*. Retrieved June 14, 2019, from https://ssir.org/articles/entry/in_search_of_the_hybrid_ideal.

---

[338] Wexler, R. A. (2009). Effective Social Enterprise — A Menu of Legal Structures. *The Exempt Organization Tax Review, 63*(3). Retrieved June 14, 2019, from https://www.adlercolvin.com/wp-content/uploads/2017/12/Effective-Social-Enterprise-A-Menu-of-Legal-Structures-00216840xA3536.pdf.

[339] Alexanderson, P. (2015, February 27). Exit Through the Gift Shop, Enter Tax Complexity. Retrieved June 14, 2019, from https://mossadams.com/articles/2015/february/gift-shop-income-and-ubi.

[340] Fundraising Portal. (n.d.). Case Study: Mindful Monsters. Retrieved June 14, 2019, from http://www.fundraisingportal.org.uk/resource/case-study-mindful-monsters.

[341] Chandler, J., Hilton, N., & Whitney, C. (n.d.). *Putting the Individual back into Individual Giving with Mindful Monsters* (Rep.). Retrieved June 14, 2019, from http://www.fundraisingportal.org.uk/sites/default/files/resource-files/iof-supporter-journey-conference-2018-mindful-monsters.pdf.

[342] WARC. (2017). Scope: Mindful Monsters. Retrieved June 14, 2019, from https://www.warc.com/content/paywall/article/dmauk/scope_mindful_monsters/117364.

[343] Chandler, J., Hilton, N., & Whitney, C. (n.d.). *Putting the Individual back into Individual Giving with Mindful Monsters* (Rep.). Retrieved June 14, 2019, from http://www.fundraisingportal.org.uk/sites/default/files/resource-files/iof-supporter-journey-conference-2018-mindful-monsters.pdf.

[344] Friedman, M. (1970, September 13). The Social Responsibility of Business is to Increase its Profits. *The New York Times Magazine*. Retrieved June 14, 2019, from http://umich.edu/~thecore/doc/Friedman.pdf.

[345] Waldron, B. (2019, January 4). Agents Of Change: 4Ocean; 4Ocean Is Paying Fishermen With Empty Nets To Catch Plastic Pollution Instead. *Surfer*. Retrieved June 14, 2019, from https://www.surfer.com/blogs/agents-of-change/agents-of-change-4ocean/.

[346] Waldron, B. (2019, January 4). Agents Of Change: 4Ocean; 4Ocean Is Paying Fishermen With Empty Nets To Catch Plastic Pollution Instead. *Surfer*. Retrieved June 14, 2019, from https://www.surfer.com/blogs/agents-of-change/agents-of-change-4ocean/.

[347] Foster, W., & Bradach, J. (2005). Should nonprofits seek profits?. *Harvard Business Review, 83*(2), 92-100. Retrieved June 14, 2019, from https://hbr.org/2005/02/should-nonprofits-seek-profits.

[348] Cryder, C. E., Loewenstein, G., & Seltman, H. (2013). Goal gradient in helping behavior. *Journal of Experimental Social Psychology, 49*(6), 1078-1083. Retrieved June 14, 2019, from https://www.cmu.edu/dietrich/sds/docs/loewenstein/GoalGradient.pdf.

[349] SocialFinance.org. (n.d.). What is Pay for Success? Retrieved June 14, 2019, from https://socialfinance.org/what-is-pay-for-success/.

[350] Rosenberg, T. (2018, March 6). Issuing Bonds to Invest in People. *New York Times*. Retrieved June 14, 2019, from https://www.nytimes.com/2018/03/06/opinion/social-projects-investing-bonds.html.

---

[351] McHugh, N., Sinclair, S., Roy, M., Huckfield, L., & Donaldson, C. (2013). Social impact bonds: a wolf in sheep's clothing?. *Journal of Poverty and Social Justice*, *21*(3), 247-257.Retrieved June 14, 2019, from http://citeseerx.ist.psu.edu/viewdoc/download?doi=10.1.1.686.2162&rep=rep1&type=pdf.
[352] Gustafsson-Wright, E., Gardiner, S., & Putcha, V. (2015, July). *The Potential And Limitations Of Impact Bonds: Lessons From The First Five Years Of Experience Worldwide* (Rep.). Retrieved June 14, 2019, from Global Economy and Development at Brookings website: https://www.brookings.edu/wp-content/uploads/2016/07/Impact-Bondsweb.pdf.
[353] Edmiston, D., & Nicholls, A. (2018). Social Impact Bonds: The Role of Private Capital in Outcome-Based Commissioning. *Journal of Social Policy*, *47*(1), 57-76. Retrieved June 14, 2019, from https://www.cambridge.org/core/journals/journal-of-social-policy/article/social-impact-bonds-the-role-of-private-capital-in-outcomebased-commissioning/83B92D884934604E21EE2A963EB4E11C.
[354] Pratt, J. (2013). Flaws in the Social Impact Bond/Pay for Success Craze. *Nonprofit Quarterly*. Retrieved June 14, 2019, from https://nonprofitquarterly.org/2013/04/17/flaws-in-the-social-impact-bond-craze/.
[355] Miller, Z. (2019, January 22). GOP Unveils Fundraising Tool to Rival Democrats' ActBlue. *Associated Press*. Retrieved June 14, 2019, from https://www.apnews.com/f845d66c4dd94fb8ae2cd94a3c1aed40.
[356] Bird, B., & Pinkava, J. (Directors). (2007). *Ratatouille*[Motion picture]. United States: Pixar Animation Studios.
[357] Fruhlinger, J. (2018, February 20). Tracking the Slow, Sad Death of Barnes & Noble via Data. Retrieved June 14, 2019, from https://web.archive.org/web/20180223001828/http://media.thinknum.com/articles/tracking-the-slow-death-of-barnes-noble-via-data/.
[358] Sago, R. (2018, December 31). Independent bookstores are thriving, but a threat looms. *Marketplace*. Retrieved June 14, 2019, from https://www.marketplace.org/2018/12/31/business/independent-bookstores-are-thriving-threat-looms.
[359] Shatzkin, M. (2018, March 27). What We are Seeing Today is Actually the Second Renaissance of Indie Bookselling, Not the First. Retrieved June 14, 2019, from https://www.idealog.com/blog/what-we-are-seeing-today-is-actually-the-second-renaissance-of-indie-bookselling-not-the-first/.
[360] For example, the third-stage antiretroviral treatment for HIV in the United States costs over $40,000 per year, per Solem, C. T., Snedecor, S. J., Khachatryan, A., Nedrow, K., Tawadrous, M., Chambers, R., ... & Simpson, K. (2014). Cost of treatment in a US commercially insured, HIV-1–Infected Population. *PLOS One*, *9*(5), e98152.
[361] Pulkki-Brännström, A. M., Wolff, C., Brännström, N., & Skordis-Worrall, J. (2012). Cost and cost effectiveness of long-lasting insecticide-treated bed nets-a

model-based analysis. *Cost Effectiveness and Resource Allocation, 10*(1), 5. Retrieved June 14, 2019, from https://www.ncbi.nlm.nih.gov/pmc/articles/PMC3348006/ .
[362] Whitman, A. (1972, March 10). Basil O'Connor, Polio Crusader, Dies. *New York Times*. Retrieved June 14, 2019, from https://www.nytimes.com/1972/03/10/archives/basil-oconnor-polio-crusader-dies.html.
[363] Gautam, K. (n.d.). *A History of Global Polio Eradication* (Rep.). Retrieved June 14, 2019, from UNICEF website: https://www.unicef.org/immunization/files/the_history_of_polio.pdf.
[364]World Health Organization. (2019, March 1). Poliomyelitis. Retrieved June 14, 2019, from https://www.who.int/news-room/fact-sheets/detail/poliomyelitis.
[365] Nocera, J. (2019, January 23). The Michael J. Fox Foundation Gets Results. *Bloomberg*. Retrieved June 14, 2019, from https://www.bloomberg.com/opinion/articles/2019-01-23/parkinson-s-inhaler-the-michael-j-fox-foundation-gets-results.

Made in the USA
Middletown, DE
26 August 2019